From Mathematics to Generic Programming

From Mathematics to Generic Programming

Alexander A. Stepanov

Daniel E. Rose

✦Addison-Wesley

Upper Saddle River, NJ • Boston • Indianapolis • San Francisco
New York • Toronto • Montreal • London • Munich • Paris • Madrid
Capetown • Sydney • Tokyo • Singapore • Mexico City

For information about buying this title in bulk quantities, or for special sales opportunities (which may include electronic versions; custom cover designs; and content particular to your business, training goals, marketing focus, or branding interests), please contact our corporate sales department at corpsales@pearsoned.com or (800) 382-3419.

For government sales inquiries, please contact governmentsales@pearsoned.com.

For questions about sales outside the United States, please contact international@pearsoned.com.

Visit us on the Web: informit.com/aw

Library of Congress Cataloging-in-Publication Data
Stepanov, Alexander A.
  From mathematics to generic programming / Alexander A. Stepanov, Daniel E. Rose.
     pages   cm
  Includes bibliographical references and index.
  ISBN 978-0-321-94204-3 (pbk. : alk. paper)
  1. Generic programming (Computer science)—Mathematics. 2. Computer algorithms. I. Rose, Daniel E. II. Title.
  QA76.6245.S74 2015
  005.1'1—dc23

                                                                        2014034539

ISBN-13: 978-0-321-94204-3
ISBN-10: 0-321-94204-3
Text printed in the United States on recycled paper at RR Donnelley in Crawfordsville, Indiana.
Third printing, August 2015

Contents

Acknowledgments

We would like to thank all the people who contributed to making this book a reality. Our management at A9.com actively supported this project from the beginning. Bill Stasior initiated the creation of the course this book is based on, and selected the topic from among several options we offered. Brian Pinkerton not only attended the course, but also strongly encouraged our idea of turning the material into a book. We also would like to thank Mat Marcus, who collaborated with Alex on a similar course at Adobe in 2004–2005.

The other members of the Fundamental Data Structures and Algorithms for Search team played important roles throughout the process. Anil Gangolli helped shape the content of the course, Ryan Ernst provided much of the programming infrastructure, and Paramjit Oberoi gave invaluable feedback during the writing stage. We have enjoyed working with all of them and are grateful for their input.

We are grateful to our editors, Peter Gordon and Greg Doench, and to the team of experts assembled by Addison-Wesley, including managing editor John Fuller, production editor Mary Kesel Wilson, copyeditor Jill Hobbs, and compositor/LaTeX expert Lori Hughes for all their work in turning our rough manuscript into a polished book.

Finally, we'd like to thank the many friends, family members, and colleagues who read earlier drafts of the book and/or gave us comments, corrections, suggestions, advice, or other help: Gašper Ažman, John Banning, Cynthia Dwork, Hernan Epelman, Ryan Ernst, Anil Gangolli, Susan Gruber, Jon Kalb, Robert Lehr, Dmitry Leshchiner, Tom London, Mark Manasse, Paul McJones, Nicolas Nicolov, Gor Nishanov, Paramjit Oberoi, Sean Parent, Fernando Pelliccioni, John Reiser, Robert Rose, Stefan Vargyas, and Adam Young. The book is much better as a result of their contributions.

Several careful readers sent corrections to errors that occurred in the first and second printings of this book, or in the digital editions. Thanks to the following people for reporting these errors: Abutalib Aghayev, Vladimir Burenkov, Greg

Ives, Nitin Kumar, John Lakos, Andy Lawman, Jeremy Murphy, Anil Pal, Miguel Pinkas, Daniel Roldán, Alexander Slinkin, Saul Tamari, and Boris Vassilev. Additional errors may be reported at errata@fm2gp.com, and future corrections may be found at www.fm2gp.com/errata.html.

About the Authors

Alexander A. Stepanov studied mathematics at Moscow State University from 1967 to 1972. He has been programming since 1972: first in the Soviet Union and, after emigrating in 1977, in the United States. He has programmed operating systems, programming tools, compilers, and libraries. His work on foundations of programming has been supported by GE, Polytechnic University, Bell Labs, HP, SGI, Adobe, and, since 2009, A9.com, Amazon's search technology subsidiary. In 1995 he received the *Dr. Dobb's Journal* Excellence in Programming Award for the design of the C++ Standard Template Library.

Daniel E. Rose is a research scientist who has held management positions at Apple, AltaVista, Xigo, Yahoo, and A9.com. His research focuses on all aspects of search technology, ranging from low-level algorithms for index compression to human–computer interaction issues in web search. Rose led the team at Apple that created desktop search for the Macintosh. He holds a Ph.D. in cognitive science and computer science from University of California, San Diego, and a B.A. in philosophy from Harvard University.

Authors' Note

The separation of computer science from mathematics greatly impoverishes both. The lectures that this book is based on were my attempt to show how these two activities—an ancient one going back to the very beginnings of our civilization and the most modern one—can be brought together.

I was very fortunate that my friend Dan Rose, under whose management our team was applying principles of generic programming to search engine design, agreed to convert my rather meandering lectures into a coherent book. Both of us hope that our readers will enjoy the result of our collaboration.

—A.A.S.

The book you are about to read is based on notes from an "Algorithmic Journeys" course taught by Alex Stepanov at A9.com during 2012. But as Alex and I worked together to transform the material into book form, we realized that there was a stronger story we could tell, one that centered on generic programming and its mathematical foundations. This led to a major reorganization of the topics, and removal of the entire section on set theory and logic, which did not seem to be part of the same story. At the same time, we added and removed details to create a more coherent reading experience and to make the material more accessible to less mathematically advanced readers.

While Alex comes from a mathematical background, I do not. I've tried to learn from my own struggles to understand some of the material and to use this experience to identify ideas that require additional explanation. If in some cases we describe something in a slightly different way than a mathematician would, or using slightly different terminology, or using more simple steps, the fault is mine.

—D.E.R.

1
one

What This Book Is About

*It is impossible to know things of this world
unless you know mathematics.*

Roger Bacon, *Opus Majus*

This book is about programming, but it is different from most programming books. Along with algorithms and code, you'll find mathematical proofs and historical notes about mathematical discoveries from ancient times to the 20th century.

More specifically, the book is about *generic programming*, an approach to programming that was introduced in the 1980s and started to become popular following the creation of the C++ Standard Template Library (STL) in the 1990s. We might define it like this:

Definition 1.1. Generic programming is an approach to programming that focuses on designing algorithms and data structures so that they work in the most general setting without loss of efficiency.

If you've used STL, at this point you may be thinking, "Wait a minute, that's all there is to generic programming? What about all that stuff about templates and iterator traits?" Those are tools that enable the language to support generic programming, and it's important to know how to use them effectively. But generic programming itself is more of an *attitude* toward programming than a particular set of tools.

We believe that this attitude—trying to write code in this general way—is one that all programmers should embrace. The components of a well-written generic program are easier to use and modify than those of a program whose data structures, algorithms, and interfaces hardcode unnecessary assumptions about

1

a specific application. Making a program more generic renders it simultaneously both simpler and more powerful.

1.1   Programming and Mathematics

So where does this generic programming attitude come from, and how do you learn it? It comes from mathematics, and especially from a branch of mathematics called *abstract algebra*. To help you understand the approach, this book will introduce you to a little bit of abstract algebra, which focuses on how to reason about objects in terms of abstract properties of operations on them. It's a topic normally studied only by university students majoring in math, but we believe it's critical in understanding generic programming.

In fact, it turns out that many of the fundamental ideas in programming came from mathematics. Learning how these ideas came into being and evolved over time can help you think about software design. For example, Euclid's *Elements*, a book written more than 2000 years ago, is still one of the best examples of how to build up a complex system from small, easily understood pieces.

Although the essence of generic programming is abstraction, abstractions do not spring into existence fully formed. To see how to make something more general, you need to start with something concrete. In particular, you need to understand the specifics of a particular domain to discover the right abstractions.

The abstractions that appear in abstract algebra largely come from concrete results in one of the oldest branches of mathematics, called *number theory*. For this reason, we will also introduce some key ideas from number theory, which deals with properties of integers, especially divisibility.

The thought process you'll go through in learning this math can improve your programming skills. But we'll also show how some of the mathematical results themselves turn out to be crucial to some modern software applications. In particular, by the end of the book we'll show how some of these results are used in cryptographic protocols underlying online privacy and online commerce.

The book will move back and forth between talking about math and talking about programming. In particular, we'll interweave important ideas in mathematics with a discussion of both specific algorithms and general programming techniques. We'll mention some algorithms only briefly, while others will be refined and generalized throughout the book. A couple of chapters will contain only mathematical material, and a couple will contain only programming material, but most have a mixture of both.

1.2   A Historical Perspective

We've always found that it's easier and more interesting to learn something if it's part of a story. What was going on at the time? Who were the people involved, and how did they come to have these ideas? Was one person's work an attempt to build on another's—or an attempt to reject what came before? So as we introduce the mathematical ideas in this book, we'll try to tell you the story of those ideas and of the people who came up with them. In many cases, we've provided short biographical sketches of the mathematicians who are the main characters in our story. These aren't comprehensive encyclopedia entries, but rather an attempt to give you some context for who these people were.

Although we take a historical perspective, that doesn't mean that the book is intended as a history of mathematics or even that all the ideas are presented in the order in which they were discovered. We'll jump around in space and time when necessary, but we'll try to give a historical context for each of the ideas.

1.3   Prerequisites

Since a lot of the book is about mathematics, you may be concerned that you need to have taken a lot of math classes to understand it. While you'll need to be able to think logically (something you should already be good at as a programmer), we don't assume any specific mathematical knowledge beyond high school algebra and geometry. In a couple of sections, we show some applications that use a little linear algebra (vectors and matrices), but you can safely skip these if you haven't been exposed to the background material before. If you're unfamiliar with any of the notation we use, it's explained in Appendix A.

An important part of mathematics is being able to prove something formally. This book contains quite a few proofs. You'll find the book easier to understand if you've done some proofs before, whether in high school geometry, in a computer science class on automata theory, or in logic. We've described some of the common proof techniques we use, along with examples, in Appendix B.

We assume that if you're reading this book, you're already a programmer. In particular, you should be reasonably proficient in a typical imperative programming language like C, C++, or Java. Our examples will use C++, but we expect you'll be able to understand them even if you've never programmed in that language before. When we make use of a construct unique to C++, we explain it in Appendix C. Irrespective of our use of C++, we believe that the principles discussed in this book apply to programming in general.

Many of the programming topics in this book are also covered from a different perspective, and more formally, in *Elements of Programming* by Stepanov and McJones. Readers interested in additional depth may find that book to be a useful companion to this one. Throughout this book, we occasionally refer interested readers to a relevant section of *Elements of Programming*.

1.4   Roadmap

Before diving into the details, it's useful to see a brief overview of where we're headed:

- Chapter 2 tells the story of an ancient algorithm for multiplication, and how to improve it.

- Chapter 3 looks at some early observations about properties of numbers, and an efficient implementation of an algorithm for finding primes.

- Chapter 4 introduces an algorithm for finding the greatest common divisor (GCD), which will be the basis for some of our abstractions and applications later on.

- Chapter 5 focuses on mathematical results, introducing a couple of important theorems that will play a critical role by the end of the book.

- Chapter 6 introduces the mathematical field of abstract algebra, which provides the core idea for generic programming.

- Chapter 7 shows how these mathematical ideas allow us to generalize our multiplication algorithm beyond simple arithmetic to a variety of practical programming applications.

- Chapter 8 introduces new abstract mathematical structures, and shows some new applications they enable.

- Chapter 9 talks about axiom systems, theories, and models, which are all building blocks of generic programming.

- Chapter 10 introduces concepts in generic programming, and examines the subtleties of some apparently simple programming tasks.

- Chapter 11 continues the exploration of some fundamental programming tasks, examining how different practical implementations can exploit theoretical knowledge of the problem.

- Chapter 12 looks at how hardware constraints can lead to a new approach for an old algorithm, and shows new applications of GCD.

- Chapter 13 puts the mathematical and algorithmic results together to build an important cryptography application.

- Chapter 14 is a summary of some of the principal ideas in the book.

The strands of programming and mathematics are interwoven throughout, though one or the other may lie hidden for a chapter or two. But every chapter plays a part in the overall chain of reasoning that summarizes the entire book:

To be a good programmer, you need to understand the principles of generic programming. To understand the principles of generic programming, you need to understand abstraction. To understand abstraction, you need to understand the mathematics on which it's based.

That's the story we're hoping to tell.

The First Algorithm

> *Moses speedily learned arithmetic, and geometry.*
> *…This knowledge he derived from the Egyptians,*
> *who study mathematics above all things.*
> Philo of Alexandria, *Life of Moses*

An algorithm is a terminating sequence of steps for accomplishing a computational task. Algorithms are so closely associated with the notion of computer programming that most people who know the term probably assume that the idea of algorithms comes from computer science. But algorithms have been around for literally thousands of years. Mathematics is full of algorithms, some of which we use every day. Even the method schoolchildren learn for long addition is an algorithm.

Despite its long history, the notion of an algorithm didn't always exist; it had to be invented. While we don't know when algorithms were first invented, we do know that some algorithms existed in Egypt at least as far back as 4000 years ago.

* * *

Ancient Egyptian civilization was centered on the Nile River, and its agriculture depended on the river's floods to enrich the soil. The problem was that every time the Nile flooded, all the markers showing the boundaries of property were washed away. The Egyptians used ropes to measure distances, and developed procedures so they could go back to their written records and reconstruct the property boundaries. A select group of priests who had studied these mathematical techniques were responsible for this task; they became known as "rope-stretchers." The Greeks would later call them *geometers*, meaning "Earth-measurers."

Unfortunately, we have little written record of the Egyptians' mathematical knowledge. Only two mathematical documents survived from this period. The one we are concerned with is called the Rhind Mathematical Papyrus, named after the 19th-century Scottish collector who bought it in Egypt. It is a document from about 1650 BC written by a scribe named Ahmes, which contains a series of arithmetic and geometry problems, together with some tables for computation. This scroll contains the first recorded algorithm, a technique for fast multiplication, along with a second one for fast division. Let's begin by looking at the fast multiplication algorithm, which (as we shall see later in the book) is still an important computational technique today.

2.1 Egyptian Multiplication

The Egyptians' number system, like that of all ancient civilizations, did not use positional notation and had no way to represent zero. As a result, multiplication was extremely difficult, and only a few trained experts knew how to do it. (Imagine doing multiplication on large numbers if you could only manipulate something like Roman numerals.)

How do we define multiplication? Informally, it's "adding something to itself a number of times." Formally, we can define multiplication by breaking it into two cases: multiplying by 1, and multiplying by a number larger than 1.

We define multiplication by 1 like this:

$$1a = a \tag{2.1}$$

Next we have the case where we want to compute a product of one more thing than we already computed. Some readers may recognize this as the process of induction; we'll use that technique more formally later on.

$$(n+1)a = na + a \tag{2.2}$$

One way to multiply n by a is to add instances of a together n times. However, this could be extremely tedious for large numbers, since $n-1$ additions are required. In C++, the algorithm looks like this:

```
int multiply0(int n, int a) {
    if (n == 1) return a;
    return multiply0(n - 1, a) + a;
}
```

The two lines of code correspond to equations 2.1 and 2.2. Both a and n must be positive, as they were for the ancient Egyptians.

The algorithm described by Ahmes—which the ancient Greeks knew as "Egyptian multiplication" and which many modern authors refer to as the "Russian Peasant Algorithm"[1]—relies on the following insight:

$$4a = ((a + a) + a) + a$$
$$= (a + a) + (a + a)$$

This optimization depends on the law of associativity of addition:

$$a + (b + c) = (a + b) + c$$

It allows us to compute $a + a$ only once and reduce the number of additions.

The idea is to keep halving n and doubling a, constructing a sum of power-of-2 multiples. At the time, algorithms were not described in terms of variables such as a and n; instead, the author would give an example and then say, "Now do the same thing for other numbers." Ahmes was no exception; he demonstrated the algorithm by showing the following table for multiplying $n = 41$ by $a = 59$:

1	✓	59
2		118
4		236
8	✓	472
16		944
32	✓	1888

Each entry on the left is a power of 2; each entry on the right is the result of doubling the previous entry (since adding something to itself is relatively easy). The checked values correspond to the 1-bits in the binary representation of 41. The table basically says that

$$41 \times 59 = (1 \times 59) + (8 \times 59) + (32 \times 59)$$

where each of the products on the right can be computed by doubling 59 the correct number of times.

The algorithm needs to check whether n is even and odd, so we can infer that the Egyptians knew of this distinction, although we do not have direct proof. But ancient Greeks, who claimed that they learned their mathematics from the

---

[1] Many computer scientists learned this name from Knuth's *The Art of Computer Programming*, which says that travelers in 19th-century Russia observed peasants using the algorithm. However, the first reference to this story comes from a 1911 book by Sir Thomas Heath, which actually says, "I have been told that there is a method in use today (some say in Russia, but *I have not been able to verify this*), ..."

Egyptians, certainly did. Here's how they defined[2] even and odd, expressed in modern notation:[3]

$$n = \frac{n}{2} + \frac{n}{2} \implies \text{even}(n)$$

$$n = \frac{n-1}{2} + \frac{n-1}{2} + 1 \implies \text{odd}(n)$$

We will also rely on this requirement:

$$\text{odd}(n) \implies \text{half}(n) = \text{half}(n-1)$$

This is how we express the Egyptian multiplication algorithm in C++:

```
int multiply1(int n, int a) {
    if (n == 1) return a;
    int result = multiply1(half(n), a + a);
    if (odd(n)) result = result + a;
    return result;
}
```

We can easily implement `odd(x)` by testing the least significant bit of x, and `half(x)` by a single right shift of x:

```
bool odd(int n) { return n & 0x1; }
int half(int n) { return n >> 1; }
```

How many additions is `multiply1` going to do? Every time we call the function, we'll need to do the addition indicated by the + in `a + a`. Since we are halving the value as we recurse, we'll invoke the function $\log n$ times.[4] And some of the time, we'll need to do another addition indicated by the + in `result + a`. So the total number of additions will be

$$\#_+(n) = \lfloor \log n \rfloor + (\nu(n) - 1)$$

where $\nu(n)$ is the number of 1s in the binary representation of n (the *population count* or *pop count*). So we have reduced an $O(n)$ algorithm to one that is $O(\log n)$.

---

[2] The definition appears in the 1st-century work *Introduction to Arithmetic*, Book I, Chapter VII, by Nicomachus of Gerasa. He writes, "The even is that which can be divided into two equal parts without a unit intervening in the middle; and the odd is that which cannot be divided into two equal parts because of the aforesaid intervention of a unit."

[3] The arrow symbol " $\implies$ " is read "implies." See Appendix A for a summary of the mathematical notation used in this book.

[4] Throughout this book, when we write "log," we mean the base 2 logarithm, unless specified otherwise.

Is this algorithm optimal? Not always. For example, if we want to multiply by 15, the preceding formula would give this result:

$$\#_+(15) = 3 + 4 - 1 = 6$$

But we can actually multiply by 15 with only 5 additions, using the following procedure:

```
int multiply_by_15(int a) {
    int b = (a + a) + a;      // b == 3*a
    int c = b + b;            // c == 6*a
    return (c + c) + b;       // 12*a + 3*a
}
```

Such a sequence of additions is called an *addition chain*. Here we have discovered an optimal addition chain for 15. Nevertheless, Ahmes's algorithm is good enough for most purposes.

Exercise 2.1. Find optimal addition chains for $n < 100$.

At some point the reader may have observed that some of these computations would be even faster if we first reversed the order of the arguments when the first is greater than the second (for example, we could compute 3×15 more easily than 15×3). That's true, and the Egyptians knew this. But we're not going to add that optimization here, because as we'll see in Chapter 7, we're eventually going to want to generalize our algorithm to cases where the arguments have different types and the order of the arguments matters.

2.2   Improving the Algorithm

Our `multiply1` function works well as far as the number of additions is concerned, but it also does $\lfloor \log n \rfloor$ recursive calls. Since function calls are expensive, we want to transform the program to avoid this expense.

One principle we're going to take advantage of is this: *It is often easier to do more work rather than less.* Specifically, we're going to compute

$$r + na$$

where r is a running result that accumulates the partial products na. In other words, we're going to perform *multiply-accumulate* rather than just multiply. This principle turns out to be true not only in programming but also in hardware design and in mathematics, where it's often easier to prove a general result than a specific one.

Here's our multiply-accumulate function:

```
int mult_acc0(int r, int n, int a) {
    if (n == 1) return r + a;
    if (odd(n)) {
        return mult_acc0(r + a, half(n), a + a);
    } else {
        return mult_acc0(r, half(n), a + a);
    }
}
```

It obeys the invariant: $r + na = r_0 + n_0 a_0$, where r_0, n_0 and a_0 are the initial values of those variables.

We can improve this further by simplifying the recursion. Notice that the two recursive calls differ only in their first argument. Instead of having two recursive calls for the odd and even cases, we'll just modify the value of r before we recurse, like this:

```
int mult_acc1(int r, int n, int a) {
    if (n == 1) return r + a;
    if (odd(n)) r = r + a;
    return mult_acc1(r, half(n), a + a);
}
```

Now our function is *tail-recursive*—that is, the recursion occurs only in the return value. We'll take advantage of this fact shortly.

We make two observations:

- n is rarely 1.

- If n is even, there's no point checking to see if it's 1.

So we can reduce the number of times we have to compare with 1 by a factor of 2, simply by checking for oddness first:

```
int mult_acc2(int r, int n, int a) {
    if (odd(n)) {
        r = r + a;
        if (n == 1) return r;
    }
    return mult_acc2(r, half(n), a + a);
}
```

Some programmers think that compiler optimizations will do these kinds of transformations for us, but that's rarely true; they do not transform one algorithm into another.

What we have so far is pretty good, but we're eventually going to want to eliminate the recursion to avoid the function call overhead. This is easier if the function is strictly tail-recursive.

Definition 2.1. A **strictly tail-recursive** procedure is one in which all the tail-recursive calls are done with the formal parameters of the procedure being the corresponding arguments.

Again, we can achieve this simply by assigning the desired values to the variables we'll be passing before we do the recursion:

```
int mult_acc3(int r, int n, int a) {
    if (odd(n)) {
        r = r + a;
        if (n == 1) return r;
    }
    n = half(n);
    a = a + a;
    return mult_acc3(r, n, a);
}
```

Now it is easy to convert this to an iterative program by replacing the tail recursion with a while(true) construct:

```
int mult_acc4(int r, int n, int a) {
    while (true) {
        if (odd(n)) {
            r = r + a;
            if (n == 1) return r;
        }
        n = half(n);
        a = a + a;
    }
}
```

With our newly optimized multiply-accumulate function, we can write a new version of multiply. Our new version will invoke our multiply-accumulate helper function:

```
int multiply2(int n, int a) {
    if (n == 1) return a;
    return mult_acc4(a, n - 1, a);
}
```

Notice that we skip one iteration of mult_acc4 by calling it with result already set to *a*.

This is pretty good, except when *n* is a power of 2. The first thing we do is subtract 1, which means that mult_acc4 will be called with a number whose binary representation is all 1s, the worst case for our algorithm. So we'll avoid this by doing some of the work in advance when *n* is even, halving it (and doubling *a*) until *n* becomes odd:

```
int multiply3(int n, int a) {
    while (!odd(n)) {
        a = a + a;
        n = half(n);
    }
    if (n == 1) return a;
    return mult_acc4(a, n - 1, a);
}
```

But now we notice that we're making mult_acc4 do one unnecessary test for odd(n), because we're calling it with an even number. So we'll do one halving and doubling on the arguments before we call it, giving us our final version:

```
int multiply4(int n, int a) {
    while (!odd(n)) {
        a = a + a;
        n = half(n);
    }
    if (n == 1) return a;
    // even(n − 1) ⟹ n − 1 ≠ 1
    return mult_acc4(a, half(n - 1), a + a);
}
```

Rewriting Code

As we have seen with our transformations of the multiply algorithm, rewriting code is important. No one writes good code the first time; it takes many iterations to find the most efficient or general way to do something. No programmer should have a single-pass mindset.

At some point during the process you may have been thinking, "One more operation isn't going to make a big difference." But it may turn out that your code will be reused many times for many years. (In fact, a temporary hack often becomes the code that lives the longest.) Furthermore, that inexpensive operation you're saving now may be replaced by a very costly one in some future version of the code.

Another benefit of striving for efficiency is that the process forces you to understand the problem in more depth. At the same time, this increased depth of understanding leads to more efficient implementations; it's a virtuous circle.

2.3 Thoughts on the Chapter

Students of elementary algebra learn how to keep transforming expressions until they can be simplified. In our successive implementations of the Egyptian multiplication algorithm, we've gone through an analogous process, rearranging the code to make it clearer and more efficient. Every programmer needs to get in the habit of trying code transformations until the final form is obtained.

We've seen how mathematics emerged in ancient Egypt, and how it gave us the first known algorithm. We're going to return to that algorithm and expand on it quite a bit later in the book. But for now we're going to move ahead more than a thousand years and take a look at some mathematical discoveries from ancient Greece.

Ancient Greek Number Theory

Pythagoreans applied themselves to the study of mathematics....
They thought that its principles must be the principles of all existing things.

Aristotle, *Metaphysics*

In this chapter, we're going to look at some of the problems studied by ancient Greek mathematicians. Their work on patterns and "shapes" of numbers led to the discovery of prime numbers and the beginnings of a field of mathematics called *number theory*. They also discovered paradoxes that ultimately produced some mathematical breakthroughs. Along the way, we'll examine an ancient algorithm for finding primes, and see how to optimize it.

3.1   Geometric Properties of Integers

Pythagoras, the Greek mathematician and philosopher who most of us know only for his theorem, was actually the person who came up with the idea that understanding mathematics is necessary to understand the world. He also discovered many interesting properties of numbers; he considered this understanding to be of great value in its own right, independent of any practical application. According to Aristotle's pupil Aristoxenus, "He attached supreme importance to the study of arithmetic, which he advanced and took out of the region of commercial utility."

Pythagoras (ca. 570 BC–ca. 490 BC)

Pythagoras was born on the Greek island of Samos, which was a major naval power at the time. He came from a prominent family, but chose to pursue wisdom rather than wealth. At some point in his youth he traveled to Miletus to study with Thales, the founder of philosophy (see Section 9.2), who advised him to go to Egypt and learn the Egyptians' mathematical secrets.

During the time Pythagoras was studying abroad, the Persian empire conquered Egypt. Pythagoras followed the Persian army eastward to Babylon (in what is now Iraq), where he learned Babylonian mathematics and astronomy. While there, he may have met travelers from India; what we know is that he was exposed to and began espousing ideas we typically associate with Indian religions, including the transmigration of souls, vegetarianism, and asceticism. Prior to Pythagoras, these ideas were completely unknown to the Greeks.

After returning to Greece, Pythagoras started a settlement in Croton, a Greek colony in southern Italy, where he gathered followers—both men and women—who shared his ideas and followed his ascetic lifestyle. Their lives were centered on the study of four things: astronomy, geometry, number theory, and music. These four subjects, later known as the *quadrivium*, remained a focus of European education for 2000 years. Each of these disciplines was related: the motion of the stars could be mapped geometrically, geometry could be grounded in numbers, and numbers generated music. In fact, Pythagoras was the first to discover the numerical structure of frequencies in musical octaves. His followers said that he could "hear the music of the celestial spheres."

After the death of Pythagoras, the Pythagoreans spread to several other Greek colonies in the area and developed a large body of mathematics. However, they kept their teachings secret, so many of their results may have been lost. They also eliminated competition within their ranks by crediting all discoveries to Pythagoras himself, so we don't actually know which individuals did what.

Although the Pythagorean communities were gone after a couple of hundred years, their work remains influential. As late as the 17th century, Leibniz (one of the inventors of calculus) described himself as a Pythagorean.

Unfortunately, Pythagoras and his followers kept their work secret, so none of their writings survive. However, we know from contemporaries what some of his discoveries were. Some of these come from a first-century book called *Introduction to Arithmetic* by Nicomachus of Gerasa. These included observations about geometric properties of numbers; they associated numbers with particular shapes.

Triangular numbers, for example, which are formed by stacking rows representing the first n positive integers, are those that formed the following geometric pattern:

| 1 | 3 | 6 | 10 | 15 | 21 |

Oblong numbers are those that look like this:

| 2 | 6 | 12 | 20 | 30 | 42 |

It is easy to see that the nth oblong number is represented by an $n \times (n+1)$ rectangle:

$$\square_n = n(n+1)$$

It's also clear geometrically that each oblong number is twice its corresponding triangular number. Since we already know that triangular numbers are the sum of the first n positive integers, we have

$$\square_n = 2\triangle_n = 2\sum_{i=1}^{n} i = n(n+1)$$

So the geometric representation gives us the formula for the sum of the first n positive integers:

$$\triangle_n = \sum_{i=1}^{n} i = \frac{n(n+1)}{2}$$

Another geometric observation is that the sequence of odd numbers forms the shape of what the Greeks called *gnomons* (the Greek word for a carpenter's square; a gnomon is also the part of a sundial that casts the shadow):

1   3   5   7   9   11

Combining the first n gnomons creates a familiar shape—a square:

1   4   9   16   25   36

This picture also gives us a formula for the sum of the first n positive odd numbers:

$$\square_n = \sum_{i=1}^{n} (2i - 1) = n^2$$

Exercise 3.1. Find a geometric proof for the following: take any triangular number, multiply it by 8, and add 1. The result is a square number. (This problem comes from Plutarch's *Platonic Questions*.)

3.2 Sifting Primes

Pythagoreans also observed that some numbers could not be made into any non-trivial rectangular shape (a shape where both sides of the rectangle are greater than 1). These are what we now call *prime numbers*—numbers that are not products of smaller numbers:

$$2, 3, 5, 7, 11, 13, \ldots$$

("Numbers" for the Greeks were always whole numbers.) Some of the earliest observations about primes come from Euclid. While he is usually associated with geometry, several books of Euclid's *Elements* actually discuss what we now call number theory. One of his results is this theorem:

Theorem 3.1 (Euclid VII, 32): *Any number is either prime or divisible by some prime.*

The proof, which uses a technique called "impossibility of infinite descent," goes like this:[1]

Proof. Consider a number A. If it is prime, then we are done. If it is composite (i.e., nonprime), then it must be divisible by some smaller number B. If B is prime, we are done (because if A is divisible by B and B is prime, then A is divisible by a prime). If B is composite, then it must be divisible by some smaller number C, and so on. Eventually, we will find a prime or, as Euclid remarks in his proof of the previous proposition, "an infinite sequence of numbers will divide the number, each of which is less than the other; and this is impossible."   □

This Euclidean principle that *any descending sequence of natural numbers terminates* is equivalent to the induction axiom of natural numbers, which we will encounter in Chapter 9.

*   *   *

Another result, which some consider the most beautiful theorem in mathematics, is the fact that there are infinitely many primes:

Theorem 3.2 (Euclid IX, 20): *For any sequence of primes $\{p_1, \ldots, p_n\}$, there is a prime p not in the sequence.*

Proof. Consider the number

$$q = 1 + \prod_{i=1}^{n} p_i$$

---

[1] Euclid's proof of VII, 32 actually relies on his proposition VII, 31 (any composite number is divisible by some prime), which contains the reasoning shown here.

where p_i is the ith prime in the sequence. Because of the way we constructed q, we know it is not divisible by any p_i. Then either q is prime, in which case it is itself a prime not in the sequence, or q is divisible by some new prime, which by definition is not in the sequence. Therefore, there are infinitely many primes.

□

One of the best-known techniques for finding primes is the *Sieve of Eratosthenes*. Eratosthenes was a 3rd-century Greek mathematician who is remembered in part for his amazingly accurate measurement of the circumference of the Earth. Metaphorically, the idea of Eratosthenes' sieve is to "sift" all the numbers so that the nonprimes "fall through" the sieve and the primes remain at the end. The actual procedure is to start with a list of all the candidate numbers and then cross out the ones known not to be primes (since they are multiples of primes found so far); whatever is left are the primes. Today the Sieve of Eratosthenes is often shown starting with all positive integers up to a given number, but Eratosthenes already knew that even numbers greater than 2 were not prime, so he didn't bother to include them.

Following Eratosthenes' convention, we'll also include only odd numbers, so our sieve will find primes greater than 2. Each value in the sieve is a candidate prime up to whatever value we care about. If we want to find primes up to a maximum of $m = 53$, our sieve initially looks like this:

$$3 \quad 5 \quad 7 \quad 9 \quad 11 \quad 13 \quad 15 \quad 17 \quad 19 \quad 21 \quad 23 \quad 25 \quad 27$$
$$29 \quad 31 \quad 33 \quad 35 \quad 37 \quad 39 \quad 41 \quad 43 \quad 45 \quad 47 \quad 49 \quad 51 \quad 53$$

In each iteration, we take the first number (which must be a prime) and cross out all the multiples except itself that have not previously been crossed out. We'll highlight the numbers being crossed out in the current iteration by boxing them. Here's what the sieve looks like after we cross out the multiples of 3:

$$③ \quad 5 \quad 7 \quad \boxed{9} \quad 11 \quad 13 \quad \boxed{15} \quad 17 \quad 19 \quad \boxed{21} \quad 23 \quad 25 \quad \boxed{27}$$
$$29 \quad 31 \quad \boxed{33} \quad 35 \quad 37 \quad \boxed{39} \quad 41 \quad 43 \quad \boxed{45} \quad 47 \quad 49 \quad \boxed{51} \quad 53$$

Next we cross out the multiples of 5 that have not yet been crossed out:

$$3 \quad ⑤ \quad 7 \quad 9\!\!\!/ \quad 11 \quad 13 \quad 1\!\!\!/5 \quad 17 \quad 19 \quad 2\!\!\!/1 \quad 23 \quad \boxed{25} \quad 2\!\!\!/7$$
$$29 \quad 31 \quad 3\!\!\!/3 \quad \boxed{35} \quad 37 \quad 3\!\!\!/9 \quad 41 \quad 43 \quad \boxed{45} \quad 47 \quad 49 \quad 5\!\!\!/1 \quad 53$$

And then the remaining multiples of 7:

$$3 \quad 5 \quad ⑦ \quad 9\!\!\!/ \quad 11 \quad 13 \quad 1\!\!\!/5 \quad 17 \quad 19 \quad 2\!\!\!/1 \quad 23 \quad 2\!\!\!/5 \quad 2\!\!\!/7$$
$$29 \quad 31 \quad 3\!\!\!/3 \quad 3\!\!\!/5 \quad 37 \quad 3\!\!\!/9 \quad 41 \quad 43 \quad 4\!\!\!/5 \quad 47 \quad \boxed{49} \quad 5\!\!\!/1 \quad 53$$

We need to repeat this process until we've crossed out all the multiples of factors less than or equal to $\lfloor \sqrt{m} \rfloor$, where m is the highest candidate we're considering.

In our example, $m = 53$, so we are done. All the numbers that have not been crossed out are primes:

$$3 \quad 5 \quad 7 \quad \not{9} \quad 11 \quad 13 \quad \not{15} \quad 17 \quad 19 \quad \not{21} \quad 23 \quad \not{25} \quad \not{27}$$
$$29 \quad 31 \quad \not{33} \quad \not{35} \quad 37 \quad \not{39} \quad 41 \quad 43 \quad \not{45} \quad 47 \quad \not{49} \quad \not{51} \quad 53$$

Before we write our implementation of the algorithm, we'll make a few observations. Let's go back to what the sieve looked like in the middle of the process (say, when we were crossing out multiples of 5) and add some information—namely, the index, or position in the list, of each candidate being considered:

```
index:  0   1   2  3   4   5   6   7   8   9   10   11   12  13  14  15   16   17  18  ...
values: 3  (5)  7  9  11  13  15  17  19  21  23  [25] 27  29  31  33  [35] 37  39  ...
```

Notice that when we're considering multiples of factor 5, the *step size*—the number of entries between two numbers being crossed out, such as 25 and 35—is 5, the same as the factor. Another way to say this is that the difference between the *indexes* of any two candidates being crossed out in a given iteration is the same as the factor being used. Also, since the list of candidates contains only odd numbers, the difference between two values is twice as much as the difference between two indexes. So the difference between two numbers being crossed out in a given iteration (e.g., between 25 and 35) is twice the step size or, equivalently, twice the factor being used. You'll see that this pattern holds for all the factors we considered in our example as well.

Finally, we observe that the first number crossed out in each iteration is the square of the prime factor being used. That is, when we're crossing out multiples of 5, the first one that wasn't previously crossed out is 25. This is because all the other multiples were already accounted for by previous primes.

3.3   Implementing and Optimizing the Code

At first glance it seems like our algorithm will need to maintain two arrays: one containing the candidate numbers we're sifting—the "values"—and another containing Boolean flags indicating whether the corresponding number is still there or has been crossed out. However, after a bit of thought it becomes clear that we don't actually need to store the values at all. Most of the values (namely, all the nonprimes) are never used. When we do need a value, we can compute it from its position; we know that the first value is 3 and that each successive value is 2 more than the previous one, so the ith value is $2i + 3$.

So our implementation will store just the Boolean flags in the sieve, using `true` for prime and `false` for composite. We call the process of "crossing out" nonprimes *marking* the sieve. Here's a function we'll use to mark all the non-primes for a given factor:

```
template <RandomAccessIterator I, Integer N>
void mark_sieve(I first, I last, N factor) {
    // assert(first != last)
    *first = false;
    while (last - first > factor) {
        first = first + factor;
        *first = false;
    }
}
```

We are using the convention of "declaring" our template arguments with a description of their requirements. We will discuss these requirements, known as *concepts*, in detail later on in Chapter 10; for now, readers can consult Appendix C as a reference. (If you are not familiar with C++ templates, these are also explained in this appendix.)

As we'll see shortly, we'll call this function with `first` pointing to the Boolean value corresponding to the first "uncrossed-out" multiple of `factor`, which as we saw is always `factor`'s square. For `last`, we'll follow the STL convention of passing an iterator that points just past the last element in our table, so that `last - first` is the number of elements.

*   *   *

Before we see how to sift, we observe the following sifting lemmas:

- The square of the smallest prime factor of a composite number c is less than or equal to c.

- Any composite number less than p^2 is sifted by (i.e., crossed out as a multiple of) a prime less than p.

- When sifting by p, start marking at p^2.

- If we want to sift numbers up to m, stop sifting when $p^2 \geq m$.

We will use the following formulas in our computation:

$$\text{value at index } i: \ \text{value}(i) = 3 + 2i = 2i + 3$$

$$\text{index of value } v: \ \text{index}(v) = \frac{v - 3}{2}$$

step between multiple k and multiple $k + 2$ of value at i:

$$\begin{aligned} \text{step}(i) &= \text{index}((k + 2)(2i + 3)) - \text{index}(k(2i + 3)) \\ &= \text{index}(2ki + 3k + 4i + 6) - \text{index}(2ki + 3k) \\ &= \frac{(2ki + 3k + 4i + 6) - 3}{2} - \frac{(2ki + 3k) - 3}{2} \\ &= \frac{4i + 6}{2} = 2i + 3 \end{aligned}$$

index of square of value at i:

$$\begin{aligned} \text{index}(\text{value}(i)^2) &= \frac{(2i + 3)^2 - 3}{2} \\ &= \frac{4i^2 + 12i + 9 - 3}{2} \\ &= 2i^2 + 6i + 3 \end{aligned}$$

We can now make our first attempt at implementing the sieve:

```
template <RandomAccessIterator I, Integer N>
void sift0(I first, N n) {
    std::fill(first, first + n, true);
    N i(0);
    N index_square(3);
    while (index_square < n) {
        // invariant: index_square = 2i^2 + 6i + 3
        if (first[i]) {                 // if candidate is prime
            mark_sieve(first + index_square,
                       first + n,   // last
                       i + i + 3); // factor
        }
        ++i;
        index_square =  2*i*(i + 3) + 3;
    }
}
```

It might seem that we should pass in a reference to a data structure containing the Boolean sequence, since the sieve works only if we sift the whole thing. But by instead passing an iterator to the beginning of the range, together with its length, we don't constrain which kind of data structure to use. The data could be in an STL container or in a block of memory; we don't need to know. Note that we use the size of the table n rather than the maximum value to sift m.

The variable `index_square` is the index of the first value we want to mark—that is, the square of the current factor. One thing we notice is that we're computing the factor we use to mark the sieve ($i + i + 3$) and other quantities (shown in *slanted text*) every time through the loop. We can hoist common subexpressions out of the loop; the changes are shown in **bold**:

```
template <RandomAccessIterator I, Integer N>
void sift1(I first, N n) {
    I last = first + n;
    std::fill(first, last, true);
    N i(0);
    N index_square(3);
    N factor(3);
    while (index_square < n) {
        // invariant: index_square = 2i^2 + 6i + 3,
        //            factor = 2i + 3
        if (first[i]) {
            mark_sieve(first + index_square, last, factor);
        }
        ++i;
        factor = i + i + 3;
        index_square =  2*i*(i + 3) + 3;
    }
}
```

The astute reader will notice that the `factor` computation is actually slightly worse than before, since it happens every time through the loop, not just on iterations when the `if` test is true. However, we shall see later why making `factor` a separate variable makes sense. A bigger issue is that we still have a relatively expensive operation—the computation of `index_square`, which involves two multiplications. So we will take a cue from compiler optimization and use a technique known as *strength reduction*, which was designed to replace more expensive operations like multiplication with equivalent code that uses less expensive operations like addition.[2] If a compiler can do this automatically, we can certainly do it manually.

Let's look at these computations in more detail. Suppose we replaced

```
factor = i + i + 3;
index_square = 3 + 2*i*(i + 3);
```

with

```
factor += δ_factor;
```

factor += δ_{factor};

---

[2]While multiplication is not necessarily slower than addition on modern processors, the general technique can still lead to using fewer operations.

```
index_square += δindex_square;
```

where δ_{factor} and δ_{index_square} are the differences between successive (ith and $i+1$st) values of `factor` and `index_square`, respectively:

$$\delta_{factor} : \quad (2(i+1)+3) - (2i+3) = 2$$

$$
\begin{aligned}
\delta_{index\_square} : \quad & (2(i+1)^2 + 6(i+1) + 3) - (2i^2 + 6i + 3) \\
& = 2i^2 + 4i + 2 + 6i + 6 + 3 - 2i^2 - 6i - 3 \\
& = 4i + 8 = (2i+3) + (2i+2+3) \\
& = (2i+3) + (2(i+1)+3) \\
& = \text{factor}(i) + \text{factor}(i+1)
\end{aligned}
$$

δ_{factor} is easy; the variables cancel and we get the constant 2. But how did we simplify the expression for δ_{index_square}? We observe that by rearranging the terms, we can express it using something we already have, `factor(i)`, and something we need to compute anyway, `factor(i + 1)`. (When you know you need to compute multiple quantities, it's useful to see if one can be computed in terms of another. This might allow you to do less work.)

With these substitutions, we get our final version of `sift`; again, our improvements are shown in bold:

```
template <RandomAccessIterator I, Integer N>
void sift(I first, N n) {
    I last = first + n;
    std::fill(first, last, true);
    N i(0);
    N index_square(3);
    N factor(3);
    while (index_square < n) {
        // invariant: index_square = 2i^2 + 6i + 3,
        //            factor = 2i + 3
        if (first[i]) {
            mark_sieve(first + index_square, last, factor);
        }
        ++i;
        index_square += factor;
        factor += N(2);
        index_square += factor;
    }
}
```

Exercise 3.2. Time the sieve using different data sizes: bit (using `std::vector<bool>`), `uint8_t`, `uint16_t`, `uint32_t`, `uint64_t`.

Exercise 3.3. Using the sieve, graph the function

$$\pi(n) = \text{number of primes} < n$$

for n up to 10^7 and find its analytic approximation.

We call primes that read the same backward and forward *palindromic primes*. Here we've highlighted the ones up to 1000:

$\boxed{2}\,\boxed{3}\,\boxed{5}\,\boxed{7}\,\boxed{11}$ 13 17 19 23 29 31 37 41 43 47 53 59 61 67 71 73 79 83 89 97 $\boxed{101}$ 103 107 109 113 127 $\boxed{131}$ 137 139 149 $\boxed{151}$ 157 163 167 173 179 $\boxed{181}$ $\boxed{191}$ 193 197 199 211 223 227 229 233 239 241 251 257 263 269 271 277 281 283 293 307 311 $\boxed{313}$ 317 331 337 347 349 $\boxed{353}$ 359 367 $\boxed{373}$ 379 $\boxed{383}$ 389 397 401 409 419 421 431 433 439 443 449 457 461 463 467 479 487 491 499 503 509 521 523 541 547 557 563 569 571 577 587 593 599 601 607 613 617 619 631 641 643 647 653 659 661 673 677 683 691 701 709 719 $\boxed{727}$ 733 739 743 751 $\boxed{757}$ 761 769 773 $\boxed{787}$ 797 809 811 821 823 827 829 839 853 857 859 863 877 881 883 887 907 911 $\boxed{919}$ $\boxed{929}$ 937 941 947 953 967 971 977 983 991 997

Interestingly, there are no palindromic primes between 1000 and 2000:

1009 1013 1019 1021 1031 1033 1039 1049 1051 1061 1063 1069 1087 1091 1093 1097 1103 1109 1117 1123 1129 1151 1153 1163 1171 1181 1187 1193 1201 1213 1217 1223 1229 1231 1237 1249 1259 1277 1279 1283 1289 1291 1297 1301 1303 1307 1319 1321 1327 1361 1367 1373 1381 1399 1409 1423 1427 1429 1433 1439 1447 1451 1453 1459 1471 1481 1483 1487 1489 1493 1499 1511 1523 1531 1543 1549 1553 1559 1567 1571 1579 1583 1597 1601 1607 1609 1613 1619 1621 1627 1637 1657 1663 1667 1669 1693 1697 1699 1709 1721 1723 1733 1741 1747 1753 1759 1777 1783 1787 1789 1801 1811 1823 1831 1847 1861 1867 1871 1873 1877 1879 1889 1901 1907 1913 1931 1933 1949 1951 1973 1979 1987 1993 1997 1999

Exercise 3.4. Are there palindromic primes > 1000? What is the reason for the lack of them in the interval [1000, 2000]? What happens if we change our base to 16? To an arbitrary n?

3.4 Perfect Numbers

As we saw in Section 3.1, the ancient Greeks were interested in all sorts of properties of numbers. One idea they came up with was that of a *perfect* number—

a number that is the sum of its proper divisors.[3] They knew of four perfect numbers:

$$6 = 1 + 2 + 3$$
$$28 = 1 + 2 + 4 + 7 + 14$$
$$496 = 1 + 2 + 4 + 8 + 16 + 31 + 62 + 124 + 248$$
$$8128 = 1 + 2 + 4 + 8 + 16 + 32 + 64 + 127 + 254 + 508 + 1016 + 2032 + 4064$$

Perfect numbers were believed to be related to nature and the structure of the universe. For example, the number 28 was the number of days in the lunar cycle.

What the Greeks really wanted to know was whether there was a way to predict other perfect numbers. They looked at the prime factorizations of the perfect numbers they knew:

$$6 = 2 \cdot 3 = 2^1 \cdot 3$$
$$28 = 4 \cdot 7 = 2^2 \cdot 7$$
$$496 = 16 \cdot 31 = 2^4 \cdot 31$$
$$8128 = 64 \cdot 127 = 2^6 \cdot 127$$

and noticed the following pattern:

$$6 = 2 \cdot 3 = 2^1 \cdot (2^2 - 1)$$
$$28 = 4 \cdot 7 = 2^2 \cdot (2^3 - 1)$$
$$120 = 8 \cdot 15 = 2^3 \cdot (2^4 - 1) \text{ not perfect}$$
$$496 = 16 \cdot 31 = 2^4 \cdot (2^5 - 1)$$
$$2016 = 32 \cdot 63 = 2^5 \cdot (2^6 - 1) \text{ not perfect}$$
$$8128 = 64 \cdot 127 = 2^6 \cdot (2^7 - 1)$$

The result of this expression is perfect when the second term is prime. It was Euclid who presented the proof of this fact around 300 BC.

Theorem 3.3 (Euclid IX, 36):

$$\text{If } \sum_{i=0}^{n} 2^i \text{ is prime then } 2^n \sum_{i=0}^{n} 2^i \text{ is perfect.}$$

---

[3] A proper divisor of a number n is a divisor of n other than n itself.

Useful Formulas

Before we look at the proof, it is useful to remember a couple of algebraic formulas. The first is the *difference of powers*:

$$x^2 - y^2 = (x - y)(x + y)$$
$$x^3 - y^3 = (x - y)(x^2 + xy + y^2)$$
$$\vdots$$
$$x^{n+1} - y^{n+1} = (x - y)(x^n + x^{n-1}y + \cdots + xy^{n-1} + y^n) \qquad (3.1)$$

This result can easily be derived using these two equations:

$$x(x^n + x^{n-1}y + \cdots + xy^{n-1} + y^n) = x^{n+1} + x^n y + x^{n-1}y^2 + \cdots + xy^n \qquad (3.2)$$
$$y(x^n + x^{n-1}y + \cdots + xy^{n-1} + y^n) = \qquad x^n y + x^{n-1}y^2 + \cdots + xy^n + y^{n+1} \quad (3.3)$$

The left and right sides of 3.2 and 3.3 are equal by the distributive law. If we then subtract 3.3 from 3.2, we get 3.1.

The second useful formula is for the *sum of odd powers*:

$$x^{2n+1} + y^{2n+1} = (x + y)(x^{2n} - x^{2n-1}y + \cdots - xy^{2n-1} + y^{2n}) \qquad (3.4)$$

which we can derive by converting the sum to a difference and relying on our previous result:

$$x^{2n+1} + y^{2n+1} = x^{2n+1} - -y^{2n+1}$$
$$= x^{2n+1} - (-y)^{2n+1}$$
$$= (x - (-y))(x^{2n} + x^{2n-1}(-y) + \cdots + (-y)^{2n})$$
$$= (x + y)(x^{2n} - x^{2n-1}y + \cdots - xy^{2n-1} + y^{2n})$$

We can get away with this because -1 to an odd power is still -1. We will rely heavily on both of these formulas in the proofs ahead.

Now we know that for $n > 0$

$$\sum_{i=0}^{n-1} 2^i = 2^n - 1 \qquad (3.5)$$

by the difference of powers formula:

$$2^n - 1 = (2 - 1)(2^{n-1} + 2^{n-2} + \cdots + 2 + 1)$$

(or just think of the binary number you get when you add powers of 2).

Exercise 3.5. Using Equation 3.1, prove that if $2^n - 1$ is prime, then n is prime.

We are going to prove Euclid's theorem the way the great German mathematician Carl Gauss did. (We'll learn more about Gauss in Chapter 8.) First, we will use Equation 3.5, substituting $2^n - 1$ for both occurrences of $\sum_{i=0}^{n-1} 2^i$ in Euclid's theorem, to restate the theorem like this:

If $2^n - 1$ is prime, then $2^{n-1}(2^n - 1)$ is perfect.

Next, we define $\sigma(n)$ to be the sum of the divisors of n. If the prime factorization of n is

$$n = p_1^{a_1} p_2^{a_2} \cdots p_m^{a_m}$$

then the set of all divisors consists of every possible combination of the prime divisors raised to every possible power up to a_i. For example, $24 = 2^3 \cdot 3^1$, so the divisors are $\{2^0 3^0, 2^1 3^0, 2^2 3^0, 2^3 3^0, 2^0 3^1, 2^1 3^1, 2^2 3^1, 2^3 3^1\}$. Their sum is

$$2^0 3^0 + 2^1 3^0 + 2^2 3^0 + 2^3 3^0 + 2^0 3^1 + 2^1 3^1 + 2^2 3^1 + 2^3 3^1 = (2^0 + 2^1 + 2^2 + 2^3)(3^0 + 3^1)$$

That is, we can write the sum of the divisors for any number n as a product of sums:

$$\sigma(n) = \prod_{i=1}^{m}(1 + p_i + p_i^2 + \cdots + p_i^{a_i})$$

$$= \prod_{i=1}^{m} \frac{p_i - 1}{p_i - 1}(1 + p_i + p_i^2 + \cdots + p_i^{a_i})$$

$$= \prod_{i=1}^{m} \frac{(p_i - 1)(1 + p_i + p_i^2 + \cdots + p_i^{a_i})}{p_i - 1}$$

$$= \prod_{i=1}^{m} \frac{p_i^{a_i+1} - 1}{p_i - 1} \tag{3.6}$$

where the last line relies on using the difference of powers formula to simplify the numerator. (In this example, and for the rest of the book, when we use p as an integer variable in our proofs, we assume it's a prime, unless we say otherwise.)

Exercise 3.6. Prove that if n and m are *coprime* (have no common prime factors), then

$$\sigma(nm) = \sigma(n)\sigma(m)$$

(Another way to say this is that σ is a *multiplicative function*.)

We now define $\alpha(n)$, the *aliquot sum*, as follows:

$$\alpha(n) = \sigma(n) - n$$

In other words, the aliquot sum is the sum of all *proper* divisors of n—all the divisors except n itself.

Now we're ready for the proof of Theorem 3.3, also known as Euclid IX, 36:

$$\text{If } 2^n - 1 \text{ is prime, then } 2^{n-1}(2^n - 1) \text{ is perfect.}$$

Proof. Let $q = 2^{n-1}(2^n - 1)$. We know 2 is prime, and the theorem's condition is that $2^n - 1$ is prime, so $2^{n-1}(2^n - 1)$ is already a prime factorization of the form $n = p_1^{a_1} p_2^{a_2} \cdots p_m^{a_m}$, where $m = 2, p_1 = 2, a_1 = n - 1, p_2 = 2^n - 1$, and $a_2 = 1$. Using the sum of divisors formula (Equation 3.6):

$$\sigma(q) = \frac{2^{(n-1)+1} - 1}{1} \cdot \frac{(2^n - 1)^2 - 1}{(2^n - 1) - 1}$$

$$= (2^n - 1) \cdot \frac{(2^n - 1)^2 - 1}{(2^n - 1) - 1} \cdot \frac{(2^n - 1) + 1}{(2^n - 1) + 1}$$

$$= (2^n - 1) \cdot \frac{((2^n - 1)(2^n - 1) - 1)((2^n - 1) + 1)}{((2^n - 1)(2^n - 1) - 1)}$$

$$= (2^n - 1)((2^n - 1) + 1)$$

$$= 2^n(2^n - 1) = 2 \cdot 2^{n-1}(2^n - 1) = 2q$$

Then

$$\alpha(q) = \sigma(q) - q = 2q - q = q$$

That is, q is perfect. □

We can think of Euclid's theorem as saying that if a number has a certain form, then it is perfect. An interesting question is whether the converse is true: if a number is perfect, does it have the form $2^{n-1}(2^n - 1)$? In the 18th century, Euler proved that if a perfect number is even, then it has this form. He was not able to prove the more general result that *every* perfect number is of that form. Even today, this is an unsolved problem; we don't know if any odd perfect numbers exist.

Exercise 3.7. Prove that every even perfect number is a triangular number.

Exercise 3.8. Prove that the sum of the reciprocals of the divisors of a perfect number is always 2. Example:

$$1 + \frac{1}{2} + \frac{1}{3} + \frac{1}{6} = 2$$

3.5 The Pythagorean Program

For Pythagoreans, mathematics was not about abstract symbol manipulation, as it is often viewed today. Instead, it was the science of numbers and space—the two fundamental perceptible aspects of our reality. In addition to their focus on understanding *figurate* numbers (such as square, oblong, and triangular numbers), they believed that there was discrete structure to space. Their challenge, then, was to provide a way to ground geometry in numbers—essentially, to have a unified theory of mathematics based on positive integers.

To do this, they came up with the idea that one line segment could be "measured" by another:

Definition 3.1. A segment *V* is a **measure** of a segment *A* if and only if *A* can be represented as a finite concatenation of copies of *V*.

A measure must be small enough that an exact integral number of copies produces the desired segment; there are no "fractional" measures. Of course, different measures might be used for different segments. If one wanted to use the same measure for two segments, it had to be a *common measure*:

Definition 3.2. A segment *V* is a **common measure** of segments *A* and *B* if and only if it is a measure of both.

For any given situation, the Pythagoreans believed there is a common measure for all the objects of interest. Therefore, space could be represented discretely.

$$*\quad*\quad*$$

Since there could be many common measures, they also came up with the idea of the *greatest common measure*:

Definition 3.3. A segment *V* is the **greatest common measure** of *A* and *B* if it is greater than any other common measure of *A* and *B*.

The Pythagoreans also recognized several properties of greatest common measure (GCM), which we represent in modern notation as follows:

$$\gcm(a, a) = a \tag{3.7}$$
$$\gcm(a, b) = \gcm(a, a + b) \tag{3.8}$$
$$b < a \implies \gcm(a, b) = \gcm(a - b, b) \tag{3.9}$$
$$\gcm(a, b) = \gcm(b, a) \tag{3.10}$$

Using these properties, they came up with the most important procedure in Greek mathematics—perhaps in all mathematics: a way to compute the greatest common measure of two segments. The computational machinery of the Greeks consisted of ruler and compass operations on line segments. Using C++ notation, we might write the procedure like this, using `line_segment` as a type:

```
line_segment gcm(line_segment a, line_segment b) {
    if (a == b)      return a;
    if (b < a)       return gcm(a - b, b);
 /* if (a < b) */    return gcm(a, b - a);
}
```

This code makes use of the *trichotomy law*: the fact that if you have two values a and b of the same totally ordered type, then either $a = b$, $a < b$, or $a > b$.

Let's look at an example. What's gcm(196, 42)?

a	b					
$196 > 42,$	gcm(196, 42)	$=$	gcm(196 − 42, 42)	$=$	gcm(154, 42)
$154 > 42,$	gcm(154, 42)	$=$	gcm(154 − 42, 42)	$=$	gcm(112, 42)
$112 > 42,$	gcm(112, 42)	$=$	gcm(112 − 42, 42)	$=$	gcm(70, 42)
$70 > 42,$	gcm(70, 42)	$=$	gcm(70 − 42, 42)	$=$	gcm(28, 42)
$28 < 42,$	gcm(28, 42)	$=$	gcm(28, 42 − 28)	$=$	gcm(28, 14)
$28 > 14,$	gcm(28, 14)	$=$	gcm(28 − 14, 14)	$=$	gcm(14, 14)
$14 = 14,$	gcm(14, 14)	$=$	14

So we're done: gcm(196, 42) = 14.

Of course, when we say gcm(196, 42), we really mean GCM of segments with length 196 and 42, but for the examples in this chapter, we'll just use the integers as shorthand.

We're going to use versions of this algorithm for the next few chapters, so it's important to understand it and have a good feel for how it works. You may want to try computing a few more examples by hand to convince yourself.

3.6   A Fatal Flaw in the Program

Greek mathematicians found that the *well-ordering principle*—the fact that any set of natural numbers has a smallest element—provided a powerful proof technique. To prove that something does not exist, prove that if it did exist, a smaller one would also exist.

Using this logic, the Pythagoreans discovered a proof that undermined their entire program.[4] We're going to use a 19th-century reconstruction of this proof by George Chrystal.

Theorem 3.4: *There is no segment that can measure both the side and the diagonal of a square.*

---

[4]We don't know if Pythagoras himself made this discovery, or one of his early followers.

Proof. Assume the contrary, that there were a segment that could measure both the side and the diagonal of some square.[5] Let us take the smallest such square for this segment:

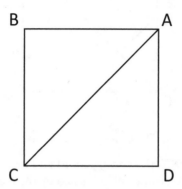

Using a ruler and compass,[6] we can construct a segment $\overline{AF}$ with the same length as $\overline{AB}$, and then create a segment starting at F and perpendicular to $\overline{AC}$.

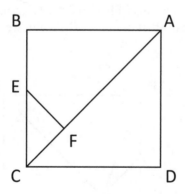

$$\overline{AB} = \overline{AF} \ \wedge \ \overline{AC} \perp \overline{EF}$$

Now we construct two more perpendicular segments, $\overline{CG}$ and $\overline{EG}$:

---

[5]This is an example of proof by contradiction. For more about this proof technique, see Appendix B.1.

[6]Although modern readers may think of a ruler as being used to measure distances, for Euclid it was only a way to draw straight lines. For this reason, some people prefer the term *straightedge* to describe Euclid's instrument. Similarly, although a modern compass can be fixed to measure equal distances, Euclid's compass was used only to draw circles with a given radius; it was collapsible, so it did not preserve distances once lifted.

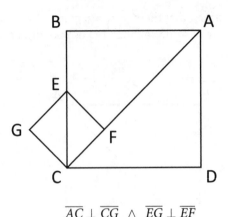

$$\overline{AC} \perp \overline{CG} \ \wedge \ \overline{EG} \perp \overline{EF}$$

We know that $\angle CFE = 90°$ (by construction) and that $\angle ECF = 45°$ (since it's the same as $\angle BCA$, which is the angle formed by the diagonal of a square, and therefore is half of $90°$). We also know that the three angles of a triangle sum to $180°$. Therefore

$$\angle CEF = 180° - \angle CFE - \angle ECF = 180° - 90° - 45° = 45°$$

So $\angle CEF = \angle ECF$, which means CEF is an isosceles triangle, so the sides opposite equal angles are equal—that is, $\overline{CF} = \overline{EF}$. Finally, we add one more segment $\overline{BF}$:

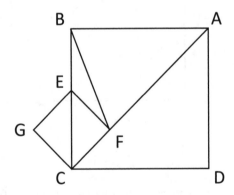

Triangle ABF is also isosceles, with $\angle ABF = \angle AFB$, since we constructed $\overline{AB} = \overline{AF}$. And $\angle ABC = \angle AFE$, since both were constructed with perpendiculars. So

$$\angle ABC - \angle ABF = \angle AFE - \angle AFB$$
$$\angle EBF = \angle EFB$$
$$\implies \overline{BE} = \overline{EF}$$

Now, we know $\overline{AC}$ is measurable since that's part of our premise, and we know $\overline{AF}$ is measurable, since it's the same as $\overline{AB}$, which is also measurable by our premise. So their difference $\overline{CF} = \overline{AC} - \overline{AF}$ is also measurable. Since we just showed that $\triangle CEF$ and $\triangle BEF$ are both isosceles,

$$\overline{CF} = \overline{EF} = \overline{BE}$$

we know $\overline{BC}$ is measurable, again by our premise, and we've just shown that $\overline{CF}$, and therefore $\overline{BE}$, is measurable. So $\overline{EC} = \overline{BC} - \overline{BE}$ is measurable.

We now have a smaller square whose side ($\overline{EF}$) and diagonal ($\overline{EC}$) are both measurable by our common unit. But our original square was chosen to be the smallest for which the relationship held—a contradiction. So our original assumption was wrong, and *there is no segment that can measure both the side and the diagonal of a square.* If you try to find one, you'll be at it forever—our `line_segment_gcm(a, b)` procedure will not terminate. □

To put it another way, the ratio of the diagonal and the side of a square cannot be expressed as a rational number (the ratio of two integers). Today we would say that with this proof, the Pythagoreans had discovered irrational numbers, and specifically that $\sqrt{2}$ is irrational.

The discovery of irrational numbers was unbelievably shocking. It undermined the Pythagoreans's entire program; it meant that geometry could not be grounded in numbers. So they did what many organizations do when faced with bad news: they swore everyone to secrecy. When one of the order leaked the story, legend has it that the gods punished him by sinking the ship carrying him, drowning all on board.

* * *

Eventually, Pythagoras' followers came up with a new strategy. If they couldn't unify mathematics on a foundation of numbers, they would unify it on a foundation of geometry. This was the origin of the ruler-and-compass constructions still used today to teach geometry; no numbers are used or needed.

Later mathematicians came up with an alternate, number-theoretic proof of the irrationality of $\sqrt{2}$. One version was included as proposition 117 in some editions of Book X of Euclid's *Elements*. While the proof predates Euclid, it was added to *Elements* some time after the book's original publication. In any case, it is an important proof:

Theorem 3.5: $\sqrt{2}$ *is irrational.*

Proof. Assume $\sqrt{2}$ is rational. Then it can be expressed as the ratio of two integers m and n, where m/n is irreducible:

$$\frac{m}{n} = \sqrt{2}$$

$$\left(\frac{m}{n}\right)^2 = 2$$

$$m^2 = 2n^2$$

m^2 is even, which means that m is also even,[7] so we can write it as 2 times some number u, substitute the result into the preceding equation, and do a bit more algebraic manipulation:

$$m = 2u$$

$$(2u)^2 = 2n^2$$

$$4u^2 = 2n^2$$

$$2u^2 = n^2$$

n^2 is even, which means that n is also even. But if m and n are both even, then m/n is not irreducible—a contradiction. So our assumption is false; there is no way to represent $\sqrt{2}$ as the ratio of two integers.   □

3.7   Thoughts on the Chapter

The ancient Greeks' fascination with "shapes" of numbers and other properties such as prime and perfect were the basis of the mathematical field of number theory. Some of the algorithms they used, such as the Sieve of Eratosthenes, are still very elegant, though we saw how to improve their efficiency further by using some modern optimization techniques.

*   *   *

Toward the end of the chapter, we saw two different proofs that $\sqrt{2}$ is irrational, one geometric and one algebraic. The fact that we have two completely different proofs of the same result is good. It is actually essential for mathematicians to look for multiple proofs of the same mathematical fact, since it increases their confidence in the result. For example, Gauss spent much of his career coming up with multiple proofs for one important theorem, the quadratic reciprocity law.

---

[7]This is easily shown: The product of two odd numbers is an odd number, so if m were not even, m^2 could not be even. Euclid proved this and many other results about odd and even numbers earlier in *Elements*.

The discovery of irrational numbers emerged from the Pythagoreans' attempts to represent continuous reality with discrete numbers. While at first glance we might think they were naive to believe that they could accomplish this, computer scientists do the same thing today—we approximate the real world with binary numbers. In fact, the tension between continuous and discrete has remained a central theme in mathematics through the present day, and will probably be with us forever. But rather than being a problem, this tension has actually been the source of great progress and revolutionary insights.

4

four

Euclid's Algorithm

The whole structure of number theory rests on a single foundation,
namely the algorithm for finding the greatest common divisor.

Dirichlet, *Lectures on Number Theory*

In the previous chapter, we met Pythagoras and the secretive order he founded to study astronomy, geometry, number theory, and music. While the Pythagoreans' failure to find a common measure of the side and the diagonal of a square ended the dream of reducing the world to numbers, the idea of a greatest common measure (GCM) turned out to be an important one for mathematics—and eventually for programming. In this chapter, we'll introduce an ancient algorithm for GCM that we'll be exploring throughout the rest of the book.

4.1 Athens and Alexandria

To set the stage for the discovery of this algorithm, we now turn to one of the most amazing times and places in history: Athens in the 5th century BC. For 150 years following the miraculous defeat of the invading Persians in the battles of Marathon, Salamis, and Platea, Athens became the center of culture, learning, and science, laying the foundations for much of Western civilization.

It was in the middle of this period of Athenian cultural dominance that Plato founded his famous Academy. Although we think of Plato today as a philosopher, the center of the Academy's program was the study of mathematics. Among Plato's discoveries were what we now call the five *Platonic solids*—the only convex three-dimensional shapes in which every face is an identical regular polygon.

Plato (429 BC–347 BC)

Plato was born into one of the ancient noble families of Athens. As a young man, he became a follower of Socrates, one of the founders of philosophy, who taught and learned by questioning, especially examining one's own life and assumptions.

Socrates was ugly, bug-eyed, shabbily dressed, old, and only a lowly stonemason by trade, but his ideas were revolutionary. At the time, self-proclaimed wise men ("Sophists") promised to teach their students to take any side of an argument and manipulate the voters. Socrates challenged the Sophists, questioning their supposed wisdom and making them look foolish. While the Sophists charged substantial fees to share their knowledge, Socrates' followers received his training for free. To this day, the technique Socrates introduced of asking questions to get at the truth is known as the Socratic method. Although Socrates was admired by some, and some of his followers went on to be prominent leaders, he was generally considered to be a notorious troublemaker, and was publicly ridiculed in Aristophanes' famous play *Clouds*. Eventually, in 399 BC, Socrates was put on trial for corrupting the city's youth, and was condemned to death by poisoning.

Plato was profoundly influenced by Socrates, and most of his own writings take the form of dialogues between Socrates and various opponents. Plato was devastated by Socrates' execution, and by the fact that a society would destroy its wisest and most just member. He left Athens in despair, studying for a while with the priests in Egypt, and later learning mathematics from the Pythagoreans in southern Italy. A decade or so later, he returned to Athens and founded what is essentially the world's first university at a place called the *Academy*, named after an ancient hero Academus. Unlike the secret teachings of the Pythagoreans, the Academy's program of study was public and available to everyone: men and women, Greeks and barbarians, free and slave.

Many of Plato's dialogues, such as *Apology*, *Phaedo*, and *Symposium*, are as beautifully written as any poetry. Although Plato's best-known works today are concerned with a variety of ethical and metaphysical issues, mathematics played a central role in the curriculum of the Academy. In fact, Plato had the inscription "Let no one ignorant of geometry enter" written over the entrance. He gathered many top mathematicians of the time to teach at the Academy and develop a uniform course of study. While Plato did not leave us any mathematical works, many mathematical ideas are spread throughout his dialogues, and one of them, *Meno*, is designed to demonstrate that mathematical reasoning is innate.

On several occasions, Plato traveled to Syracuse to influence the local ruler to introduce a just society. He was unsuccessful; in fact, one of the trips annoyed the ruler so much that he arranged for Plato to be sold into slavery. Fortunately, the philosopher was quickly ransomed by an admirer.

It is hard to exaggerate the influence of Plato on European thought. As the prominent British philosopher Whitehead said, "The safest general characterization of the European philosophical tradition is that it consists of a series of footnotes to Plato."

Athenian culture spread throughout the Mediterranean, especially during the reign of Alexander the Great. Among his achievements, Alexander founded the Egyptian city of Alexandria (named for himself), which became the new center of research and learning. More than a thousand scholars worked in what we would now think of as a research institute, the *Mouseion*—the "Institution of the Muses"—from which we get our word "museum." The scholars' patrons were the Greek kings of Egypt, the Ptolemys, who paid their salaries and provided free room and board. Part of the Mouseion was the Library of Alexandria, which was given the task of collecting all the world's knowledge. Supposedly containing 500,000 scrolls, the library kept a large staff of scribes busy copying, translating, and editing scrolls.

*   *   *

It was during this period that Euclid, one of the scholars at the Mouseion, wrote his *Elements*, one of the most important books in the history of mathematics. *Elements* includes derivations of fundamental results in geometry and number theory, as well as the ruler-and-compass constructions that students still learn today.

Euclid (flourished ca. 300 BC)

We know very little about Euclid—not even exactly when he lived. What we do know is that he took geometry very seriously. According to a story told by the philosopher Proclus Diadochus, one of Plato's later successors as head of the Academy: "Ptolemy [the king of Egypt] once asked Euclid whether there was any shorter way to a knowledge of geometry than by study of the *Elements*, whereupon Euclid answered that there was no royal road to geometry." It is probable that Euclid studied at the Academy some time after Plato's death and brought the mathematics he learned to Alexandria.

Although we know almost nothing else about Euclid's life, we do know about his work. His *Elements* incorporated mathematical results and proofs from several existing texts. A careful reading reveals some of these layers; for example, since ancient times the work on the theory of proportions in Book V has generally been believed to be based on the work of Plato's student, Eudoxus. But it was Euclid who wove these ideas together to form a carefully crafted coherent story. In Book I, he starts with the fundamental tools for geometric construction with ruler and compass and ends with what we now call the Pythagorean Theorem (Proposition I, 47). In the 13th and final book, he shows how to construct the five Platonic solids, and proves that they are the only convex regular polyhedra (bodies whose faces are congruent, regular polygons) that exist.

Euclid's *Elements* shows a sense of purpose unique in the history of mathematics. Each proposition and proof is there for a reason; no unnecessary results are presented. However beautiful, no theorem is presented unless it is needed for the larger story. Euclid also prefers proofs that construct as many useful results as possible with the fewest ruler-and-compass operations. His approach is reminiscent of a modern programmer striving for minimal elegant algorithms.

From its publication around 300 BC until the beginning of the 20th century, Euclid's *Elements* was used as the basis of mathematical education. It was not only scientists and mathematicians who studied Euclid; great political leaders such as Thomas Jefferson and Abraham Lincoln also admired and studied *Elements* throughout their lives. Even now, many people believe that students would still benefit from this approach.

4.2   Euclid's Greatest Common Measure Algorithm

Book X of Euclid's *Elements* contained a concise treatment of *incommensurable quantities*:

> **Proposition 2.** *If, when the less of two unequal magnitudes is continually subtracted in turn from the greater, that which is left never measures the one before it, then the two magnitudes are incommensurable.*

Essentially, Euclid is saying what we observed earlier in the chapter: if our procedure for computing greatest common measure never terminates, then there is no common measure.

Euclid then goes on to explicitly describe the algorithm and prove that it computes the GCM. This diagram may be useful in following the proof:

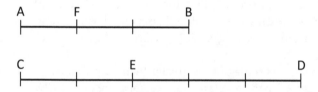

Since this is the first algorithm termination proof in history, we're including the entire text, using Sir Thomas Heath's translation:

> **Proposition 3.** *Given two commensurable magnitudes, to find their greatest common measure.*

Proof.

> Let the two given commensurable magnitudes be AB, CD of which AB is the less; thus it is required to find the greatest common measure of AB, CD.
>
> Now the magnitude AB either measures CD or it does not.
>
> If then it measures it—and it measures itself also—AB is a common measure of AB, CD.
>
> And it is manifest that it is also the greatest; for a greater magnitude than the magnitude AB will not measure AB.
>
> Next, let AB not measure CD.

Then, if the less be continually subtracted in turn from the greater, that which is left over will sometime measure the one before it, because AB, CD are not incommensurable; [cf. X. 2] let AB, measuring ED, leave EC less than itself, let EC, measuring FB, leave AF less than itself, and let AF measure CE.

Since, then, AF measures CE, while CE measures FB, therefore AF will also measure FB.

But it measures itself also; therefore AF will also measure the whole AB.

But AB measures DE; therefore AF will also measure ED.

But it measures CE also; therefore it also measures the whole CD.

Therefore AF is a common measure of AB, CD.

I say next that it is also the greatest.

For, if not, there will be some magnitude greater than AF which will measure AB, CD.

Let it be G.

Since then G measures AB, while AB measures ED, therefore G will also measure ED.

But it measures the whole CD also; therefore G will also measure the remainder CE.

But CE measures FB; therefore G will also measure FB.

But it measures the whole AB also, and it will therefore measure the remainder AF, the greater [measuring] the less: which is impossible.

Therefore no magnitude greater than AF will measure AB, CD; therefore AF is the greatest common measure of AB, CD.

Therefore the greatest common measure of the two given commensurable magnitudes AB, CD has been found.   □

This "continual subtraction" approach to GCM is known as *Euclid's algorithm* (or sometimes *the Euclidean algorithm*). It's an iterative version of the gcm function we saw in Chapter 3. As we did before, we will use C++-like notation to show its implementation:

```
line_segment gcm0(line_segment a, line_segment b) {
    while (a != b) {
        if (b < a) a = a - b;
        else       b = b - a;
    }
    return a;
}
```

In Euclid's world, segments cannot be zero, so we do not need this as a precondition.

Exercise 4.1. gcm0 is inefficient when one segment is much longer than the other. Come up with a more efficient implementation. Remember you can't introduce operations that couldn't be done by ruler-and-compass construction.

Exercise 4.2. Prove that if a segment measures two other segments, then it measures their greatest common measure.

To work toward a more efficient version of line_segment_gcm, we'll start by rearranging, checking for $b < a$ as long as we can:

```
line_segment gcm1(line_segment a,  line_segment b) {
    while (a != b) {
        while (b < a) a = a - b;
        std::swap(a, b);
    }
    return a;
}
```

We could avoid a swap in the case where $a = b$, but that would require an extra test, and we're not quite ready to optimize the code anyway. Instead, we observe that the inner while loop is computing the *remainder* of a and b. Let's factor out that piece of functionality:

```
line_segment segment_remainder(line_segment a, line_segment b) {
    while (b < a) a = a - b;
    return a;
}
```

How do we know the loop will terminate? It's not as obvious as it might appear. For example, if our definition of line_segment included the half line starting at a point and continuing infinitely in one direction, the code would not terminate. The required assumptions are encapsulated in the following axiom:

Axiom of Archimedes: *For any quantities a and b, there is a natural number n such that $a \leq nb$.*

Essentially, what this says is that there are no infinite quantities.

*   *   *

Now we can rewrite our GCM function with a call to `segment_remainder`:

```
line_segment gcm(line_segment a, line_segment b) {
    while (a != b) {
        a = segment_remainder(a, b);
        std::swap(a, b);
    }
    return a;
}
```

So far we have refactored our code but not improved its performance. Most of the work is done in `segment_remainder`. To speed up that function, we will use the same idea as in Egyptian multiplication—doubling and halving our quantities. This requires knowing something about the relationship of doubled segments to remainder:

Lemma 4.1 (Recursive Remainder Lemma): *If $r = $ segment_remainder$(a, 2b)$, then*

$$\text{segment\_remainder}(a, b) = \begin{cases} r & \text{if } r \le b \\ r - b & \text{if } r > b \end{cases}$$

Suppose, for example, that we wanted to find the remainder of some number n divided by 10. We'll try to take the remainder of n divided by 20. If the result is less than 10, we're done. If the result is between 11 and 20, we'll take away 10 from the result and get the remainder that way.

Using this strategy, we can write our faster function:

```
line_segment fast_segment_remainder(line_segment a,
                                     line_segment b) {
    if (a <= b) return a;
    if (a - b <= b) return a - b;
    a = fast_segment_remainder(a, b + b);
    if (a <= b) return a;
    return a - b;
}
```

It's recursive, but it's a less intuitive form of *upward* recursion. In most recursive programs, we go down from n to $n - 1$ when we recurse; here, we're making our argument *bigger* every time, going from n to $2n$. It's not obvious where the work is done, but it works.

Let's look at an example. Suppose we have a segment *a* of length 45 and a segment *b* of length 6, and we want to find the remainder of *a* divided by *b*:

> $a = 45, b = 6.$
> $a \leq b?$ (45 ≤ 6?) No.
> $a - b \leq b?$ (39 ≤ 6?) No.
> Recurse:
>> $a = 45, b = 12$
>> $a \leq b?$ (45 ≤ 12?) No.
>> $a - b \leq b?$ (33 ≤ 12?) No.
>> Recurse:
>>> $a = 45, b = 24$
>>> $a \leq b?$ (45 ≤ 24?) No.
>>> $a - b \leq b?$ (21 ≤ 24?) Yes, return $a - b = 21$
>> $a \leftarrow 21$
>> $a \leq b?$ (21 ≤ 12?) No.
>> return $a - b = 9$
> $a \leftarrow 9$
> $a \leq b?$ (9 ≤ 6?) No.
> return $a - b = 9 - 6 = 3$

Remember that since the Greeks had no notion of a zero-length segment, their remainders were in the range $[1, n]$.

We still have the overhead of recursion, so we'll eventually want to come up with an iterative solution, but we'll put that aside for now.

Finally, we can plug this code into our GCM function, providing a solution to Exercise 4.1:

```
line_segment fast_segment_gcm(line_segment a, line_segment b) {
    while (a != b) {
        a = fast_segment_remainder(a, b);
        std::swap(a, b);
    }
    return a;
}
```

Of course, no matter how fast it is, this code will still never terminate if *a* and *b* do not have a common measure.

4.3   A Millennium without Mathematics

As we have seen, ancient Greece was a source of several centuries of astonishing mathematical developments. By the 3rd century BC, mathematics was a flourishing field of study, with Archimedes (best known today for a story about discovering the principle of buoyancy in his bathtub) its most dominant figure. Unfortunately, the rise of Roman power led to a stagnation in Western mathematics that would last for almost 1500 years. While the Romans built great works of engineering, they were generally uninterested in advancing the mathematics that made these structures possible. As the great Roman statesman Cicero said in his *Tusculan Disputations*:

> Among the Greeks geometry was held in highest honor; nothing could outshine mathematics. But we have limited the usefulness of this art to measuring and calculating.

While there were Greek mathematicians working in Roman times, it is a remarkable fact that there is no record of any original mathematical text written in Latin (the language of ancient Rome) at that time.

The period of history that followed was not kind to the formerly great societies of Europe. In Byzantium, the Greek-speaking Eastern remnant of the former Roman Empire, mathematics was still studied, but innovation declined. By the 6th to 7th centuries, scholars still read Euclid, but usually just the first book of *Elements*; Latin translations didn't even bother to include the proofs. By the end of the first millennium, if you were a European who wanted to study mathematics, you had to go to cities like Cairo, Baghdad, or Cordoba in the realm of the Arabs.

Other Mathematical Traditions

Throughout ancient times, mathematics developed in many parts of the world. Civilization depends on mathematics. All major civilizations developed number systems, which were a fundamental requirement for two critical civic activities: collecting taxes and computing calendars to determine cultivation dates.

Furthermore, all major civilizations developed common mathematical concepts, such as Pythagorean triples (sets of three integers a, b, c where $a^2 + b^2 = c^2$). While some have argued that this implies a common Neolithic source of mathematical knowledge that spread throughout the world, there is no evidence for this claim. Today it seems more likely that this is simply the mathematical equivalent of convergent evolution in biology, where the same characteristics evolve independently in unrelated species. The fact that these same mathematical ideas were rediscovered independently suggests their fundamental nature.

Many civilizations developed important mathematical traditions at some point in their history. For example, in China, 3rd-century mathematician and poet Liu Hui wrote important commentaries on an earlier book, *Nine Chapters on the Mathematical Art*, and extended the work. Among other discoveries, he demonstrated that the value of π must be greater than 3, and provided several geometric techniques for surveying. In India, 5th-century mathematician and astronomer Aryabhata wrote a foundational text called the *Aryabhatiya*, which included algorithms for computing square and cube roots, as well as geometric techniques. Ideas of Indian mathematics were further developed by Arab, Persian, and Jewish scholars, all writing in Arabic, who in turn heavily influenced the rebirth of European mathematics in the early 13th century.

Computer science emerged from this reinvigorated European mathematics, so this is what we are focusing on. As programmers, we are all heirs of this tradition.

4.4   The Strange History of Zero

The next development in the history of Euclid's algorithm required something the Greeks didn't have: zero. You may have heard that ancient societies had no notion of zero, and that it was invented by Indians or Arabs, but this is only partially correct. In fact, Babylonian astronomers were using zero as early as 1500 BC, together with a positional number system. However, their number system used base 60. The rest of their society used base 10—for example, in commerce—without either zero or positional notation. Amazingly, this state of affairs persisted for *centuries*. Greek astronomers eventually learned the Babylonian system and used it (still in base 60) for their trigonometric computations, but again, this approach was used only for this one application and was unknown to the rest of society. (It was also these Greek astronomers who started using the Greek letter omicron, which looks just like our letter "O," to represent zero.)

What is particularly surprising about the lack of zero outside of astronomy is that it persisted despite the fact that the *abacus* was well known and commonly used for commerce in nearly every ancient civilization. Abaci consist of stones or beads arranged in columns; the columns correspond to 1s, 10s, 100s, and so on, and each bead represents one unit of a given power of 10. In other words, ancient societies used a device that represented numbers in base 10 positional notation, yet there was no commonly used written representation of zero until 1000 years later.

The unification of a written form of zero with a decimal positional notation is due to early Indian mathematicians sometime around the 6th century AD. It then spread to Persia between the 6th and 9th centuries AD. Arab scholars learned the technique and spread it across their empire, from Baghdad in the east to Cordoba in the west. There is no evidence that zero was known anywhere in Europe outside this empire (even in the rest of Spain); 300 years would pass before this innovation crossed from one culture to the other.

The breakthrough came in 1203 when Leonardo Pisano, also known as Fibonacci, published *Liber Abaci* ("The Book of Calculation"). In addition to introducing zero and positional decimal notation, this astonishing book described to Europeans, for the first time, the standard algorithms for doing arithmetic that we are now taught in elementary school: long addition, long subtraction, long multiplication, and long division. With one stroke, Leonardo brought mathematics back to Europe.

Leonardo Pisano (1170–ca. 1240)

The Italian city of Pisa, which today is landlocked, was a major port and naval power in the 12th and 13th century. It competed with Venice as the dominant trading center in the Mediterranean. Thousands of Pisan traders crisscrossed the sea routes to the Middle East, Byzantium, North Africa, and Spain, and the Pisan government sent trade representatives to major cities to ensure their success. One of these representatives, Guglielmo Bonacci, was posted to Algeria. He decided to bring his son Leonardo along, a decision that changed the course of mathematical history.

Leonardo learned "Hindu digits" from the Arabs, and continued his studies during business trips to Egypt, Syria, Sicily, Greece, and Provence. In his book *Liber Abaci*, he would go on to introduce their innovations (including zero) to Europe. But *Liber Abaci* was not just a translation of other people's work: it was a first-class mathematical treatise with many fundamental new contributions. Leonardo would go on to write several more books on various branches of mathematics, including some of the most important mathematical developments in centuries.

He called himself Leonardo Pisano ("Leonardo the Pisan"), although since the 19th century he has usually been known as Fibonacci, an abbreviation of *filius Bonacci* ("son of Bonacci").

Leonardo's fame reached the Holy Roman Emperor, Frederick II, a great intellectual conversant in many languages and a patron of science and mathematics, whose court was in Palermo, Sicily. Frederick came to Pisa and organized a challenge to Leonardo by his court mathematicians. Leonardo performed well and impressed the visiting dignitaries. Toward the end of his life, the city of Pisa gave him a salary as a reward for his great contributions.

Leonardo Pisano's later work *Liber Quadratorum* ("The Book of Squares"), published in 1225, is probably the greatest work on number theory in the time span between Diophantus 1000 years earlier and the great French mathematician Pierre de Fermat 400 years later. Here is one of the problems from the book:

Exercise 4.3 (easy). Prove that $\sqrt[3]{16} + \sqrt[3]{54} = \sqrt[3]{250}$.

Why was a problem like this difficult for the Greeks? They had no terminating procedure for computing cube roots (in fact, it was later proven that no such process exists). So from their perspective, the problem starts out: "First, execute a nonterminating procedure...."

Leonardo's insight will be familiar to any middle-school algebra student, but it was revolutionary in the 13th century. Basically, what he said was, "Even though I don't know how to compute $\sqrt[3]{2}$, I'll just pretend I do and assign it an arbitrary symbol."

Here's another example of the kind of problem Leonardo solved:

Exercise 4.4. Prove the following proposition from *Liber Quadratorum*: For any odd square number x, there is an even square number y, such that $x + y$ is a square number.

Exercise 4.5 (hard). Prove the following proposition from *Liber Quadratorum*: If x and y are both sums of two squares, then so is their product xy. (This is an important result that Fermat builds on.)

4.5 Remainder and Quotient Algorithms

Once zero was widely used in mathematics, it actually took centuries longer before it occurred to anyone that a segment could have zero length—specifically, the segment $\overline{AA}$.

Zero-length segments force us to rethink our GCM and remainder procedures, because Archimedes' axiom no longer holds—we can add a zero-length segment forever, and we'll never exceed a nonzero segment. So we'll allow the first argument a to be zero, but we need a precondition to ensure that the second argument b is not zero. Having zero also lets us shift our remainders to the range $[0, n-1]$, which will be crucial for modular arithmetic and other developments. Here's the code:

```
line_segment fast_segment_remainder1(line_segment a,
                                     line_segment b) {
    // precondition: b != 0
    if (a < b) return a;
    if (a - b < b) return a - b;
    a = fast_segment_remainder1(a, b + b);
    if (a < b) return a;
    return a - b;
}
```

The only thing we've changed are the conditions; everywhere we used to say a <= b, we now check a < b.

Let's see if we can get rid of the recursion. Every time we recurse down, we double b, so in the iterative version, we'd like to precompute the maximum amount of doubling we'll need. We can define a function that finds the first repeated doubling of b that exceeds the difference $a - b$:

```
line_segment largest_doubling(line_segment a, line_segment b) {
    // precondition: b != 0
    while (a - b >= b) b = b + b;
    return b;
}
```

Now we need our iterative function to do the same computation that happens on the way out of the recursion. Each time it returns, the value of b has the value it had before the most recent recursive call (i.e., the most recent doubling). So to simulate this, the iterative version needs to repeatedly "undouble" the value, which it will do by calling a function half. Remember, we're still "computing" with ruler and compass. Fortunately, there is a Euclidean procedure for "halving" a segment,[1] so we can use a half function. Now we can write an iterative version of remainder:

```
line_segment remainder(line_segment a, line_segment b) {
    // precondition: b != 0
    if (a < b) return a;
    line_segment c = largest_doubling(a, b);
```

[1] Draw a circle with the center at one end of the segment and radius equal to the segment; repeat for the other end. Use ruler to connect the two points where the circles intersect. The resulting line will bisect the original segment.

```
    a = a - c;
    while (c != b) {
        c = half(c);
        if (c <= a) a = a - c;
    }
    return a;
}
```

The first part of the function, which finds the largest doubling value, does what the "downward" recursion does, while the last part does what happens on the way back up out of the recursive calls. Let's look again at our example of finding the remainder of 45 divided by 6, this time with the new remainder function:

$a = 45, b = 6$

$a < b?$ $(45 < 6?)$ No.

$c \leftarrow$ `largest_doubling`$(45, 6) = 24$

$a \leftarrow a - c = 45 - 24 = 21$

loop :

    $c \neq b?$ $(24 \neq 6)?$ Yes, keep going.

        $c \leftarrow$ `half`$(c) =$ `half`$(24) = 12$

        $c \leq a?$ $(12 \leq 21)?$ Yes. $a \leftarrow a - c = 21 - 12 = 9$

    $c \neq b?$ $(12 \neq 6)?$ Yes, keep going.

        $c \leftarrow$ `half`$(c) =$ `half`$(12) = 6$

        $c \leq a?$ $(6 \leq 9)?$ Yes. $a \leftarrow a - c = 9 - 6 = 3$

    $c \neq b?$ $(6 \neq 6)?$ No, done with loop.

return $a = 3$

Notice that the successive values of c in the iterative implementation are the same as the values of b following each recursive call in the recursive implementation. Also, compare this to the trace of our earlier version of the algorithm at the end of Section 4.2. Observe how the results of the first part ($c = 24$ and $a = 21$) here are the same as the innermost recursion in the old example.

This is an extremely efficient algorithm, nearly as fast as the hardware implemented remainder operation in modern processors.

* * *

What if we wanted to compute *quotient* instead of remainder? It turns out that the code is almost the same. All we need are a couple of minor modifications, shown in bold:

```
integer quotient(line_segment a, line_segment b) {
    // Precondition: b > 0
    if (a < b) return integer(0);
    line_segment c = largest_doubling(a, b);
    integer n(1);
    a = a - c;
    while (c != b) {
        c = half(c); n = n + n;
        if (c <= a) { a = a - c; n = n + 1; }
    }
    return n;
}
```

Quotient is the number of times one line segment fits into another, so we use the type integer to represent this count. Basically, we are going to count multiples of b. If $a < b$, then we don't have any multiples of b and we return 0. But if $a \geq b$, we initialize the counter to 1, then double it each time we halve c, adding one more multiple for each iteration when it fits. Again, let's work through an example. This time, instead of finding the remainder of 45 divided by 6, we'll find the quotient of 45 divided by 6.

$a = 45, b = 6$

$a < b?$ (45 < 6?) No.

$c \leftarrow$ largest_doubling(45, 6) = 24

$n \leftarrow 1$

$a \leftarrow a - c = 45 - 24 = 21$

loop :

   $c \neq b?$ (24 ≠ 6)? Yes, keep going.

   $c \leftarrow$ half(c) = half(24) = 12; $n \leftarrow n + n = 1 + 1 = 2$

   $c \leq a?$ (12 ≤ 21)? Yes. $a \leftarrow a - c = 21 - 12 = 9$;

$n \leftarrow n + 1 = 2 + 1 = 3$

   $c \neq b?$ (12 ≠ 6)? Yes, keep going.

   $c \leftarrow$ half(c) = half(12) = 6; $n \leftarrow n + n = 3 + 3 = 6$

   $c \leq a?$ (6 ≤ 9)? Yes. $a \leftarrow a - c = 9 - 6 = 3$;

$n \leftarrow n + 1 = 6 + 1 = 7$

   $c \neq b?$ (6 ≠ 6)? No, done with loop.

return $n = 7$

Essentially, this is the Egyptian multiplication algorithm in reverse. And Ahmes knew it: a primitive variant of this algorithm, known to the Greeks as *Egyptian division*, appears in the Rhind papyrus.

4.6 Sharing the Code

Since the majority of the code is shared between quotient and remainder, it would make much more sense to combine them into a single function that returns both values; the complexity of the combined function is the same as either individual function. Note that C++11 allows us to use initializer list syntax {x, y} to construct the pair that the function returns:

```
std::pair<integer, line_segment>
quotient_remainder(line_segment a, line_segment b) {
    // Precondition: b > 0
    if (a < b) return {integer(0), a};
    line_segment c = largest_doubling(a, b);
    integer n(1);
    a = a - c;
    while (c != b) {
        c = half(c); n = n + n;
        if (c <= a) { a = a - c; n = n + 1; }
    }
    return {n, a};
}
```

In fact, any quotient or remainder function does nearly all the work of the other.

Programming Principle: The Law of Useful Return

Our quotient_remainder function illustrates an important programming principle, which we call the *law of useful return*:

> *If you've already done the work to get some useful result,*
> *don't throw it away. Return it to the caller.*

This may allow the caller to get some extra work done "for free" (as in the quotient_remainder case) or to return data that can be used in future invocations of the function.

Unfortunately, this principle is not always followed. For example, the C and C++ programming languages have separate quotient and remainder operators;

there is no way for a programmer to get both results with one call—despite the fact that many processors have an instruction that returns both.

Most computing architectures, whether ruler-and-compass or modern CPUs, provide an easy way to compute half; for us, it's just a 1-bit right shift. However, if you should happen to be working with an architecture that doesn't support this functionality, there is a remarkable version of the remainder function developed by Robert Floyd and Donald Knuth that does not require halving. It's based on the idea of the Fibonacci sequence—another of Leonardo Pisano's inventions, which we will discuss more in Chapter 7. Instead of the next number being double the previous one, we'll make the next number be the sum of the two previous ones:[2]

```
line_segment remainder_fibonacci(line_segment a, line_segment b) {
    // Precondition: b > 0
    if (a < b) return a;
    line_segment c = b;
    do {
        line_segment tmp = c; c = b + c; b = tmp;
    } while (a >= c);
    do {
        if (a >= b) a = a - b;
        line_segment tmp = c - b; c = b; b = tmp;
    } while (b < c);
    return a;
}
```

The first loop is equivalent to computing largest_doubling in our previous algorithm. The second loop corresponds to the "halving" part of the code. But instead of halving, we use subtraction to get back the earlier number in the Fibonacci sequence. This works because we always keep one previous value around in a temporary variable.

Exercise 4.6. Trace the remainder_fibonacci algorithm as it computes the remainder of 45 and 6, in the way we traced the remainder algorithm in Section 4.5.

Exercise 4.7. Design quotient_fibonacci and quotient_remainder_fibonacci.

Now that we have an efficient implementation of the remainder function, we can return to our original problem, the greatest common measure. Using our new remainder function from p. 54, we can rewrite Euclid's algorithm like this:

---

[2]Note that this sequence starts at b, so the values will not be the same as the traditional Fibonacci sequence.

```
line_segment gcm_remainder(line_segment a, line_segment b) {
    while (b != line_segment(0)) {
        a = remainder(a, b);
        std::swap(a, b);
    }
    return a;
}
```

Since we now allow `remainder` to return zero, the termination condition for the main loop is when b (the previous iteration's remainder) is zero, instead of comparing a and b as we did originally.

We will use this algorithm for the next few chapters, leaving its structure intact but exploring how it applies to different types. We will leave our ruler-and-compass constructions behind and implement the algorithm with a digital computer in mind. For example, for integers, the equivalent function is the *greatest common divisor* (GCD):

```
integer gcd(integer a, integer b) {
    while (b != integer(0)) {
        a = a % b;
        std::swap(a, b);
    }
    return a;
}
```

The code is identical, except that we have replaced `line_segment` with `integer` and used the modulus operator `%` to compute the remainder. Since computers have instructions to compute the integer remainder (as invoked by the C++ modulus operator), it's better to use them than to rely on doubling and halving.

4.7   Validating the Algorithm

How do we know that the integer GCD algorithm works? We need to show two things: first, that the algorithm terminates, and second, that it computes the GCD.

To prove that the algorithm terminates, we rely on the fact that

$$0 \le (a \bmod b) < b$$

Therefore, in each iteration, the remainder gets smaller. Since any decreasing sequence of positive integers is finite, the algorithm must terminate.

To prove that the algorithm computes the GCD, we start by observing that in each iteration, the algorithm computes a remainder of a and b, which by definition is

$$r = a - bq$$

where q is the integer quotient of a divided by b. Since $gcd(a, b)$ by definition divides a and also divides b (and therefore bq), it must also divide r. We can rewrite the remainder equation as follows:

$$a = bq + r$$

By the same reasoning, since $gcd(b, r)$ by definition divides b (and therefore bq), and also divides r, it must also divide a. Since pairs (a, b) and (b, r) have the same common divisors, they have the same greatest common divisor. Therefore we have shown that

$$a = bq + r \implies gcd(a, b) = gcd(b, r) \tag{4.1}$$

At each iteration, the algorithm replaces $gcd(a, b)$ with $gcd(b, r)$ by taking the remainder and swapping the arguments. Here is the list of remainders, starting with a_0 and b_0, the initial arguments to the function:

$$r_1 = \text{remainder}(a_0, b_0)$$
$$r_2 = \text{remainder}(b_0, r_1)$$
$$r_3 = \text{remainder}(r_1, r_2)$$
$$\cdots$$
$$r_n = \text{remainder}(r_{n-2}, r_{n-1})$$

Using the definition of remainder, we rewrite the sequence computed by the algorithm like this:

$$r_1 = a_0 - b_0 q_1$$
$$r_2 = b_0 - r_1 q_2$$
$$r_3 = r_1 - r_2 q_3$$
$$\cdots$$
$$r_n = r_{n-2} - r_{n-1} q_n$$

What Equation 4.1 guarantees is that the GCD stays the same each time. In other words:

$$gcd(a_0, b_0) = gcd(b_0, r_1) = gcd(r_1, r_2) = \cdots = gcd(r_{n-1}, r_n)$$

But we know that the remainder of r_{n-1} and r_n is 0, because that's what triggers the termination of the algorithm. And $gcd(x, 0) = x$. So

$$gcd(a_0, b_0) = \cdots = gcd(r_{n-1}, r_n) = gcd(r_n, 0) = r_n$$

which is the value returned by the algorithm. Therefore, the algorithm computes the GCD of its original arguments.

4.8   Thoughts on the Chapter

We've seen how an ancient algorithm for computing the greatest common measure of two line segments could be turned into a modern function for computing the GCD of integers. We've looked at variants of the algorithm and seen its relationship to functions for finding the quotient and the remainder. Does the GCD algorithm work for other things besides line segments and integers? In other words, is there a way to make the algorithm more general? We'll come back to that question later in the book.

5

five

The Emergence of
Modern Number Theory

*Mathematicians have tried in vain to this day
to discover some order in the sequence of prime numbers,
and we have reason to believe that it is a mystery
into which the human mind will never penetrate.*

Leonhard Euler

In the previous chapter, we saw how the fledging field of number theory, which
had fascinated the ancient Greeks, was revived in medieval Europe after a long
period of dormancy. But number theory in its modern sense really emerged a
few hundred years later, in 17th-century France. For this chapter, we are going to
put programming aside for a bit and learn some of the results discovered by 17th-
century French mathematicians, which we'll use for some important computer
applications later on.

5.1   Mersenne Primes and Fermat Primes

Mathematicians of the Renaissance rekindled the ancient Greeks' fascination
with prime numbers. They wondered whether there were certain predictable
patterns of primes. They were particularly interested in primes of the form $2^n - 1$,
since (as we saw in Section 3.4) this was the source of perfect numbers. Mathematicians from the 15th to the 18th centuries, like the Greeks before them, felt
that these numbers had special importance. Letters of the 17th-century mathematicians Fermat, Mersenne, and Descartes contain many references to perfect
numbers, as well as a closely related concept, *amicable* numbers. In the 18th

century, the great mathematician Leonhard Euler still found the subject to be of primary importance.

As we saw in Chapter 3, the Greeks knew that they could generate perfect numbers from primes of the form $2^n - 1$. They knew that numbers of that form are prime for $n = 2, 3, 5$, and 7, and possibly 13. In 1536, Hudalricus Regius showed that the expression was nonprime for $n = 11$, by finding

$$2^{11} - 1 = 2047 = 23 \times 89$$

Pietro Cataldi added several more values of n to the list in 1603—17, 19, (23), (29), 31, and (37)—but half of these (shown in parentheses) were incorrect. Pierre de Fermat discovered that

$$2^{23} - 1 = 8388607 = 47 \times 178481$$
$$2^{37} - 1 = 137438953471 = 223 \times 61631877$$

In his 1644 book *Cogitata Physico Mathematica*, the French mathematician Mersenne states that for $n \leq 257$, $2^n - 1$ is prime if and only if

$$n = 2, 3, 5, 7, 13, 17, 19, 31, (67), 117, (257)$$

Two of these were wrong (shown in parentheses), and he missed 89 and 107. Because of Mersenne's conjecture, primes of this form became known as *Mersenne primes*. We still do not know whether there is an infinite number of them, but even today Mersenne numbers are still used to search for large primes.

Marin Mersenne (1588–1648)

Starting around 1624, when Cardinal Richelieu became chief minister, France began to rise as a military, political, cultural, and scientific power. While scholars at traditional universities still interpreted Aristotle's ancient works, philosophers like Descartes in France, working outside of the university system, were revolutionizing the way people thought about the world. Richelieu created the first modern state, with a carefully organized central bureaucracy and military, and even official control of the French language. By 1660, France had become the undisputed leader of

Europe, and French became the dominant language for diplomats and aristocrats in most Western countries for the next 250 years.

It was during this period that Marin Mersenne, a French polymath and a member of the strict religious order of Minims, had an enormous impact on science. Although educated by the intellectual Jesuits and an accomplished classical scholar and mathematician, Mersenne chose the extreme asceticism of the Minims, who held no property (even in common), ate a strict vegan diet, and drank no alcohol. Mersenne's humility extended to his professional life; while other scientists proclaimed their own importance, his cause was to help others disseminate their work and learn about each other's results. Mersenne did some important work on the theory of sound and other areas, but his greatest contribution was the creation of a shared scientific community.

Scientific journals did not yet exist, but Mersenne served as a "virtual scientific journal," by exchanging letters with friends and informing them of each other's results. Mersenne's friends included people like Galileo, Huygens, Torricelli, Descartes, Fermat, and Pascal. In fact, Mersenne arranged for publication of Galileo's work in Protestant Holland, despite Galileo's condemnation by the Catholic Church. Later in Mersenne's life, scholars would meet together in his cell in a kind of informal weekly conference. When his letters were published after his death, they were in essence the world's first scientific proceedings.

In a letter to Mersenne in June 1640, Fermat wrote that his factorization of $2^{37} - 1$ depends on the following three discoveries:

1. If n is not a prime, $2^n - 1$ is not a prime.

2. If n is a prime, $2^n - 2$ is a multiple of $2n$.

3. If n is a prime, and p is a prime divisor of $2^n - 1$, then $p - 1$ is a multiple of n.

We'll look at the proof of discovery 1 in a bit, but for now let's assume that all three statements are true.

Fermat reasoned that if $2^{37} - 1$ is not prime, it must have a prime factor p, which must be odd. By observation 3, $p-1$ is a multiple of 37, which is equivalent to saying that

$$p = 37u + 1$$

Also, since p is odd, $p - 1 = 37u$ must be even, so u must be even. That means we can express u as $2v$, which gives us:

$$p = 74v + 1$$

Fermat therefore narrowed the factoring task from trying all possible numbers to just those primes produced by this formula. Testing these in sequence:

What about $v = 1$? No, 75 is not a prime.
What about $v = 2$? No, 149 is prime, but is not a divisor of $2^{37} - 1$.
What about $v = 3$? Yes! 223 is prime, and is a divisor of $2^{37} - 1$.
So $2^{37} - 1$ is not prime.

*　　*　　*

Now let's look at Fermat's proof of discovery 1, which we state in its contrapositive[1] form.

Theorem 5.1: *If $2^n - 1$ is prime, then n is prime.*

Proof. Suppose n is not prime. Then there must be factors u and v such that

$$n = uv, \quad u > 1, \quad v > 1$$

Then

$$
\begin{aligned}
2^n - 1 &= 2^{uv} - 1 \\
&= (2^u)^v - 1 \\
&= (2^u - 1)((2^u)^{v-1} + (2^u)^{v-2} + \cdots + (2^u) + 1) \quad (5.1)
\end{aligned}
$$

where the last step uses Equation 3.1, the difference of powers formula. Since $u > 1$, we know that both of the following are true:

$$1 < 2^u - 1$$
$$1 < (2^u)^{v-1} + (2^u)^{v-2} + \cdots + (2^u) + 1$$

So 5.1 shows that we have factored $2^n - 1$ into two numbers each greater than 1. But this contradicts the condition of the theorem is that $2^n - 1$ is prime. So the initial assumption in our proof must be false, and n must be prime. □

As for discoveries 2 and 3, Fermat never shared the proofs. In a letter to his friend Frenicle, Fermat wrote that "he would send [the proof] if he did not fear being too long." We shall return to them soon.

---

[1] Any implication $p \implies q$ is logically equivalent to its *contrapositive*, which is the expression $\neg q \implies \neg p$. See "Implication and the Contrapositive" in Appendix A for more details.

Pierre de Fermat (1601–1665)

Pierre de Fermat was a lawyer and provincial magistrate from Toulouse in the south of France. He was a Renaissance man in the tradition of Montaigne, interested in a variety of subjects including classical literature, and fluent in Latin and Greek. The last of the great amateur mathematicians, Fermat became interested in number theory after reading Bachet's translation of Diophantus' ancient Greek text *Arithmetic*. Although he made enormous contributions to mathematics, he never personally interacted with  other mathematicians. In fact, Mersenne repeatedly invited him to visit Paris, but as far as we know, Fermat never went.

Fermat often boasted of his results while keeping his methods secret. He would often say that he had a proof of something, yet come up with an excuse not to provide it. When he did publicize a result, he would try to divulge as little as possible about how he did it.

During his life, Fermat never published his work, although he corresponded with Mersenne and others through letters. After Fermat's death, his son published the edition of Diophantus with Fermat's marginal notes. These notes contained many theorems, which were gradually confirmed by other mathematicians in later years. The last to be solved—which became known as Fermat's Last Theorem—was the statement that $a^n + b^n = c^n$ has no solutions in positive integers for $n > 2$. It was finally proved in 1994 by Andrew Wiles.

Fermat notoriously wrote "the proof is too large to fit in the margin" next to his statement of the Last Theorem. As mentioned earlier, this was his common pattern; he often gave similar excuses to avoid sharing his proofs. Although all but one of his conjectures have been confirmed, some of the proofs are so complex and lengthy that later mathematicians such as Gauss have been skeptical that Fermat actually discovered them.

In addition to his work on number theory, Fermat made major contributions to other areas of mathematics. He invented analytic geometry—the study of equations of curves—before Descartes, but described the work in an unpublished manuscript. He also co-invented probability theory in the course of a lengthy correspondence with Blaise Pascal.

Fermat made a lot of conjectures for which he left no proofs, but every one has since been proven true except one:

$$2^n + 1 \text{ is prime} \iff n = 2^i$$

(The double-arrow symbol is read "if and only if"; see Appendix A for details.) Since then, numbers of this form ($2^{2^i} + 1$) have been known as *Fermat primes*. It's easy to prove a part of his conjecture:

Theorem 5.2: $2^n + 1$ *is prime* $\implies n = 2^i$.

Proof. Suppose $n \neq 2^i$. Then one of n's factors must be odd, so we can express that factor as $2q + 1$. This is > 1, so we can express n as

$$n = m(2q + 1)$$

Substituting $m(2q + 1)$ for n and then using the formula for sum of odd powers (Equation 3.4), we factor $2^n + 1$:

$$
\begin{aligned}
2^n + 1 &= 2^{m(2q+1)} + 1 \\
&= 2^{m(2q+1)} + 1^{m(2q+1)} \\
&= (2^m)^{2q+1} + 1^{2q+1} \\
&= (2^m + 1)((2^m)^{2q} - (2^m)^{2q-1} + \cdots + 1)
\end{aligned}
$$

But factoring $2^n + 1$ contradicts the premise of the conjecture; it can't have non-trivial factors if it's prime. So our initial assumption in the proof is false, and $n = 2^i$. □

What about other primes of the form $2^{2^i} + 1$? Fermat states that 3, 5, 17, 257, 65537, 4294967297, and 18446744073709551617 are prime, and so are all the rest of this form. Unfortunately, he was wrong about two of his examples—only the first five are prime—and about his conjecture. In 1732, Euler showed that

$$2^{32} + 1 = 4294967297 = 641 \times 6700417$$

In fact, we know that for $5 \leq i \leq 32$, the numbers are composite. Are there any more Fermat primes besides these five? As of this writing, no one knows.

5.2   Fermat's Little Theorem

We now come to one of the most important results in number theory.

Theorem 5.3 (Fermat's Little Theorem):

If p is prime, $a^{p-1} - 1$ is divisible by p for any $0 < a < p$.

Fermat claimed to have a proof of the theorem in 1640, but did not publish it. Leibniz discovered a proof some time between 1676 and 1680, but did not publish it either. Finally, Euler published two different proofs in 1742 and 1750. We will prove the theorem here, but first we need to derive several other results. While these may at first seem to be unrelated, we will see shortly how they come together.

Leonhard Euler (1707–1783)

Leonhard Euler (pronounced "OILer") was born in a well-educated middle-class family in Switzerland. A talented and well-rounded student with an amazing memory, he studied with Johann Bernoulli, the greatest mathematician of the time and a friend of Euler's father. (Bernoulli himself was a student of Leibniz, the co-inventor of calculus.)

For most of the 18th century, Czar Peter the Great and his successors conducted a period of dramatic reform that "Europeanized" Russian society and culture. One of the results of these reforms was the creation of the Imperial Academy of Sciences in St. Petersburg, which recruited European scholars. It was there in 1727 that Euler, at age 20, got a job doing mathematical research. Within 10 years, his results in mathematics, mechanics, and even shipbuilding established his reputation as one of the top scientific minds in Europe. By the time Frederick the Great recruited him to come to Berlin in 1741, Euler was an international superstar. At the time, kings and queens considered associating with scientists and other intellectuals to be an important way to increase their own status. Throughout Euler's years in Berlin, the French and Russian royal courts competed to woo him away. Eventually, in 1766, he returned to St. Petersburg, where he spent the rest of his career.

Euler's contributions to mathematics (and physics) were enormous. He worked in many areas; he founded modern graph theory and made fundamental discoveries in number theory. However, his greatest achievement was the development of modern analysis—calculus and differential equations—from the individual techniques invented by Newton and Leibniz to a systematic discipline. His three books on calculus (*Introduction to Analysis of the Infinite*, *Differential Calculus*, and *Integral Calculus*) were the definitive texts for nearly a century and still deserve careful study.

Euler wrote the first book on popular science, *Letters to a German Princess*, in which he explains the Newtonian view of the world to a lay person. He also wrote an elementary algebra textbook intended for non-mathematicians, which is still in print.

Euler was so prolific that after his death, the Russian Academy of Sciences took 60 years to publish all the additional work he had submitted. He was generally regarded as the greatest mathematician in the world in his time, and after 200 years, we still share Laplace's view that "he is the master of us all."

Our first step is another proposition from Euclid:

Theorem 5.4 (Euclid VII, 30): *The product of two integers smaller than a prime p is not divisible by p.*

(Another way to say this is that if p is prime and a and b are smaller than p, then ab is not divisible by p.) If some number x is divisible by some other number y, then x is a multiple of y: $x = my$. If x is **not** divisible by y, then dividing x by y leaves a remainder r: $x = my + r$. So we can restate the proposition like this:

$$p \text{ is prime } \land\ 0 < a, b < p \implies ab = mp + r\ \land\ 0 < r < p$$

Proof. Assume the contrary, that ab is a multiple of p. Then for a given a, let b be the smallest integer such that $ab = mp$. Then since p is prime, we know dividing p by b leaves a remainder $v < b$:

$$p = bu + v\ \land\ 0 < v < b$$

Multiplying both sides of the equation by a and then substituting with $ab = mp$ gives

$$ap = abu + av$$
$$ap - abu = av$$
$$ap - mpu = av$$
$$av = (a - mu)p \;\wedge\; 0 < v < b$$

But this means that v is an integer smaller than b such that av is a multiple of p. That's a contradiction, since we chose b to be the smallest such number. So our assumption is false, and ab is not divisible by p. □

This approach was actually a common pattern for proofs in ancient Greek mathematics: choose the smallest of something, and then show that certain assumptions would lead to a smaller one.

$$\star \quad \star \quad \star$$

Next, we prove a result about remainders:

Lemma 5.1 (Permutation of Remainders Lemma): *If p is prime, then for any $0 < a < p$,*

$$a \cdot \{1, \ldots, p-1\} =$$
$$\{a, \ldots, a(p-1)\} = \{q_1 p + r_1, \ldots, q_{p-1} p + r_{p-1}\}$$

where

$$0 < r_i < p \;\wedge\; i \neq j \implies r_i \neq r_j$$

In other words, if we take all the multiples of a from $1a$ to $(p-1)a$, and express each multiple in the form $qp + r$, every remainder r will be unique and the set of remainders will be a permutation of $\{1, \ldots, p-1\}$. (We know each remainder is less than p, so we have $p-1$ unique numbers in the range $[1, p-1]$.)

Example: If $p = 7$ and $a = 4$, then the lemma says that

$$\{4, 8, 12, 16, 20, 24\} = \{0 \cdot 7 + 4, \; 1 \cdot 7 + 1, \; 1 \cdot 7 + 5, \; 2 \cdot 7 + 2, \; 2 \cdot 7 + 6, \; 3 \cdot 7 + 3\}$$

so the remainders are

$$\{4, 1, 5, 2, 6, 3\}$$

which is a permutation of $\{1, \ldots, 7 - 1\}$.

Proof. Suppose $r_i = r_j$ and $i < j$; that is, two of the remainders are equal. Then we could take the difference of the two corresponding elements in the set, and the remainders r_i and r_j would cancel:

$$(q_j p + r_j) - (q_i p + r_i) = q_j p - q_i p$$
$$= (q_j - q_i)p$$

Since the ith and jth elements of the set are the products ai and aj, we could equivalently write the difference of these two elements as $aj - ai$. That is:

$$aj - ai = (q_j - q_i)p$$
$$a(j - i) = (q_j - q_i)p$$

But this is of the form $ab = mp$, which implies that the product of two integers smaller than p is divisible by p. Since this contradicts Euclid VII, 30, which we just proved, our assumption must be false, and the remainders must be unique.

$\square$

5.3   Cancellation

Now we will look at some results that deal with the notion of *cancellation*. If we are multiplying two numbers x and y, they cancel (i.e., their product is 1) when one is the multiplicative inverse of the other.

Cancellation and Modular Arithmetic

One way to view cancellation is in the context of *modular arithmetic*, which was introduced by Carl Gauss, whom we shall meet in Chapter 8. Although Euler did not use this technique in his proof of Fermat's Little Theorem, you may find it useful to understand the logic.

A good analogy for modular arithmetic is a standard 12-hour clock. If it's 10 o'clock, and you have to do something that's going to take 5 hours, you'll be done at 3 o'clock. In a sense, you're saying that 10 + 5 = 3. More precisely, you're saying that (10 + 5) mod 12 = 3. (Mathematicians would call noon "0," though.) Of course, we can do modular arithmetic in any base. Here are a couple of examples using 7:

$$(6 + 4) \bmod 7 = 3$$

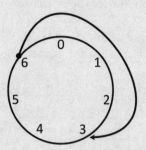

$$(3 \times 3) \bmod 7 = (3 + 3 + 3) \bmod 7 = 2$$

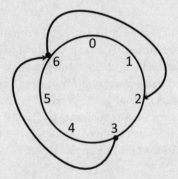

Notice in the latter case that we could also calculate our product in the traditional way, then express it in terms of multiples of the modular base and a remainder:

$$(3 \times 3) = 9 = (1 \times 7) + 2$$

In other words, **a value modulo n is equivalent to the remainder after using n as a divisor.**

In elementary arithmetic (for example, arithmetic of rational numbers), if the product of two terms x and y is 1, then they are said to *cancel*, and x and y are called *inverses* of each other. The same is true in modular arithmetic, only the inverses will both be integers. For example,

$$(2 \times 4) \bmod 7 = 1$$

so 2 and 4 cancel, and are each other's inverse.

A negative number x mod n is equal to the positive number $n - x$; it's the position you'd get to if you "turned the clock back" by x hours. In particular, -1 mod $n = n - 1$.

Just as with elementary arithmetic, we can write multiplication tables for modular arithmetic. Here's one for integers modulo 7:

×	1	2	3	4	5	6
1	1	2	3	4	5	6
2	2	4	6	1	3	5
3	3	6	2	5	1	4
4	4	1	5	2	6	3
5	5	3	1	6	4	2
6	6	5	4	3	2	1

First we express the product as a multiple of 7 and a remainder; the modular product is then just the remainder. For example, $5 \times 4 = 20 = (2 \times 7) + 6 = 6$ mod 7, so there is a 6 in the table at the intersection of row 5 and column 4. Observe that every row is a permutation of every other row, and that every row contains a 1. Recall that if the product is 1, the two factors are inverses. In the table above, we see, for example, that 2 and 4 are inverses since $2 \times 4 = 1$ mod 7. Here's a version of the table with the inverse of each factor on the left shown in the column on the right:

×	1	2	3	4	5	6	
1	1	2	3	4	5	6	1
2	2	4	6	1	3	5	4
3	3	6	2	5	1	4	5
4	4	1	5	2	6	3	2
5	5	3	1	6	4	2	3
6	6	5	4	3	2	1	6

Formally, for integer $n > 1$ and integer $u > 0$, we call v a *multiplicative inverse modulo n* if there is an integer q such that $uv = 1 + qn$. In other words, u and v are inverses if their product divided by n yields a remainder of 1. We will rely heavily on this in the following proofs.

* * *

The next result relies on this generalized notion of cancellation:

Lemma 5.2 (Cancellation Law): *If p is prime, then for any $0 < a < p$ there is a number $0 < b < p$ such that $ab = mp + 1$.*

In other words, a and b cancel modulo p.

Example: Suppose again that $p = 7$ and $a = 4$. Is there a value of b that satisfies the equation $ab = mp + 1$? Let's try all the values of b until we find one that works:

$$b = 1 \quad 4 \cdot 1 = 7m + 1? \quad \text{No.}$$
$$b = 2 \quad 4 \cdot 2 = 7m + 1? \quad \text{Yes, when } m = 1.$$

Proof. By the Permutation of Remainders Lemma, we know that one of the possible products in the set

$$a \cdot \{1, \ldots, p - 1\}$$

will have a remainder of 1. In this case we have $p - 1$ unique remainders greater than 0 and less than p, so one of them must be 1. Therefore, there must be another element b that cancels a. □

Note that 1 and $p - 1$ are *self-canceling* elements—that is, if you multiply each by itself, the result is 1 mod p, or (equivalently) the result can be expressed in the form $mp + 1$. It's obvious that $1 \cdot 1$ can be expressed in this form, since it's $0p + 1$. What about $p - 1$?

$$(p - 1)^2 = p^2 - 2p + 1 = (p - 2)p + 1 = mp + 1$$

In fact, 1 and $p - 1$ are the *only* self-canceling elements, which we'll now demonstrate.

Lemma 5.3 (Self-Canceling Law):

$$\text{For any } 0 < a < p, \quad a^2 = mp + 1 \implies a = 1 \ \lor \ a = p - 1$$

Proof. Assume there is a self-canceling a that's neither 1 nor $p - 1$:

$$a \neq 1 \land a \neq p - 1 \implies 1 < a < p - 1$$

Rearranging the condition of the proof, we have

$$a^2 - 1 = mp$$

Factoring the expression on the left, we have

$$(a - 1)(a + 1) = mp$$

But since by our assumption $0 < a - 1, a + 1 < p$, which means we have a product of two integers smaller than p that is divisible by p, a contradiction with Euclid VII, 30 (see p. 70). So our assumption is false, and the only self-canceling elements are 1 and $p - 1$. □

We are almost ready to prove Fermat's Little Theorem, but we still need one more result: Wilson's theorem, announced by Edward Waring in 1770, who attributed it to his student, John Wilson. At the time, Waring stated that he was unable to prove the theorem since he did not have the right notation—in response to which Gauss later remarked, "One needs notion, not notation."

Theorem 5.5 (Wilson's Theorem): *If p is prime, there exists an integer m such that*

$$(p - 1)! = mp + (p - 1)$$

or in other words

$$(p - 1)! = (p - 1) \bmod p$$

Proof. By definition,

$$(p - 1)! = 1 \cdot 2 \cdot 3 \ldots (p - 1)$$

By the Cancellation Law, every number a between 1 and $p - 1$ has a number b in that range that's its inverse; by the Self-Canceling Law, only 1 and $p - 1$ are their own inverses. So every other number in the product except 1 and $p - 1$ is cancelled by its inverse; that is, their product divided by p has remainder 1. In other words, we could express all the cancelled terms together—all the terms between 1 and $p - 1$—as $np + 1$ for some n. We still have our uncanceled terms 1 and $p - 1$, so our product now becomes

$$\begin{aligned}(p - 1)! &= 1 \cdot (np + 1) \cdot (p - 1) \\ &= np \cdot p - np + p - 1 \\ &= (np - n)p + (p - 1)\end{aligned}$$

Then $m = np - n$ satisfies the theorem. □

Exercise 5.1. Prove that if $n > 4$ is composite, then $(n - 1)!$ is a multiple of n.

5.4   Proving Fermat's Little Theorem

Finally, using the results we've just derived, we can prove Fermat's Little Theorem:

If p is prime, $a^{p-1} - 1$ is divisible by p for any $0 < a < p$.

Proof. Consider the expression $\prod_{i=1}^{p-1} ai$. We can move the a terms outside the product, so we have

$$\prod_{i=1}^{p-1} ai = a^{p-1} \prod_{i=1}^{p-1} i \tag{5.2}$$

Wilson's Theorem can be written as

$$\prod_{i=1}^{p-1} i = (p-1) + mp$$

Therefore we can make the above substitution into Equation 5.2, giving

$$\prod_{i=1}^{p-1} ai = a^{p-1}((p-1) + mp)$$

$$= a^{p-1}p - a^{p-1} + a^{p-1}mp$$

$$= (a^{p-1} + a^{p-1}m)p - a^{p-1} \tag{5.3}$$

Now let's return to the expression $\prod_{i=1}^{p-1} ai$. Its expansion contains all the terms $\{a, 2a, 3a, \ldots, (p-1)a\}$, which by the Permutation of Remainders Lemma (p. 71) is the same as $\{q_1 p + r_1, \ldots, q_{p-1} p + r_{p-1}\}$. So we can write

$$\prod_{i=1}^{p-1} ai = \prod_{i=1}^{p-1} (q_i p + r_i)$$

When we expand the product on the right, we get a sum containing many terms with p, and one that is the product of all r_i. We group all the p terms together; they give us some multiple up. What remains is the product of all r_i:

$$\prod_{i=1}^{p-1} ai = up + \prod_{i=1}^{p-1} r_i$$

Now we can apply Wilson's Theorem again to the product on the right, then again group multiples of p:

$$\prod_{i=1}^{p-1} ai = up + vp + (p-1)$$

$$= wp - 1 \tag{5.4}$$

where $w = u + v + 1$. We know expressions 5.3 and 5.4 are equal, and need only some simple rearrangement:

$$wp - 1 = (a^{p-1} + a^{p-1}m)p - a^{p-1}$$
$$a^{p-1} + wp - 1 = (a^{p-1} + a^{p-1}m)p$$
$$a^{p-1} - 1 = (a^{p-1} + a^{p-1}m)p - wp$$

Again, we can combine multiples of p on the right, giving our desired result:

$$a^{p-1} - 1 = np$$

So $a^{p-1} - 1$ is divisible by p. □

We also observe that a^{p-2} is an inverse of a, since $a^{p-2} \cdot a = a^{p-1}$, which Fermat's Little Theorem tells us is $mp + 1$. (Remember that being an inverse with respect to p means having a remainder of 1 after dividing by p.)

* * *

What about the converse of Fermat's Little Theorem? To prove that, we need one more intermediate result:

Lemma 5.4 (Non-invertibility Lemma): *If $n = uv \ \land \ u, v > 1$, then u is not invertible modulo n.*

Proof. Let $n = uv$ and w be an inverse of u (i.e., $wu = mn + 1$). Then

$$wn = wuv$$
$$= (mn + 1)v$$
$$= mvn + v$$
$$wn - mvn = v$$

So if we define $z = (w - mv)$, then

$$(w - mv)n = zn = v$$

Since $n > v$, then $zn > v$, which is a contradiction with $zn = v$. So u cannot have an inverse. □

Definition 5.1. Two numbers m and n are **coprime** if $\gcd(m, n) = 1$. Equivalently, m and n are coprime if they have no common factors greater than 1.

The Non-invertibility Lemma tells us that when we are dealing with numbers modulo n, where n is not prime, there are invertible elements and non-invertible elements; elements that are not coprime to n are not invertible.

Theorem 5.6 (Converse of Fermat's Little Theorem): *If for all $a, 0 < a < n$,*

$$a^{n-1} = 1 + q_a n$$

then n is prime.

Proof. Suppose n is not prime; that is, $n = uv$. Then by the Non-invertibility Lemma, u is not invertible. But by the condition of the theorem, $u^{n-1} = u^{n-2}u = 1 + q_u n$. In other words, u has an inverse u^{n-2}, which is a contradiction. So n must be prime. $\square$

5.5 Euler's Theorem

Like any great mathematician, Euler was not satisfied with just proving Fermat's Little Theorem; he wanted to see if it could be generalized. Since Fermat's Little Theorem was only for primes, Euler wondered whether there was a similar result that would include composite numbers. But composite numbers do strange things in modular arithmetic. To illustrate this, let's take a look at the multiplication table modulo 10, which we've annotated by showing inverses of the left-hand factor on the right-hand side of the table:

×	1	2	3	4	5	6	7	8	9	
1	1	2	3	4	5	6	7	8	9	1
2	2	4	6	8	0	2	4	6	8	
3	3	6	9	2	5	8	1	4	7	7
4	4	8	2	6	0	4	8	2	6	
5	5	0	5	0	5	0	5	0	5	
6	6	2	8	4	0	6	2	8	4	
7	7	4	1	8	5	2	9	6	3	3
8	8	6	4	2	0	8	6	4	2	
9	9	8	7	6	5	4	3	2	1	9

The table should look a bit familiar, because it's just like the traditional 10×10 multiplication table, if you keep only the last digit of each product. For example, $7 \times 9 = 63$, which is 3 mod 10. Immediately we can see differences from the table we did for 7, which was prime (see p. 74). For one thing, the rows are no longer permutations of each other. More importantly, some rows now contain 0. That's a problem for multiplication—how can the product of two things be 0? That would mean that we get into a situation where we can never escape zero—any product of the result will be zero.

The other property we noted earlier about primes—that only 1 and −1 are self-canceling—happens to be true for 10 as well, but is not always true for composite numbers. (The integer 8, for example, has four self-canceling elements: 1, 3, 5, and 7.)

Let's look at the multiplication table for 10 again, focusing on certain entries:

×	1	2	3	4	5	6	7	8	9	
[1]	1	2	3	4	5	6	7	8	9	1
2	2	4	6	8	0	2	4	6	8	
[3]	3	6	9	2	5	8	1	4	7	7
4	4	8	2	6	0	4	8	2	6	
5	5	0	5	0	5	0	5	0	5	
6	6	2	8	4	0	6	2	8	4	
[7]	7	4	1	8	5	2	9	6	3	3
8	8	6	4	2	0	8	6	4	2	
[9]	9	8	7	6	5	4	3	2	1	9

The rows that contain only "good" products (i.e., no zeros) are the ones whose first factor is shown in a rectangular box on the left—which also happen to be the rows where that factor has an inverse, shown on the right side of the table. Which rows have this property? Those that represent numbers that are coprime with 10. (Remember, being coprime means having no common factors greater than 1.)

So could we just use the good rows and leave out the rest? Not quite, because some of the results in good rows would themselves lead to bad rows if used in a successive product. (For example, 3 is a good row, but $(3 \times 5) \times 2 = 0$.) Euler's idea was to use only the entries in good *columns* as well as good rows—the numbers in shaded cells. Notice that those numbers have all the nice properties we saw for primes: the shaded numbers in each row are permutations of each other, each set of shaded numbers contains a 1, and so on.

*   *   *

To extend Fermat's Little Theorem for composite numbers, Euler uses only these bold values. He starts by defining the size of the set of coprimes:

Definition 5.2. The **totient** of a positive integer n is the number of positive integers less than n that are coprime with n. It is given by the formula:

$$\phi(n) = |\{0 < i < n \wedge \text{coprime}(i, n)\}|$$

This is known as the **Euler totient function** or **Euler ϕ function**.

$\phi(n)$ gives us the number of rows containing shaded entries in the multiplication table modulo n. For example, $\phi(10) = 4$, and $\phi(7) = 6$, as we can see from the multiplication tables given earlier.

Since primes by definition don't share any prime factors with smaller numbers, the totient of a prime number is

$$\phi(p) = p - 1$$

In other words, all numbers less than a given prime are coprime with it.

What Euler realized was that the $p - 1$ in Fermat's theorem is just a special case; it's what ϕ happens to be for primes. Now we can state Euler's generalization of Fermat's Little Theorem.

Theorem 5.7 (Euler's Theorem): coprime$(a, n) \iff a^{\phi(n)} - 1$ *is divisible by* n.

Exercise 5.2. Prove Euler's Theorem by modifying the proof of Fermat's Little Theorem. Steps:

- Replace Permutation of Remainders Lemma with Permutation of Coprime Remainders Lemma. (Essentially, use the same proof but look only at "good" elements.)

- Prove that every coprime remainder has a multiplicative inverse. (We just showed that the remainders form a permutation, so 1 has to be somewhere in the permutation.)

- Use the product of all coprime remainders where the proof of Little Fermat has the product of all nonzero remainders.

∗   ∗   ∗

We would like to be able to compute the ϕ function for any integer. Since we can express any integer as the product of powers of primes, we'll start by seeing how to compute the totient of a power of a prime p. We want to know the number of coprimes of p^m. We know there are at most $p^m - 1$ of them, because that's all the possible numbers less than p^m. But we also know that those divisible by p (i.e., multiples of p) are not coprime, so we need to subtract however many of these there are from our total:

$$\phi(p^m) = (p^m - 1) - |\{p, 2p, \ldots, p^m - p\}|$$
$$= (p^m - 1) - |\{1, 2, \ldots, p^{m-1} - 1\}|$$
$$= (p^m - 1) - (p^{m-1} - 1)$$
$$= p^m - p^{m-1}$$
$$= p^m \left(1 - \frac{1}{p}\right)$$

What happens if we have $\phi(p^u q^v)$, where p and q are both primes? Again, we start with the maximum possible and then subtract off all the multiples. So we'll subtract the number of multiples of p and also the number of multiples of q, but then we have to add back multiples of both p and q, because otherwise they'd be subtracted twice. (This general technique, known as the *inclusion-exclusion principle*, is often used in combinatorics.) Let us assume $n = p^u q^v$:

$$\phi(n) = (n - 1) - \left(\frac{n}{p} - 1\right) - \left(\frac{n}{q} - 1\right) + \left(\frac{n}{pq} - 1\right)$$
$$= n - \frac{n}{p} - \frac{n}{q} + \frac{n}{pq}$$
$$= n \left(1 - \frac{1}{p} - \frac{1}{q} + \frac{1}{pq}\right)$$
$$= n \left[\left(1 - \frac{1}{p}\right) - \frac{1}{q}\left(1 - \frac{1}{p}\right)\right]$$
$$= n \left(1 - \frac{1}{p}\right)\left(1 - \frac{1}{q}\right)$$
$$= p^u \left(1 - \frac{1}{p}\right) q^v \left(1 - \frac{1}{q}\right)$$
$$= \phi(p^u)\phi(q^v)$$

As a special case when we have a simple product of two primes, p_1 and p_2, we now know that

$$\phi(p_1 p_2) = \phi(p_1)\phi(p_2) \tag{5.5}$$

For example, since $10 = 5 \times 2$,

$$\phi(10) = \phi(5)\phi(2) = 4$$

Although the case we care most about is the one given here, we can generalize the formula to handle a product of any number of primes raised to powers, not just two. For example, if we had three factors p, q, and r, we'd subtract all the multiples of each, then add back the double-counted multiples of pq, pr, and qr, and then compensate for our overcompensation by again subtracting multiples of pqr. Extending this to m primes gives this formula, where $n = \prod_{i=1}^{m} p_i^{k_i}$:

$$\phi(n) = \phi\left(\prod_{i=1}^{m} p_i^{k_i}\right)$$
$$= n\prod_{i=1}^{m}\left(1 - \frac{1}{p_i}\right)$$
$$= \prod_{i=1}^{m} \phi\left(p_i^{k_i}\right)$$

Euler's interest in proving his theorem led to his need to count coprimes. His derivation of the ϕ function gave him a tool that allowed him to efficiently compute this count in the cases where the prime decomposition is known.

5.6 Applying Modular Arithmetic

In Section 5.3, we saw how modular multiplication was related to remainders. Let's take a look at a couple of our important results from earlier in the chapter and see what some examples look like if we do them modulo 7. Wilson's Theorem states that for a prime p, there exists some m such that

$$(p - 1)! = (p - 1) + mp$$

Another way to say this is

$$(p - 1)! = (p - 1) \bmod p$$

Let's see if we can confirm that result if p is 7. $p - 1$ is 6, so we start by expanding $6!$ into its factors, rearranging them, and using our modular multiplication table to cancel inverses:

$$6! = 1 \times 2 \times 3 \times 4 \times 5 \times 6$$
$$= 1 \times (2 \times 4) \times (3 \times 5) \times 6$$
$$= (1 \times 1 \times 1 \times 6) \bmod 7$$
$$= 6 \bmod 7$$

which is what Wilson's Theorem predicts.

Similarly, let's use modular multiplication to see what Fermat's Little Theorem says. The original form is

If p is prime, $a^{p-1} - 1$ is divisible by p for any $0 < a < p$.

But with modular arithmetic, we could restate it as

$$\text{If } p \text{ is prime,} \quad a^{p-1} - 1 = 0 \bmod p \quad \text{for any } 0 < a < p.$$

or

$$\text{If } p \text{ is prime,} \quad a^{p-1} = 1 \bmod p \quad \text{for any } 0 < a < p.$$

Again, let's use $p = 7$, and try $a = 2$. This time we'll expand our expression, multiply both sides by 6!, and then use modular multiplication to cancel terms:

$$2^6 = (2 \times 2 \times 2 \times 2 \times 2 \times 2)$$
$$2^6 \times 6! = (2 \times 2 \times 2 \times 2 \times 2 \times 2) \times (1 \times 2 \times 3 \times 4 \times 5 \times 6)$$
$$= (2 \times 1) \times (2 \times 2) \times (2 \times 3) \times (2 \times 4) \times (2 \times 5) \times (2 \times 6)$$
$$= (2 \times 4 \times 6 \times 1 \times 3 \times 5) \bmod 7$$
$$= (1 \times 2 \times 3 \times 4 \times 5 \times 6) \bmod 7$$
$$= 6! \bmod 7$$
$$2^6 = 1 \bmod 7$$

which is what Fermat's Little Theorem tells us.

5.7   Thoughts on the Chapter

Earlier, we saw how the ancient Greeks were interested in perfect numbers. There wasn't any practical value to this work; they were simply interested in exploring properties of certain kinds of numbers for their own sake. Yet as we have seen in this chapter, over time the search for these "useless" perfect numbers led to the discovery of Fermat's Little Theorem, one of the most practically useful theorems in all of mathematics. We'll see why it's so useful in Chapter 13.

This chapter also gave us a first look at the process of abstraction in mathematics. Euler looked at Fermat's Little Theorem and realized that he could extend it from one specific situation (primes) to a more general one (integers). He saw that the exponent in Fermat's theorem was a special case of a more general concept, the number of coprimes. That same process of abstraction lies at the heart of generic programming. Generalizing code is like generalizing theorems and their proofs. Just as Euler saw how to extend Fermat's result from one type of mathematical object to another, so programmers can take a function that was designed for one type of computational object (say, vectors) and extend it to work equally well on another (perhaps linked lists).

6
s i x

Abstraction in Mathematics

*Mathematicians do not study objects, but the relations between objects;
to them it is a matter of indifference if these objects are replaced by others,
provided that the relations do not change. Matter does not
engage their attention, they are interested in form alone.*

Poincaré, *Science and Hypothesis*

The history of mathematics is filled with discoveries of new abstractions: finding ways to solve a more general problem. For example, we saw in Chapter 5 how Euler generalized Fermat's Little Theorem so it would work with composite numbers as well as primes. Eventually, mathematicians realized that they could generalize beyond numbers, and derive results about abstract entities called *algebraic structures*—collections of objects that follow certain rules. This led to the development of an entirely new branch of mathematics, *abstract algebra*. In this chapter, we'll introduce the first examples of these abstract entities, and prove some of their properties. As we did in the previous chapter, we're going to put programming aside while we build the foundations we need to derive a generic algorithm in Chapter 7.

6.1 Groups

The first and most important of these algebraic structures, discovered by French mathematician Évariste Galois in 1832, is called a *group*.

Definition 6.1. A **group** is a set on which the following are defined:

$$\text{operations}: \quad x \circ y, \ x^{-1}$$
$$\text{constant}: \quad e$$

and on which the following axioms hold:

$$x \circ (y \circ z) = (x \circ y) \circ z \qquad \text{associativity}$$
$$x \circ e = e \circ x = x \qquad \text{identity}$$
$$x \circ x^{-1} = x^{-1} \circ x = e \qquad \text{cancellation}$$

The constant e is the *identity element* (also sometimes written *id*), which is often written as 1 in multiplicative contexts. The operation x^{-1} is the *inverse* operation; applying the operation to an item and its inverse results in the identity element, as the last axiom shows. The group operation is *binary*, which simply means that it takes two arguments (it has nothing to do with the binary representation of numbers used in computers). The symbol $\circ$ (sometimes written $*$) can represent *any* binary operation, as long as it follows the axioms.

We often treat the group operation as multiplication, and even refer to "multiplying" two elements of a group, although what we really mean is applying the group operation, whatever it might be. Just as with multiplication, the symbol for the operation is often dropped; that is, $x \circ y$ may be written xy, and $x \circ x = xx = x^2$.

The group operation is not necessarily commutative (commutativity means that $\forall x, y : x \circ y = y \circ x$). When we want to require commutativity, we need to specify a particular kind of group:

Definition 6.2. An **abelian group** is a group whose operation is commutative.

One kind of abelian group is the *additive group*:

Definition 6.3. An **additive group** is an abelian group where the group operation is addition.

Additive groups are the exception to the naming conventions given earlier. For an additive group, the symbol $+$ is used to represent its operation and 0 its identity element. Even though the name "additive group" says nothing about commutativity, it is by convention assumed to be commutative.

Groups are *closed* under their operation. This means that if you take any two elements of the group and apply the group operation, the result will itself be a member of the group. Similarly, they are closed under the inverse function: if you take the inverse of any element of the group, the result is still an element of the group.

Some examples of groups follow:

- *Additive group of integers:* the elements are integers and the operation is addition.

- *Multiplicative group of nonzero remainders modulo 7:* the elements are the numbers 1 through 6 and the operation is multiplication modulo 7.

- *Group of rearrangements of a deck of cards:* the elements are permutations of the deck and the operation is composition of these permutations.

- *Multiplicative group of invertible matrices (those with nonzero determinants) with real coefficients:* the elements are matrices and the operation is matrix multiplication.

- *Group of rotations of the plane:* the elements are different rotations around the origin and the operation is composition of these rotations.

Note that integers do not form a multiplicative group, because the multiplicative inverse of most integers is not an integer. In other words, integers are not closed under multiplicative inverse.

Exercise 6.1. How many integers have multiplicative inverses that are integers? What are they?

Let's look at one of the examples in a bit more detail. In Chapter 5, we looked at the multiplication table for integers modulo 7:

×	1	2	3	4	5	6
1	1	2	3	4	5	6
2	2	4	6	1	3	5
3	3	6	2	5	1	4
4	4	1	5	2	6	3
5	5	3	1	6	4	2
6	6	5	4	3	2	1

The unique values in the table—the set {1, 2, 3, 4, 5, 6}—are also called "nonzero remainders modulo 7," and as we noted earlier, these form a multiplicative group. What does that mean? Since it's a multiplicative group, the group operation is multiplication, and its identity element is 1. We can see from the first row and column of the table that 1 is the identity, because the product of any element x and 1 is x.

Since groups are closed under their operation, if we multiply any two members of the group, we get another member of the group. For example:

$$2 \circ 5 = (2 \times 5) \bmod 7 = 3$$
$$4 \circ 3 = (4 \times 3) \bmod 7 = 5$$
$$5 \circ 2 = (5 \times 2) \bmod 7 = 3$$

Associativity and commutativity of modular multiplication follows from associativity and commutativity of integer multiplication. The commutativity or abelianness of the group is evident by observing that the multiplication table is symmetric with respect to the main diagonal.

Since groups are closed under inverse, if we take the inverse of any member of the group, we get another member of the group. (Recall that the inverse of an element x is the element that produces 1 when multiplied by x. From the multiplication table, you can see the pairs of inverses by looking at the rows and columns whose cells contain 1s.) For example:

$$2^{-1} = 4 \bmod 7$$
$$4^{-1} = 2 \bmod 7$$
$$5^{-1} = 3 \bmod 7$$

Évariste Galois (1811–1832)

The concept of groups started with the work of Évariste Galois, a young French college dropout involved in a revolutionary movement, and the most romantic figure in the history of mathematics.

In the early 19th century, a romantic spirit spread through Europe; young people idolized the English poet Byron, who died fighting for Greek independence, and others who were willing to give their lives for a cause. They remembered Napoleon not as a tyrant, but as a young hero who abolished feudalism throughout Europe.

Paris in the early 1830s was aflame with revolutionary activity. Galois, who was a bohemian hothead, joined the revolutionary movement. As a romantic rebel, Galois did not follow the conventional path through a university education. After failing to be admitted to one school and being expelled from another, he studied mathematics on his own, becoming an expert on Lagrange's theory of polynomials. He served brief prison sentences for various protest activities, such as marching through the streets in the uniform of a banned national guard unit while carrying several loaded weapons—but kept doing mathematics while in prison.

At age 20, Galois, defending the honor of a woman whom he apparently barely knew, issued a challenge (or was challenged) to a duel. The night before the duel, certain of his impending death, he wrote a long letter to a friend describing his mathematical ideas. This manuscript contained the seeds of the theory of groups, fields, and their automorphisms (mappings onto themselves). These ideas laid the foundations for a major new field of mathematics, abstract algebra. According to mathematician Hermann Weyl, "This letter, if judged by the novelty and profundity of ideas it contains, is perhaps the most substantial piece of writing in the whole literature of mankind."

The next day, Galois fought the duel and died as a result of his wounds. It is ironic that while he only played at being a revolutionary in politics, he was a true revolutionary in mathematics.

6.2 Monoids and Semigroups

In some situations, we are interested in algebraic structures that have fewer requirements than groups. (We'll see some of these applications in the next chapter.) For example, there are times when we don't need to require an inverse operation, but we want to maintain the other properties of a group. This is called a *monoid*. More formally:

Definition 6.4. A **monoid** is a set on which the following are defined:

$$\text{operation}: \quad x \circ y$$
$$\text{constant}: \quad e$$

and on which the following axioms hold:

$$x \circ (y \circ z) = (x \circ y) \circ z \qquad \text{associativity}$$
$$x \circ e = e \circ x = x \qquad \text{identity}$$

This definition is literally the same as the one for groups, except we've left out the inverse operation and the axiom of cancellation that uses it. As with groups, we can define particular kinds of monoids by specifying the operation, such as an *additive monoid* (where the operation is addition) and a *multiplicative monoid* (where the operation is multiplication).

Some examples of monoids follow:

- *Monoid of finite strings (free monoid)*: the elements are strings, the operation is concatenation, and the identity element is the empty string.

- *Multiplicative monoid of integers*: the elements are integers, the operation is multiplication, and the identity element is 1.

We can relax the requirements even further by dropping the identity element. This is called a *semigroup*:

Definition 6.5. A **semigroup** is a set on which the following is defined:

$$\text{operation}: \quad x \circ y$$

and on which the following axiom holds:

$$x \circ (y \circ z) = (x \circ y) \circ z \qquad\qquad \text{associativity}$$

Again, all we've done is taken the previous definition and removed something—in this case, the requirement that there be an identity element, and the axiom that uses it. And as we did with groups and monoids, we can define *additive semigroups* and *multiplicative semigroups* as semigroups that use those operations.

Some examples of semigroups follow:

- *Additive semigroup of positive integers*: the elements are positive integers and the operation is addition.

- *Multiplicative semigroup of even integers*: the elements are even integers and the operation is multiplication.

As we mentioned earlier, mathematicians write repeated applications of the semigroup, monoid, or group operation with the same conventions as ordinary multiplication. For example:

$$x \circ x \circ x = xxx = x^3$$

More formally, we define raising a semigroup to a power as follows:

$$x^n = \begin{cases} x & \text{if } n = 1 \\ xx^{n-1} & \text{otherwise} \end{cases} \qquad\qquad (6.1)$$

Exercise 6.2. Why can't we define power for semigroups starting with $n = 0$?

Equation 6.1 shows the semigroup operation happening on the left side of the power (i.e., it says xx^{n-1}, not $x^{n-1}x$). What if we wanted to write the expansion the other way? We can do that, too, as we will now prove:

Lemma 6.1: *For $n \geq 2$,* $\quad xx^{n-1} = x^{n-1}x.$

Proof. We prove this by induction.[1]
Basis: $n = 2$. It's obviously true, because

$$xx^1 = xx = x^1x$$

---

[1] For a refresher on this proof technique, see Appendix B.2.

As the induction hypothesis, we assume the statement is true for $n = k - 1$:

$$xx^{(k-1)-1} = xx^{k-2} = x^{k-2}x = x^{(k-1)-1}x$$

and then derive the result for $n = k$:

$$
\begin{aligned}
xx^{k-1} &= x(xx^{k-2}) && \text{by definition of power} \\
&= x(x^{k-2}x) && \text{by induction hypothesis} \\
&= (xx^{k-2})x && \text{by associativity of semigroup operation} \\
&= (x^{k-1})x && \text{by definition of power}
\end{aligned}
$$

$\square$

Even though a semigroup guarantees only associativity and not commutativity of its operation, it turns out that *powers* of a given semigroup element always commute, which we can also prove by generalizing this result. This is perhaps the most important theorem on semigroups.

Theorem 6.1 (Commutativity of Powers): $x^n x^m = x^m x^n = x^{n+m}$

Proof. Proof by induction on m.
Basis: $m = 1$:

$$
\begin{aligned}
x^n x &= xx^n && \text{by Lemma 6.1} \\
&= x^{n+1} && \text{by definition of power}
\end{aligned}
$$

Inductive step: Assume true for $m = k$. Show for $m = k + 1$:

$$
\begin{aligned}
x^n x^{k+1} &= x^n(xx^k) && \text{by definition of power} \\
&= (x^n x)x^k && \text{by associativity of semigroup operation} \\
&= x^{n+1}x^k && \text{by Lemma 6.1 and definition of power} \\
&= x^{n+1+k} && \text{by inductive hypothesis} \\
&= x^{n+k+1} && \text{by commutativity of integer addition}
\end{aligned}
$$

We have shown that $x^n x^m = x^{n+m}$. Therefore, it is also true that $x^m x^n = x^{m+n}$. Since integer addition is commutative, $x^{n+m} = x^{m+n}$, so $x^n x^m = x^m x^n$. $\square$

A semigroup is the weakest interesting algebraic structure. The only requirement left to relax is the associativity axiom. An algebraic structure called *magma* drops even that axiom, but it turns out not to be very useful. Since there are no axioms left, no theorems can be proved.

6.3   Some Theorems about Groups

Now let's return to groups and look at some of their properties.

An important observation is that all groups are *transformation groups*. In other words, every element a of the group G defines a transformation of G onto itself:

$$x \rightarrow ax$$

For example, with the additive group of integers, if we choose $a = 5$, then this acts as a "+5" operation, transforming the set of elements x to the set $x+5$. These transformations are one-to-one because of our invertibility axiom:

$$a^{-1}(ax) \rightarrow x$$

In our example, we can undo our +5 transformation by applying the inverse, −5.

Theorem 6.2: *A group transformation is a one-to-one correspondence.*[2]

This is equivalent to saying that for any finite set S of elements of group G and any element a of G, a set of elements aS has the same number of elements as S.

Proof. If $S = \{s_1, \ldots, s_n\}$, then $aS = \{as_1, \ldots, as_n\}$. We know that the set aS can't contain more unique elements than S, but could it contain fewer? (That would be the case if two of the elements in S were mapped to the same element in aS.) Suppose two elements of aS were the same: $as_i = as_j$. Then

$$a^{-1}(as_i) = a^{-1}(as_j)$$
$$(a^{-1}a)s_i = (a^{-1}a)s_j \qquad \text{by associativity}$$
$$es_i = es_j \qquad\qquad \text{by cancellation}$$
$$s_i = s_j \qquad\qquad\quad \text{by identity}$$

So if two results of the transformation as_k are equal, then their inputs s_k must be equal. Equivalently (by the contrapositive of the previous statement), if the inputs are not equal, then the results of the transformation must not be equal. Since we started with n distinct arguments, we will have n distinct results. In other words, the set aS has the same number of elements as S.   □

---

[2] *A one-to-one correspondence* between two sets is a mapping between them that is both *one-to-one* and *onto*.

Here are a few more simple results about groups:

Theorem 6.3: *There is a unique inverse for every element.*

$$ab = e \implies b = a^{-1}$$

Proof. Suppose $ab = e$. Then we can multiply both sides by a^{-1} on the left, like this:

$$ab = e$$
$$a^{-1}(ab) = a^{-1}e$$
$$(a^{-1}a)b = a^{-1}$$
$$eb = a^{-1}$$
$$b = a^{-1}$$
$\square$

Theorem 6.4: *The inverse of a product is the reversed product of the inverses.*

$$(ab)^{-1} = b^{-1}a^{-1}$$

Proof. The two expressions are equal if and only if multiplying one by the inverse of the other yields the identity element. We'll use the inverse of $(ab)^{-1}$, which by definition is (ab), and multiply it by $b^{-1}a^{-1}$:

$$(ab)(b^{-1}a^{-1}) = a(bb^{-1})a^{-1}$$
$$= aa^{-1}$$
$$= e$$
$\square$

Theorem 6.5: *The power of an inverse is the inverse of the power.*

$$(x^{-1})^n = (x^n)^{-1}$$

Proof by induction. Basis: $n = 1$

$$(x^{-1})^1 = x^{-1} = (x^1)^{-1}$$

Inductive step: Assume true for $n = k - 1$; that is, $(x^{-1})^{k-1} = (x^{k-1})^{-1}$. Then prove for $n = k$.

We want to show that $(x^{-1})^k = (x^k)^{-1}$; that is, the inverse of x^k is $(x^{-1})^k$. If that's true, then when we multiply them together, we should get the identity element. Using the definition of power and the commutativity of powers theorem, we'll rewrite x^k as $x^{k-1}x$ and $(x^{-1})^k$ as $x^{-1}(x^{-1})^{k-1}$, regroup the terms to get some to cancel, and then substitute using our inductive assumption:

$$
\begin{aligned}
x^k(x^{-1})^k &= (xx^{k-1})(x^{-1}(x^{-1})^{k-1}) \\
&= (x^{k-1}x)(x^{-1}(x^{-1})^{k-1}) \\
&= x^{k-1}(xx^{-1})(x^{-1})^{k-1} \\
&= x^{k-1}(x^{-1})^{k-1} \\
&= x^{k-1}(x^{k-1})^{-1} \\
&= e
\end{aligned}
$$

Therefore $(x^n)^{-1} = (x^{-1})^n$.   □

Exercise 6.3 (very easy). Prove that any group has at least one element.

Definition 6.6. If a group has $n > 0$ elements, n is called the group's **order**. If a group has infinitely many elements, its order is **infinite**.

There is also the notion of the *order of an element* in a group:

Definition 6.7. An element a has an **order** $n > 0$ if $a^n = e$ and for any $0 < k < n$, $a^k \neq e$. (In other words, the order of a is the smallest power of a that produces e.) If such n does not exist, a has an infinite order.

Exercise 6.4 (very easy). What is the order of e? Prove that e is the only element of such order.

*   *   *

We now come to an important theorem about groups:

Theorem 6.6: *Every element of a finite group has finite order.*

Proof. If n is an order of the group, then for any element a, $\{a, a^2, a^3, \ldots, a^{n+1}\}$ has at least one repetition a^i and a^j. Let us assume that $1 \leq i < j \leq n+1$, a^i is the first repeated element and a^j is its first repetition. Then

$$
\begin{aligned}
a^j &= a^i \\
a^j a^{-i} &= a^i a^{-i} = e \\
a^{j-i} &= e
\end{aligned}
$$

and $j - i > 0$ is the order of a.   □

This proof uses a version of the *pigeonhole principle*. (To learn more about the pigeonhole principle and how to use it, see Appendix B.3.) The result guarantees that this simple algorithm for computing the order of an element will terminate: just keep multiplying by itself until you get e.

Exercise 6.5. Prove that if a is an element of order n, then $a^{-1} = a^{n-1}$.

6.4 Subgroups and Cyclic Groups

Definition 6.8. A subset H of a group G is called a **subgroup** of G if

$$e \in H$$
$$a \in H \implies a^{-1} \in H$$
$$a, b \in H \implies a \circ b \in H$$

In other words, to be a subgroup, H must be a subset and a group. Associativity of the operation on G implies its associativity on H, so we do not need to explicitly state the associativity requirement in the definition; by the same reasoning, we do not need to explicitly restate the identity and cancellation axioms.

For example, the additive group of even numbers is a subgroup of the additive group of integers; so is the additive group of numbers divisible by 5.

Some groups have many subgroups, but almost all groups have at least two: the group itself and the group consisting of just the element e. These two subgroups are called *trivial* subgroups. (The only group that doesn't have at least two subgroups is the group that consists of just the identity element.)

Let's return again to the multiplicative group $\{1, 2, 3, 4, 5, 6\}$ of nonzero remainders modulo 7 and its multiplication table:

×	1	2	3	4	5	6
1	1	2	3	4	5	6
2	2	4	6	1	3	5
3	3	6	2	5	1	4
4	4	1	5	2	6	3
5	5	3	1	6	4	2
6	6	5	4	3	2	1

Our group has four multiplicative subgroups:

$$\{1\}, \{1, 6\}, \{1, 2, 4\}, \{1, 2, 3, 4, 5, 6\}$$

How can we tell? To be a subgroup, each one first needs to be a subset of the original group. Each of these is obviously a subset of $\{1, 2, 3, 4, 5, 6\}$, since all of their elements are contained in the larger set. Next, each subset also contains 1 (the identity element) and is closed under its operation (multiplication modulo 7) and its inverse operation.

For example, consider the set {1, 2, 4}: if we multiply any element of the set by itself or any other member of the set any number of times (mod 7), we will still get a result in the set.

Exercise 6.6. Find orders of every element of:

- The multiplicative group of remainders mod 7
- The multiplicative group of remainders mod 11

∗   ∗   ∗

The simplest kind of groups are *cyclic* groups.

Definition 6.9. A finite group is called **cyclic** if it has an element a such that for any element b, there is an integer n where

$$b = a^n$$

In other words, every element in the group can be generated by raising one particular element to different powers. Such an element is called a *generator* of the group; a group may have multiple generators. The additive group of remainders modulo n is an example of a cyclic group.

In our previous example of remainders modulo 7, we can tell that the generators are 3 and 5, because they are not in any nontrivial subgroup of the original group.

Exercise 6.7. Prove that any subgroup of a cyclic group is cyclic.

Exercise 6.8. Prove that a cyclic group is abelian.

Lemma 6.2: *Powers of a given element in a finite group form a subgroup.*

In other words, every element of a finite group is contained in a cyclic subgroup generated by this element.

Proof. For a set to be a subgroup, it must be a nonempty subset and it must be a group. To be a subset, it must be closed under the group operation. We know it's closed under the operation because the product of two powers is a power. To be a group, its operation needs to be associative, it must contain the identity element, and it must have an inverse operation. We know the operation is associative, because it's the same operation from the original group. We know the set of powers of a given element has an identity element, since we showed earlier (Theorem 6.6) that every element of a finite group has finite order.[3] And we

---

[3] Recall that part of the definition of an element a having a finite order is that $a^n = e$.

know that they have an inverse, because for every power a^k, a^{n-k} is its inverse, where n is the order of a. □

6.5 Lagrange's Theorem

One of the remarkable things about abstract algebra is that we can prove results for structures such as groups *without knowing anything about either the specific items in the group or the operation*. To see an important example of this, we will start by proving a few simple results about *cosets*.

Definition 6.10. If G is a group and $H \subset G$ is a subgroup of G, then for any $a \in G$ the **(left) coset** of a by H is a set

$$aH = \{g \in G \mid \exists h \in H : g = ah\}$$

In other words, a coset aH is a set of all elements in G obtainable by multiplying elements of H by a.

As an example, consider the additive group[4] of integers $\mathbb{Z}$ and its subgroup, integers divisible by 4, $4\mathbb{Z}$. (The use of $\mathbb{Z}$ as a symbol for integers comes from the German word *Zahlen*, which means "numbers.") It has four distinct cosets: $4n, 4n + 1, 4n + 2$, and $4n + 3$. Adding other integers will result only in values that are already in one of these cosets; for example, the coset $4n + 5$ will contain the same elements as the coset $4n + 1$. (The left and right cosets are the same, since integer addition is commutative.)

Lemma 6.3 (Size of Cosets): *In a finite group G, for any of its subgroups H, the number of elements in a coset aH is the same as the number of elements in the subgroup H.*

Proof. We already proved the one-to-one correspondence of transformations aS when S is a subset of G. Since a subgroup is by definition also a subset, then we know the mapping from H to aH is also a one-to-one correspondence. If there is a one-to-one correspondence between two finite sets, they are the same size. □

Lemma 6.4 (Complete Coverage by Cosets): *Every element a of a group G belongs to some coset of subgroup H.*

Proof. $a \in aH$. That is, every element a belongs to the coset aH generated by itself, because H, being a subgroup, contains the identity element. □

---

[4]Remember, in an additive group, the role of group "multiplication" is played by addition. So the coset aH consists of elements of G obtainable by *adding* a to elements of H.

Lemma 6.5 (Cosets are either disjoint or identical): *If two cosets aH and bH in a group G have a common element c, then aH = bH.*

Proof. Suppose the common element c is ah_a in one coset and bh_b in the other coset.

$$ah_a = bh_b$$

Multiplying both sides on the right by h_a^{-1}, we get

$$ah_ah_a^{-1} = bh_bh_a^{-1}$$
$$a = bh_bh_a^{-1}$$
$$a = b(h_bh_a^{-1})$$

The term on the right is b times something from H (we know it's from H because h_b is from H and h_a^{-1} is from H, and since H is a subgroup, it is closed under multiplication). Now let's multiply both sides on the right by x, an arbitrary element from H:

$$ax = b(h_bh_a^{-1})x$$

We know by definition that ax is in the coset aH. We also know that the term on the right is b times something from H, so it's also in the coset bH. Since we can do this for any x in H, $aH \subseteq bH$. We can then repeat the process from the beginning, this time using h_b^{-1} instead of h_a^{-1}, to show that $bH \subseteq aH$. So $bH = aH$. □

With these results, we can state an important theorem in group theory, which illustrates the power of abstract reasoning. If you want to learn one theorem in group theory, this is the one. While it's very simple to state, it provides the foundation for the theory of finite groups.

Theorem 6.7 (Lagrange's Theorem): *The order of a subgroup H of a finite group G divides the order of the group.*

Proof.

1. The group G is covered by cosets of H. (Proved earlier, Lemma 6.4)

2. Different cosets are disjoint. (Proved earlier, Lemma 6.5)

3. They are of the same size n, where n is the order of H. (Proved earlier, Lemma 6.3. Specifically, the result says that $|aH| = |H|$ for any a, so every coset has size $|H|$ and therefore the same size as every other coset.)

Therefore the order of G is nm, where m is the number of distinct cosets, which means that the order of G is a multiple of the order of H. In other words, the order of H divides the order of G. □

As an example, suppose a group G has two distinct cosets of its subgroup H. Then every element of G must be covered by one or the other (but not both) of those cosets, so the order of H must be $|G|/2$.

Interestingly, the converse of Lagrange's Theorem is not true: in a group of order n, not every divisor of n will have a subgroup of corresponding order.

Joseph-Louis Lagrange (1736–1813)

The leading mathematician in Europe at the end of the 18th century was Joseph-Louis Lagrange, who was a successor of Leonhard Euler both in terms of intellectual leadership and as holder of a position as director of mathematics at the Prussian Academy of Sciences in Berlin.

Lagrange was born Giuseppe Luigi Lagrancia in Turin, in the northern Italian region of Piedmont. As his original name suggests, he grew up speaking Italian, although his family claimed French ancestry. Lagrange discovered mathematics largely on his own while a student in Turin, and within a few years became an instructor and began publishing his work.

Sometime around age 20, he began corresponding with Euler, who was in Berlin at the time. Impressed by Lagrange's work, Euler acted as a mentor to the younger mathematician, encouraging him and promoting his discoveries. Euler began lobbying to bring Lagrange to Berlin, but by the time this plan came to fruition in 1766, Euler had moved back to Russia. With Euler gone, Lagrange was appointed to his mentor's former position, and soon established himself as the second most prominent mathematician in Europe.

Lagrange spent the next 20 years in Berlin, and did his most important work during this period, contributing to several areas of mathematics and physics. His book *Analytical Mechanics*, perhaps one of the 10 most important books in the history of mathematics, described a top-down approach to solving mechanical problems that was more general than using Newtonian mechanics. Much of modern physics relies on Lagrange's work. He also did extensive work on polynomial equations, realizing that coefficients could be expressed as functions of a polynomial's roots, and laid the groundwork for a later breakthrough by Galois. And in number theory, Lagrange figured out when continued fractions will be periodic, complementing Euler's earlier work on the subject.

After the death of his patron and friend, King Friedrich II of Prussia, Lagrange was approached by the French ambassador (acting on orders from King Louis XVI) to convince the great mathematician to move to France. Lagrange agreed, and would live in Paris from 1786 until his death.

Despite his prominence, Lagrange was a shy, unpretentious man with few friends and little social life. He was prone to bouts of depression, and made little progress on his work for years at a time, particularly during his first years in France. However, the French Revolution revived his interest— although he often feared he would need to flee the country due to the revolutionaries' expulsion of most foreigners. He became involved in efforts to come up with a new system of weights and measures, and was one of a committee of five prominent scientists who voted to approve what we now call the metric system. Lagrange also began teaching again, although by many accounts he was not popular with students, who had trouble understanding both his ideas and his Italian accent.

In his later years, Lagrange was favored by the new emperor Napoleon Bonaparte—himself quite an accomplished mathematician. Napoleon recognized Lagrange's genius, and made him a Count of the Empire.

*   *   *

Now we'll prove a couple of corollaries to Lagrange's Theorem:

Corollary 6.7.1: *The order of any element in a finite group divides the order of the group.*

Proof. The powers of an element of G form a subgroup of G. Since the order of an element is the order of the subgroup, and since the order of the subgroup must divide the order of the group, then the order of the element must divide the order of the group.   □

(Reminder: The order of an element is equal to the order of the cyclic group of its powers.)

Corollary 6.7.2: *Given a group G of order n, if a is an element of G, then $a^n = e$.*

Proof. If a has an order m, then m divides n (by the previous corollary), so $n = qm$. $a^m = e$ (by definition of order of an element). Therefore $(a^m)^q = e$ and $a^n = e$. ☐

Note that this doesn't say that the order of a is n; it could be smaller.

Lagrange's Theorem lets us easily prove some important results from Chapter 5 in much simpler fashion than we did the first time:

Fermat's Little Theorem: *If p is prime, $a^{p-1} - 1$ is divisible by p for any $0 < a < p$.*

Proof. Let us take the multiplicative group of remainders modulo p. It contains $p - 1$ nonzero remainders. Since $p - 1$ is the order of the group, it follows immediately from Corollary 6.7.2 that

$$a^{p-1} = e$$

Since the identity element for a multiplicative group is 1 (specifically, 1 mod p in our group of remainders), we have

$$a^{p-1} = 1 \bmod p$$

$$a^{p-1} - 1 = 0 \bmod p$$

which is what it means to be divisible by p. ☐

Euler's Theorem: *For $0 < a < n$, where a and n are coprime, $a^{\phi(n)} - 1$ is divisible by n.*

Proof. Let us take the multiplicative group of invertible remainders modulo n. Since $\phi(n)$ is by definition the number of coprimes, and every coprime is invertible, $\phi(n)$ gives us the order of the group. It follows immediately from Corollary 6.7.2 that

$$a^{\phi(n)} = e$$

$$a^{\phi(n)} = 1 \bmod n$$

or equivalently

$$a^{\phi(n)} - 1 = 0 \bmod n$$ ☐

The logic is exactly the same as the previous proof.

Exercise 6.9 (very easy). What are subgroups of a group of order 101?

Exercise 6.10. Prove that every group of prime order is cyclic.

6.6   Theories and Models

Groups, monoids, and semigroups are examples of what mathematicians call theories. People use the word "theory" in many ways, often meaning something like "conjecture"—that is, an unproven explanation. But to mathematicians, "theory" has a very specific meaning, which does not include this sense of being unproven.

Definition 6.11. A **theory** is a set of true propositions.

From now on, when we use the word "theory," we'll mean this specific mathematical sense. Here are some important facts about theories:

- A theory can be generated by a set of axioms plus a set of inference rules.

- A theory is *finitely axiomatizable* if it can be generated from a finite set of axioms.

- A set of axioms is *independent* if removing one will decrease the set of true propositions.

- A theory is *complete* if for any proposition, either that proposition or its negation is in the theory.

- A theory is *consistent* if for no proposition it contains both that proposition and its negation.

Let's look at a specific example: the notion of groups that we've been discussing throughout the chapter. A group is a theory in the sense we've just defined—specifically, a theory that, given operations $x \circ y$ and x^{-1} and the identity element e, has these axioms:

$$x \circ (y \circ z) = (x \circ y) \circ z$$
$$x \circ e = e \circ x = x$$
$$x \circ x^{-1} = x^{-1} \circ x = e$$

Starting with these, we can derive any number of true propositions (theorems), such as

$$x \circ y = x \implies y = e$$
$$(x \circ y)^{-1} = y^{-1} \circ x^{-1}$$

We aren't enumerating all the true propositions that constitute the theory of groups. Rather, we're generating the propositions by deriving them from the axioms and from previously proven propositions. For example, we can prove the first theorem by multiplying both sides of the equation by x^{-1}. Like basis vectors in linear algebra, axioms form a basis for the theory. Also like the linear algebra case, we can have more than one basis for the same theory.

*   *   *

Closely associated with the notion of a theory is that of a **model**. Again, the mathematical meaning is quite different from the everyday meaning:

Definition 6.12. A set of elements where all the operations in the theory are defined and all the propositions in the theory are true is called its **model**.

In a sense, a model is a particular *implementation* of a theory. A model gives you the specific set of elements; a theory does not. Just as there can be multiple implementations of, say, an algorithm, so there can be multiple models of a theory. For example, the additive group of integers and the multiplicative group of nonzero remainders modulo 7 are both models of the theory of abelian groups.

The more[5] propositions there are in a theory, the fewer different models there are. If we generate propositions from axioms and inference rules, then fewer axioms means fewer propositions, and therefore more models. This makes sense intuitively: axioms and propositions are *constraints* on a theory; the more of them you have, the harder it is to satisfy all of them, so the fewer models there will be that do so.

Conversely, the more models there are for a theory, the fewer propositions there are. If there are more ways to do something, there must be fewer constraints on how you can do it.

Definition 6.13. Two models are **isomorphic** if there is a one-to-one correspondence between them that preserves their operations. This means we can apply the mapping (or its inverse) before or after the operation and we'll get the same result.

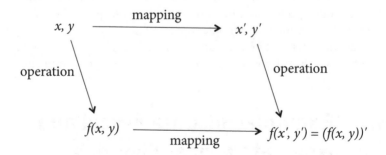

For example, we can map natural numbers to even natural numbers with the mapping "multiply by 2," and use addition as our operation. If we add two natural

---

[5]The notion of "more" that we're interested in here is that of *additional*. If the set of propositions for theory A contains all the propositions of theory B, plus some additional ones, then we say A has more, even if both have a countably infinite number of propositions.

numbers and then apply the mapping (i.e., multiply by 2), we get the same result as if we first multiply by 2 and then add the numbers:

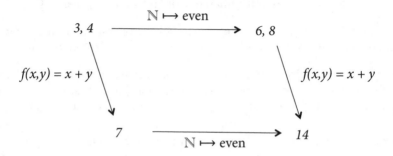

An isomorphism of a model with itself is called an *automorphism*.

Definition 6.14. A (consistent) theory is called **categorical** or **univalent** if all of its models are isomorphic.[6]

An inconsistent theory is one that has no models—there's no way to satisfy all the propositions without a contradiction.

Categorical Theories versus STL

For a long time, people believed that only categorical theories were good for programming. When the C++ Standard Template Library (STL) was first proposed, some computer scientists opposed it on the grounds that many of its fundamental concepts, such as **Iterator**, were underspecified. In fact, it is this underspecification that gives the library its generality. While linked lists and arrays are not computationally isomorphic, many STL algorithms are defined on input iterators and work on both data structures. If you can get by with fewer axioms, you allow for a wider range of implementations.

6.7 Examples of Categorical and Non-categorical Theories

Let's look at an example of a categorical theory with two isomorphic models: cyclic groups of order 4. The first model is $\mathbb{Z}_4$, the additive group of remainders

---

[6]This is the original definition by Oswald Veblen. Modern logicians talk about κ-categorical theories: all models of the cardinality κ are isomorphic. Full treatment of modern model theory is well outside the scope of this book.

modulo 4 (consisting of {0, 1, 2, 3}); the second model is $\left(\mathbb{Z}'_5, \times\right)$, the multiplicative group of nonzero remainders modulo 5 (consisting of {1, 2, 3, 4}). These groups have the following "multiplication" tables:

	0	1	2	3
0	0	1	2	3
1	1	2	3	0
2	2	3	0	1
3	3	0	1	2

	1	2	3	4
1	1	2	3	4
2	2	4	1	3
3	3	1	4	2
4	4	3	2	1

$$\mathbb{Z}_4 \qquad\qquad \left(\mathbb{Z}'_5, \times\right)$$

Even though the numbers are different, these two models are isomorphic; we could map elements of one to elements of the other. In theory, there are 4! = 12 possible mappings—0 in the first model could map to 1, 2, 3, or 4 in the second, then 1 could map to the three remaining choices, and so on. But in this case, the actual number of possibilities is much smaller.

We observe that in the first model, the values 1 and 3 are *generators* of the group—we could start with either of them, raise it to a power using the group operation, and get all the other elements. In the second model, 2 and 3 are generators. This helps us narrow the choices: a generator from one group has to map to a generator from the other group, which in this case gives us two different mappings. For example, we can say, "the role of 1 in the first model is played by 2 in the second model, and 3 in the first model corresponds to 3 in the second."

What about the other two values? We know from the multiplication tables that 0 in the first model is the identity element, a role played by 1 in the second model. Finally, we know that 2 in the first model maps to 4 in the second model, because in both cases it is the only non-identity element that gives identity when applied to itself.

So we have two possible mappings:

Value in $\mathbb{Z}_4$	Value in $\left(\mathbb{Z}'_5, \times\right)$		Value in $\mathbb{Z}_4$	Value in $\left(\mathbb{Z}'_5, \times\right)$
0	1		0	1
1	2		1	3
2	4		2	4
3	3		3	2

How do we know these mappings produce our second model? One way is to see if we can use them to transform the $\mathbb{Z}_4$ multiplication table into the $\left(\mathbb{Z}'_5, \times\right)$ multiplication table. Let's try it using the second mapping.

First, we replace the values from the $\mathbb{Z}_4$ table with the mapped values. That gives us:

	1	3	4	2
1	1	3	4	2
3	3	4	2	1
4	4	2	1	3
2	2	1	3	4

Then we permute the rows and columns so the headers are in the right order. We'll start by swapping the last two columns and the last two rows (shaded in the preceding table):

	1	3	2	4
1	1	3	2	4
3	3	4	1	2
2	2	1	4	3
4	4	2	3	1

Finally, we'll swap the middle two rows and columns:

	1	2	3	4
1	1	2	3	4
2	2	4	1	3
3	3	1	4	2
4	4	3	2	1

This is exactly the multiplication table for $\left(\mathbb{Z}_5', \times\right)$ we showed on p. 105, which is what we wanted.

*   *   *

Now let's look at an example of a non-categorical theory: all groups of order 4. While there is only one non-isomorphic group of order 1, 2, or 3, there are two non-isomorphic groups of order 4: the cyclic group $\mathbb{Z}_4$, which we just described, and a group called the *Klein group*. There are two important models of the Klein group: the multiplicative group of units modulo 8 (consisting of $\{1, 3, 5, 7\}$) and the group of isometries transforming a rectangle into itself (the identity transform, vertical symmetry, horizontal symmetry, and 180° rotation).

These two kinds of groups have the following multiplication tables. Since we don't know the individual elements of a theory, this time we'll write them using e to mean the identity element and a, b, and c to mean their other elements:

	e	a	b	c
e	e	a	b	c
a	a	b	c	e
b	b	c	e	a
c	c	e	a	b

	e	a	b	c
e	e	a	b	c
a	a	e	c	b
b	b	c	e	a
c	c	b	a	e

Cyclic group $\mathbb{Z}_4$ **Klein group**

In the table on the left, addition is our operation and we can think of "e" as being 0 (the additive identity) and a, b, and c as representing the integers 1, 2, and 3. So, for example, $a \circ b = 1 + 2 = 3 = c$; therefore the value at row a and column b is c.

Are these two groups really different (i.e., not isomorphic), or is there a way to transform one into the other, as we did before? In other words, is there a distinguishing proposition for groups of order 4? Yes, the proposition

$$\forall x \in G \ : \ x^2 = e$$

is true for the Klein group but false for $\mathbb{Z}_4$. We can see this by looking at the diagonal of the multiplication table. Another way to see that they are different is to notice that the cyclic group contains two generators, while the Klein group contains none.

6.8   Thoughts on the Chapter

In this chapter we introduced the idea of algebraic structures, abstract sets of elements that obey certain properties. We looked at groups, the most important of these structures, and their weaker cousins monoids and semigroups. These are summarized in the following table, which we'll be adding to later:

STRUCTURE	OPERATIONS	ELEMENTS	AXIOMS
semigroup	$x \circ y$		$x \circ (y \circ z) = (x \circ y) \circ z$
Example: positive integers under addition			
monoid	$x \circ y$	e	$x \circ (y \circ z) = (x \circ y) \circ z$
			$x \circ e = e \circ x = x$
Example: strings under concatenation			
group	$x \circ y$	e	$x \circ (y \circ z) = (x \circ y) \circ z$
	x^{-1}		$x \circ e = e \circ x = x$
			$x \circ x^{-1} = x^{-1} \circ x = e$
Example: invertible matrices under multiplication			
abelian group	$x \circ y$	e	$x \circ (y \circ z) = (x \circ y) \circ z$
	x^{-1}		$x \circ e = e \circ x = x$
			$x \circ x^{-1} = x^{-1} \circ x = e$
			$x \circ y = y \circ x$
Example: two-dimensional vectors under addition			

Each row of the table includes all the properties of the previous row, with one or more additions. We can view the relationships between the structures like this:

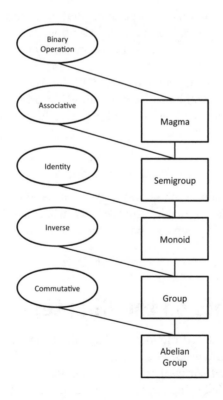

For example, the diagram shows that a monoid is a semigroup that also has an identity element (and the identity axiom).

A few additional structures we talked about are most easily defined in terms of others:

STRUCTURE	DEFINITION
additive semigroup	semigroup where operation is + and (by convention) commutes
additive monoid	additive semigroup with identity element 0
subgroup	group that is a subset of another group
cyclic group	group where all elements can be obtained by raising (at least) one element to different powers

We also saw how we could derive properties of groups (like the one stated by Lagrange's Theorem) without knowing anything about the particular elements being manipulated. In other words, we saw how to derive results about theories without specifying a particular model. Now we're ready to put these algebraic structures to practical use.

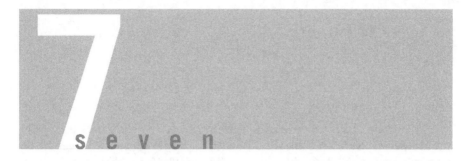

Deriving a Generic Algorithm

> To generalize something means to think it.
>
> Hegel, *Philosophy of Right*

In this chapter we'll take the Egyptian multiplication algorithm from Chapter 2 and, by using the mathematical abstractions introduced in the previous chapter, generalize it to apply to a wide variety of problems beyond simple arithmetic.

7.1 Untangling Algorithm Requirements

Two steps are required to write a good piece of code. The first step is to get the algorithm right. The second step is to figure out which sorts of things (types) it works for. Now, you might be thinking that you already know the type—it's int or float or whatever you started with. But that may not always be the case; things change. Next year someone may want the code to work with unsigned ints or doubles or something else entirely. We want to design our code so we can reuse it in these different situations.

Let's take another look at the multiply-accumulate version of the Egyptian multiplication algorithm we developed in Chapter 2. Recall that we are multiplying n by a and accumulating the result in r; also recall that we have a precondition that neither n nor a can be zero:

```
int mult_acc4(int r, int n, int a) {
    while (true) {
        if (odd(n)) {
            r = r + a;
            if (n == 1) return r;
        }
```

```
        n = half(n);
        a = a + a;
    }
}
```

This time we've written some of the code in a *slanted* typeface and some of it in a **bold** typeface. Notice that the slanted and bold parts are disjointed; there are no places where a "slanted variable" and a "bold variable" are combined or interact with each other in any way. This means that the requirements for being a slanted variable don't have to be the same as the requirements for being a bold variable—or to put it in programming language terms, they can be different types.

So what are the requirements for each kind of variable? Until now, we've declared the variables as ints, but it seems as if the algorithm would work for many other similar types as well. Slanted variables *r* and *a* must be some type that supports adding—we might say that they must be a "plusable" type. The bold variable *n* must be able to be checked for oddness, compared with 1, and must support division by 2 (it must be "halvable"). Note that division by 2 is a much more restricted operation than division in general. For example, angles can be divided by 2 with ruler-and-compass construction, while dividing them by 3 is impossible in that framework.

We've established that *r* and *a* are the same type, which we'll write using the template typename **A**. Similarly, we said that *n* is a different type, which we'll call **N**. So instead of insisting that all the arguments be of type int, we can now write the following more generic form of the program:

```
template <typename A, typename N>
A multiply_accumulate(A r, N n, A a) {
    while (true) {
        if (odd(n)) {
            r = r + a;
            if (n == 1) return r;
        }
        n = half(n);
        a = a + a;
    }
}
```

This makes the problem easier—we can figure out the requirements for **A** separately from the requirements on **N**. Let's dig a bit deeper into these types, starting with the simpler one.

7.2   Requirements on A

What are the *syntactic requirements* on **A**? In other words, which operations can we do on things belonging to **A**? Just by looking at how variables of this type are used in the code, we can see that there are three operations:

- They can be added (in C++, they must have `operator+`).

- They can be passed by value (in C++, they must have a copy constructor).

- They can be assigned (in C++, they must have `operator=`).

We also need to specify the *semantic requirements*. That is, we need to say what these operations mean. Our main requirement is that + must be *associative*, which we express as follows:

$$A(T) \implies \forall a, b, c \in T : a + (b + c) = (a + b) + c$$

(In English, we might read the part before the colon like this: "If type T is an **A**, then for any values *a*, *b*, and *c* in T, the following holds: ....")

Even though + is associative in theory (and in math generally), things are not so simple on computers. There are real-world cases where associativity of addition does not hold. For example, consider these two lines of code:

```
w = (x + y) + z;
```

```
w = x + (y + z)
```

Suppose *x*, *y*, and *z* are of type `int`, and *z* is negative. Then it is possible that for some very large values, $x + y$ will overflow, while this would not have happened if we added $y + z$ first. The problem arises because addition is not well defined for all possible values of the type `int`; we say that + is a *partial* function.

To address this problem, we clarify our requirements. We require that the axioms hold only inside the *domain of definition*—that is, the set of values for which the function is defined.[1]

*   *   *

In fact, there are a couple more syntactic requirements that we missed. They are implied by copy construction and assignment. For example, copy construction means to make a copy that is equal to the original. To do this, we need the ability to test things belonging to **A** for equality:

---

[1] For a more rigorous treatment of this topic, see Section 2.1 of *Elements of Programming* by Stepanov and McJones.

- They can be compared for equality (in C++, they must have `operator==`).

- They can be compared for inequality (in C++, they must have `operator!=`).

Accompanying these syntactic requirements are semantic requirements for what we call *equational reasoning*; equality on a type T should satisfy our expectations:

- Inequality is the negation of equality.

$$(a \neq b) \iff \neg(a = b)$$

- Equality is reflexive, symmetric, and transitive.

$$a = a$$
$$a = b \implies b = a$$
$$a = b \wedge b = c \implies a = c$$

- Equality implies substitutability.

$$\text{for any function } f \text{ on T,} \quad a = b \implies f(a) = f(b)$$

The three axioms in the middle (reflexivity, symmetry, and transitivity) provide what we call *equivalence*, but equational reasoning requires something much stronger, so we add the substitutability requirement.

We have a special name for types that behave in the "usual way"—*regular* types:

Definition 7.1. A **regular type** T is a type where the relationships between construction, assignment, and equality are the same as for built-in types such as `int`.

For example:

- `T a(b); assert(a == b); unchanged(b);`

- `a = b; assert(a == b); unchanged(b);`

- `T a(b);` is equivalent to `T a; a = b;`

For an extensive treatment of regular types, see Chapter 1 of *Elements of Programming*. All types that we use in this book are regular.

* * *

Now we can formalize the requirements on **A**:

- Regular type

- Provides associative +

As we saw in Chapter 6, algebraic structures that have a binary associative operation are called *semigroups* (see Definition 6.5). Also, a regular type guarantees the ability to compare two values for equality, which we need for our associativity axiom. Therefore we can say that **A** is a semigroup. Its operation is addition, so we might be tempted to call it an additive semigroup. But recall that by convention, additive semigroups are assumed to be commutative. Since we don't need commutativity for our algorithm, we'll say that **A** is a *noncommutative additive semigroup*. This means that commutativity is not *required*; it does not mean that commutativity is not allowed. In other words, every (commutative) additive semigroup is also a noncommutative additive semigroup.

Definition 7.2. A **noncommutative additive semigroup** is a semigroup where the associative binary operation is +.

Some examples of noncommutative additive semigroups are positive even integers, negative integers, real numbers, polynomials, planar vectors, Boolean functions, and line segments. These examples happen to also be additive semigroups, but that is not always the case. As we shall see, + may have different interpretations for these different types, but it will always be associative.

For many centuries, the symbol "+" has been used, by convention, to mean a commutative operation as well as an associative one. Many programming languages (e.g., C++, Java, Python) use + for string concatenation, a noncommutative operation. This violates standard mathematical practice, which is a bad idea. The mathematical convention is as follows:

- If a set has one binary operation and it is both associative and commutative, call it +.

- If a set has one binary operation and it is associative and not commutative, call it ∗.

20th-century logician Stephen Kleene introduced the notation *ab* to denote string concatenation (since in mathematics ∗ is usually elided).

The Naming Principle

If we are coming up with a name for something, or overloading an existing name, we should follow these three guidelines:

1. If there is an established term, use it.

2. Do not use an established term inconsistently with its accepted meaning. In particular, overload an operator or function name only when you will be preserving its existing semantics.

3. If there are conflicting usages, the much more established one wins.

The name *vector* in STL was taken from the earlier programming languages Scheme and Common Lisp. Unfortunately, this was inconsistent with the much older meaning of the term in mathematics and violates Rule 3; this data structure should have been called *array*. Sadly, if you make a mistake and violate these principles, the result might stay around for a long time.

7.3 Requirements on N

Now that we know that **A** must be a noncommutative additive semigroup, we can specify that in our template instead of just saying `typename`:

```
template <NoncommutativeAdditiveSemigroup A, typename N>
A multiply_accumulate(A r, N n, A a) {
    while (true) {
        if (odd(n)) {
            r = r + a;
            if (n == 1) return r;
        }
        n = half(n);
        a = a + a;
    }
}
```

Here we're using **NonCommutativeAdditiveSemigroup** as a C++ *concept*, a set of requirements on types that we'll discuss in Chapter 10. Instead of saying `typename`, we name the concept we wish to use. Since concepts are not yet supported in the language as of this writing, we're doing a bit of preprocessor slight-of-hand:

```
#define NonCommutativeAdditiveSemigroup typename
```

As far as the compiler is concerned, A is just a typename, but for us, it's a **NonCommutativeAdditiveSemigroup**. We'll use this trick from now on when we want to specify the type requirements in templates.

Although this behavior is not needed for abstract mathematics, in programming we need our variables to be constructible and assignable, which are also guaranteed by being regular types. From now on, when we specify an algebraic structure as a concept, we will assume that we are inheriting all of the regular type requirements.

What about the requirements on our other argument's type, **N**? Let's start with the syntactic requirements. **N** must be a regular type implementing

- `half`

- `odd`

- `== 0`

- `== 1`

Here are the semantic requirements on **N**:

- $\text{even}(n) \implies \text{half}(n) + \text{half}(n) = n$

- $\text{odd}(n) \implies \text{even}(n - 1)$

- $\text{odd}(n) \implies \text{half}(n - 1) = \text{half}(n)$

- Axiom: $n \leq 1 \ \lor \ \text{half}(n) = 1 \ \lor \ \text{half}(\text{half}(n)) = 1 \lor \ldots$

Which C++ types satisfy these requirements? There are several: `uint8_t`, `int8_t`, `uint64_t`, and so on. The concept that they satisfy is called **N Integer**.

*   *   *

Now we can finally write a fully *generic* version of our multiply-accumulate function by specifying the correct requirements for both types:

```
template <NoncommutativeAdditiveSemigroup A, Integer N>
A multiply_accumulate_semigroup(A r, N n, A a) {
    // precondition(n >= 0);
    if (n == 0) return r;
    while (true) {
        if (odd(n)) {
            r = r + a;
            if (n == 1) return r;
        }
        n = half(n);
        a = a + a;
    }
}
```

We've added one more line of code, which returns r when n is zero. We do this because when n is zero, we don't need to do anything. However, the same is not true for multiply, as we'll see in a moment.

Here's the multiply function that calls the preceding code; it has the same requirements:

```
template <NoncommutativeAdditiveSemigroup A, Integer N>
A multiply_semigroup(N n, A a) {
    // precondition(n > 0);
    while (!odd(n)) {
        a = a + a;
        n = half(n);
    }
    if (n == 1) return a;
    return multiply_accumulate_semigroup(a, half(n - 1), a + a);
}
```

We can also update our helper functions odd and half to work for any **Integer**:

```
template <Integer N>
bool odd(N n) { return bool(n & 0x1); }
```

```
template <Integer N>
N half(N n) { return n >> 1; }
```

7.4   New Requirements

Our precondition for multiply says that n must be strictly greater than zero. (We made this assumption earlier, since the Greeks had only positive integers, but now we need to make it explicit.) What should an additive semigroup multiplication function return when n is zero? It should be the value that doesn't change the result when the semigroup operator—addition—is applied. In other words, it should be the additive identity. But an additive semigroup is not required to have an identity element, so we can't depend on this property. In other words, we can't rely on there being an equivalent of zero. (Remember, a no longer has to be an integer; it can be any **NoncommutativeAdditiveSemigroup**, such as positive integers or nonempty strings.) That's why n can't be zero.

But there is an alternative: instead of having a restriction on the data requiring $n > 0$, we can require that any type we use know how to deal with 0. We do this by changing the concept requirement on n from additive semigroup to *monoid*. Recall from Chapter 6 that in addition to an associative binary operation, a monoid contains an identity element e and an identity axiom that says

$$x \circ e = e \circ x = x$$

In particular, we're going to use a *noncommutative additive monoid*, where the identity element is called "0":

$$x + 0 = 0 + x = x$$

This is the multiply function for monoids:

```
template <NoncommutativeAdditiveMonoid A, Integer N>
A multiply_monoid(N n, A a) {
    // precondition(n >= 0);
    if (n == 0) return A(0);
    return multiply_semigroup(n, a);
}
```

What if we want to allow negative numbers when we multiply? We need to ensure that "multiplying by a negative" makes sense for any type we might have. This turns out to be equivalent to saying that the type must support an *inverse operation*. Again, we find that our current requirement—noncommutative additive monoid—is not guaranteed to have this property. For this, we need a *group*. A group, as you may recall from Chapter 6, includes all of the monoid operations and axioms, plus an inverse operation x^{-1} that obeys the cancellation axiom

$$x \circ x^{-1} = x^{-1} \circ x = e$$

In our case, we want a noncommutative additive group, one where the inverse operation is unary minus and the cancellation axiom is:

$$x + -x = -x + x = 0$$

Having strengthened our type requirements, we can remove our preconditions on n to allow negative values. Again, we'll wrap the last version of our function with our new one:

```
template <NoncommutativeAdditiveGroup A, Integer N>
A multiply_group(N n, A a) {
    if (n < 0) {
        n = -n;
        a = -a;
    }
    return multiply_monoid(n, a);
}
```

7.5   Turning Multiply into Power

Now that our code has been generalized to work for any additive semigroup (or monoid or group), we can make a remarkable observation:

> *If we replace + with ∗ (thereby replacing doubling with squaring),*
> *we can use our existing algorithm to compute a^n instead of $n \cdot a$.*

Here's the C++ function we get when we apply this transformation to our code for `multiply_accumulate_semigroup`:

```
template <MultiplicativeSemigroup A, Integer N>
A power_accumulate_semigroup(A r, A a, N n) {
    // precondition(n >= 0);
    if (n == 0) return r;
    while (true) {
        if (odd(n)) {
            r = r * a;
            if (n == 1) return r;
        }
        n = half(n);
        a = a * a;
    }
}
```

The new function computes ra^n. The only things that have changed are highlighted in **bold**. Note that we've changed the order of arguments a and n, so as to match the order of arguments in standard mathematical notation (i.e., we say na, but a^n).

Here's the function that computes power:

```
template <MultiplicativeSemigroup A, Integer N>
A power_semigroup(A a, N n) {
    // precondition(n > 0);
    while (!odd(n)) {
        a = a * a;
        n = half(n);
    }
    if (n == 1) return a;
    return power_accumulate_semigroup(a, a * a, half(n - 1));
}
```

Here are the wrapped versions for multiplicative monoids and groups:

```
template <MultiplicativeMonoid A, Integer N>
A power_monoid(A a, N n) {
    // precondition(n >= 0);
    if (n == 0) return A(1);
    return power_semigroup(a, n);
}
```

```
template <MultiplicativeGroup A, Integer N>
A power_group(A a, N n) {
    if (n < 0) {
        n = -n;
        a = multiplicative_inverse(a);
    }
    return power_monoid(a, n);
}
```

Just as we needed an additive identity (0) for our monoid multiply, so we need a multiplicative identity (1) in our monoid power function. Also, just as we needed an additive inverse (unary minus) for our group multiply, so we need a multiplicative inverse for our group power function. There's no built-in multiplicative inverse (reciprocal) operation in C++, but it's easy to write one:

```
template <MultiplicativeGroup A>
A multiplicative_inverse(A a) {
    return A(1) / a;
}
```

7.6   Generalizing the Operation

We've seen examples of two semigroups—additive and multiplicative—each with its associated operation (+ and ∗, respectively). The fact that we could use the same algorithm for both is wonderful, but it was annoying to have to write different versions of the same code for each case. In reality, there could be many such semigroups, each with its associative operations (for example, multiplication mod 7) that work on the same type T. Rather than having another version for every operation we want to use, we can generalize the *operation* itself, just as we generalized the types of the arguments before. In fact, there are many situations where we need to pass an operation to an algorithm; you may have seen examples of this in STL.

Here's the accumulate version of our power function for an arbitrary semigroup. We still refer to the function it computes as "power," even though the operation it's repeatedly applying may not necessarily be multiplication.

```
template <Regular A, Integer N, SemigroupOperation Op>
// requires (Domain<Op, A>)
A power_accumulate_semigroup(A r, A a, N n, Op op) {
    // precondition(n >= 0);
    if (n == 0) return r;
    while (true) {
        if (odd(n)) {
```

```
            r = op(r, a);
            if (n == 1) return r;
        }
        n = half(n);
        a = op(a, a);
    }
}
```

Notice that we've added a "requires" comment to our template that says the domain of operation Op must be **A**. If future versions of C++ support concepts, this comment could be turned into a statement (similar to an assertion) that the compiler could use to ensure the correct relationship holds between the given types. As it is, we'll have to make sure as programmers that we call this function only with template arguments that satisfy the requirement.

Also, since we no longer know which kind of semigroup to make **A**—it could be additive, multiplicative, or something else altogether, depending on Op—we can require only that **A** be a regular type. The "semigroupness" will come from the requirement that Op be a SemigroupOperation.

We can use this function to write a version of power for an arbitrary semigroup:

```
template <Regular A, Integer N, SemigroupOperation Op>
// requires (Domain<Op, A>)
A power_semigroup(A a, N n, Op op) {
    // precondition(n > 0);
    while (!odd(n)) {
        a = op(a, a);
        n = half(n);
    }
    if (n == 1) return a;
    return power_accumulate_semigroup(a, op(a, a),
                                      half(n - 1), op);
}
```

As we did before, we can extend the function to monoids by adding an identity element. But since we don't know in advance which operation will be passed, we have to obtain the identity from the operation:

```
template <Regular A, Integer N, MonoidOperation Op>
// requires(Domain<Op, A>)
A power_monoid(A a, N n, Op op) {
    // precondition(n >= 0);
    if (n == 0) return identity_element(op);
    return power_semigroup(a, n, op);
}
```

Here are examples of `identity_element` functions for $+$ and $*$:

```
template <NoncommutativeAdditiveMonoid T>
T identity_element(std::plus<T>) { return T(0); }
```

```
template <MultiplicativeMonoid T>
T identity_element(std::multiplies<T>) { return T(1); }
```

Each of these functions specifies the type of the object it expects to be called with, but doesn't name it, since the object is never used. The first one says, "The additive identity is 0." Of course, there will be different identity elements for different monoids—for example, the maximum value of the type T for `min`.

*   *   *

To extend `power` to groups, we need an inverse operation, which is itself a function of the specified **GroupOperation**:

```
template <Regular A, Integer N, GroupOperation Op>
// requires(Domain<Op, A>)
A power_group(A a, N n, Op op) {
    if (n < 0) {
        n = -n;
        a = inverse_operation(op)(a);
    }
    return power_monoid(a, n, op);
}
```

Examples of `inverse_operation` look like this:

```
template <AdditiveGroup T>
std::negate<T> inverse_operation(std::plus<T>) {
    return std::negate<T>();
}
```

```
template <MultiplicativeGroup T>
reciprocal<T> inverse_operation(std::multiplies<T>) {
    return reciprocal<T>();
}
```

STL already has a `negate` function, but (due to an oversight) has no `reciprocal`. So we'll write our own. We'll use a *function object*—a C++ object that provides a function declared by `operator()` and is invoked like a function call, using the name of the object as the function name. To learn more about function objects, see Appendix C.

```
template <MultiplicativeGroup T>
struct reciprocal {
    T operator()(const T& x) const {
        return T(1) / x;
    }
};
```

This is just a generalization of the `multiplicative_inverse` function we wrote in the previous section.[2]

Reduction

The power algorithm is not the only important algorithm defined on semi-groups. Another key algorithm is *reduction*, in which a binary operation is applied successively to each element of a sequence and its previous result.

Two commonly seen examples of this in mathematics are the summa-tion (Σ) function for additive semigroups and the product (Π) function for multiplicative semigroups. We can generalize this to an arbitrary semigroup.

This generalized version of reduction was invented in 1962 by computer scientist Ken Iverson in his language APL. In APL terminology, the / rep-resented the reduction operator. For example, summation of a sequence is expressed as

```
+ / 1 2 3
```

The idea of reduction has appeared in many contexts since then. John Backus, inventor of the first high-level programming language, included a similar operator called *insert* in his language FP in 1977. (He called opera-tors "functional forms.") An early paper on generic programming, "Oper-ators and Algebraic Structures," by Kapur, Musser, and Stepanov, extended the idea to parallel reduction in 1981 and clarified the relationship to as-sociative operations. The language Common Lisp, popular in the 1980s for artificial intelligence applications, included a `reduce` function. Google's MapReduce system, and its open-source variant Hadoop, is a current prac-tical application of these ideas.

7.7 Computing Fibonacci Numbers

Note: This section assumes some basic knowledge of linear algebra. The rest of the book does not depend on the material covered here, and this section may be skipped without affecting the reader's understanding.

---

[2]This time we do not need a precondition preventing x from being zero, because **Multiplicative-Group** does not contain a non-invertible zero element. If in practice we have a type such as `double` that otherwise would satisfy the requirements of **MultiplicativeGroup** if it did not contain a zero, we can add a precondition to eliminate that case.

In Chapter 4 we met the early 13th-century mathematician Leonardo Pisano, often known today as Fibonacci. One of the things he's best known for is a famous problem he posed: if we start with one pair of rabbits, how many pairs will we have after a certain number of months? To simplify the problem, Leonardo made some assumptions: the original pair of rabbits and every litter afterward consists of a male and a female; female rabbits take one month to reach sexual maturity and have one litter per month after that; rabbits live forever.

Initially we have 1 pair of rabbits. At the start of month 2, the rabbits mate, but we still have only 1 pair. At the start of month 3, the female gives birth, so we have 2 pairs. At the start of month 4, the initial female gives birth another time, so we have 3 pairs. At the start of month 5, the initial female gives birth again, but so does the female born in month 3, so now we have 5 pairs, and so on. If we say that we had 0 rabbits in month 0 (before the experiment began), then the number of pairs in each month looks like this:

$$0, 1, 1, 2, 3, 5, 8, 13, 21, 34...$$

Each month's population can be obtained simply by adding the populations of each of the previous two months. Today, elements of this sequence are called *Fibonacci numbers*, and such a sequence is defined formally like this:

$$F_0 = 0$$
$$F_1 = 1$$
$$F_i = F_{i-1} + F_{i-2}$$

How long does it take to compute the nth Fibonacci number? The "obvious" answer is $n - 2$, but the obvious answer is wrong.

The naive way to implement this in C++ is something like this:

```cpp
int fib0(int n) {
    if (n == 0) return 0;
    if (n == 1) return 1;
    return fib0(n - 1) + fib0(n - 2);
}
```

However, this code does an awful lot of repeated work. Consider the calculations to compute `fib0(5)`:

$$F_5 = F_4 + F_3$$
$$= (F_3 + F_2) + (F_2 + F_1)$$
$$= ((F_2 + F_1) + (F_1 + F_0)) + ((F_1 + F_0) + F_1)$$
$$= (((F_1 + F_0) + F_1) + (F_1 + F_0)) + ((F_1 + F_0) + F_1)$$

Even in this small example, the computation does 7 additions, and just the quantity $F_1 + F_0$ is recomputed 3 times.

Exercise 7.1. How many additions are needed to compute `fib0(n)`?

Recomputing the same thing over and over is unacceptable, and there's no excuse for code like that. We can easily fix the code by keeping a running state of the previous two results:

```
int fibonacci_iterative(int n) {
    if (n == 0) return 0;
    std::pair<int, int> v = {0, 1};
    for (int i = 1; i < n; ++i) {
        v = {v.second, v.first + v.second};
    }
    return v.second;
}
```

This is an acceptable solution, which takes $O(n)$ operations. In fact, given that we want to find the nth element of a sequence, it might appear to be optimal. But the amazing thing is that we can actually compute the nth Fibonacci number in $O(\log n)$ operations, which for most practical purposes is less than 64.

Suppose we represent the computation of the next Fibonacci number from the previous two using the following matrix equation:[3]

$$\begin{bmatrix} v_{i+1} \\ v_i \end{bmatrix} = \begin{bmatrix} 1 & 1 \\ 1 & 0 \end{bmatrix} \begin{bmatrix} v_i \\ v_{i-1} \end{bmatrix}$$

Then the nth Fibonacci number may be obtained by

$$\begin{bmatrix} v_n \\ v_{n-1} \end{bmatrix} = \begin{bmatrix} 1 & 1 \\ 1 & 0 \end{bmatrix}^{n-1} \begin{bmatrix} 1 \\ 0 \end{bmatrix}$$

In other words, we can compute the nth Fibonacci number by raising a certain matrix to a power. As we will see, matrix multiplication can be used to solve many problems. Matrices are a multiplicative monoid, so *we already have an $O(\log n)$ algorithm*—our `power` algorithm from Section 7.6.

Exercise 7.2. Implement computing Fibonacci numbers using `power`.

This is a nice application of our `power` algorithm, but computing Fibonacci numbers isn't the only thing we can do. If we replace the + with an arbitrary linear recurrence function, we can use the same technique to compute any *linear recurrence*.

---

[3] A brief refresher on matrix multiplication may be found at the beginning of Section 8.5.

Definition 7.3. A **linear recurrence function** of order k is a function f such that

$$f(y_0, \ldots, y_{k-1}) = \sum_{i=0}^{k-1} a_i y_i$$

Definition 7.4. A **linear recurrence sequence** is a sequence generated by a linear recurrence from initial k values.

The Fibonacci sequence is a linear recurrence sequence of order 2.

For any linear recurrence sequence, we can compute the nth step by doing matrix multiplication using our power algorithm:

$$\begin{bmatrix} x_n \\ x_{n-1} \\ x_{n-2} \\ \vdots \\ x_{n-k+1} \end{bmatrix} = \begin{bmatrix} a_0 & a_1 & a_2 & \cdots & a_{k-2} & a_{k-1} \\ 1 & 0 & 0 & \cdots & 0 & 0 \\ 0 & 1 & 0 & \cdots & 0 & 0 \\ \vdots & \vdots & \vdots & & \vdots & \vdots \\ 0 & 0 & 0 & \cdots & 1 & 0 \end{bmatrix}^{n-k+1} \begin{bmatrix} x_{k-1} \\ x_{k-2} \\ x_{k-3} \\ \vdots \\ x_0 \end{bmatrix}$$

The line of 1s just below the diagonal provides the "shifting" behavior, so that each value in the sequence depends on the previous k.

7.8 Thoughts on the Chapter

We began this chapter by analyzing the requirements on our code from Chapter 2, abstracting the algorithms to use an associative operation on arbitrary types. We were able to rewrite the code so that it is defined on certain algebraic structures: semigroups, monoids, and groups.

Next, we demonstrated that the algorithm could be generalized, first from multiplication to power, then to arbitrary operations on our algebraic structures. We'll use this generalized power algorithm again later on in the book.

The process we went through—taking an efficient algorithm, generalizing it (without losing efficiency) so that it works on abstract mathematical concepts, and then applying it to a variety of situations—is the essence of generic programming.

More Algebraic Structures

*For Emmy Noether, relationships among numbers, functions,
and operations became transparent, amenable to generalization,
and productive only after they have been dissociated from any particular
objects and have been reduced to general conceptual relationships.*

B. L. van der Waerden

When we first introduced Euclid's algorithm in Chapter 4, it was for computing the greatest common measure of line segments. Then we showed how to extend it to work for integers. Does it work for other kinds of mathematical entities? This is the question we'll be investigating in this chapter. As we'll see, attempts to answer it led to important developments in abstract algebra. We'll also show how some of these new algebraic structures enable new programming applications.

8.1 Stevin, Polynomials, and GCD

Some of the most important contributions to mathematics were due to one of its least-known figures, the 16th-century Flemish mathematician Simon Stevin. In addition to his contributions to engineering, physics, and music, Stevin revolutionized the way we think about and operate on numbers. As Bartel van der Waerden wrote in his *History of Algebra*:

> [With] one stroke, the classical restrictions of "numbers" to integers or to rational fractions was eliminated. [Stevin's] general notion of a real number was accepted by all later scientists.

In his 1585 pamphlet *De Thiende* ("The Tenth"), published in English as *Disme: The Art of Tenths, or, Decimall Arithmetike*, Stevin introduces and explains the use of decimal fractions. This was the first time anyone in Europe proposed using positional notation in the other direction—for tenths, hundredths, and so on. *Disme* (pronounced "dime") was one of the most widely read books in the history of mathematics. It was one of Thomas Jefferson's favorites, and is the reason why U.S. currency has a coin called a "dime" and uses decimal coinage rather than the British pounds, shillings, and pence in use at the time.

Simon Stevin (1548–1620)

Simon Stevin was born in Bruges, Flanders (now part of Belgium), but later moved to Leiden in Holland. Prior to this period, the Netherlands provinces (which included both Flanders and Holland) were part of the Spanish empire, led by its Hapsburg kings and held together by its invincible professional army. In 1568, the Dutch began a war of independence, united by a common culture and language, ultimately creating a republic and then an empire of their own. Stevin, a Dutch patriot and military engineer, joined in the rebellion and became friends with Prince Maurice of Orange, its leader. In part helped by Stevin's designs for fortifications and his clever use of a system of sluices to flood invading Spanish troops, the rebellion succeeded, creating an independent Dutch nation called the United Provinces. This began the Dutch "Golden Age," when the country became a cultural, scientific, and commercial power, remembered today in the great works of artists like Rembrandt and Vermeer.

Stevin was a true Renaissance man, with many far-reaching interests beyond military engineering. While Stevin's official job for most of his career was quartermaster-general of the army, in practice he also became a kind of science advisor to Prince Maurice. In addition to his invention of decimal fractions, polynomials, and other mathematical work, Stevin made many contributions to physics. He studied statics, realizing that forces could be added using what we now call the "parallelogram of forces," and paved the way for the work of Newton and others. He discovered the relationship of frequencies in adjacent notes of a 12-tone musical scale. Stevin even demonstrated constant acceleration of falling objects, a few years before Galileo.

Stevin was also an ardent proponent of the Dutch language, which until then had been considered a sort of second-rate dialect of German. He helped Prince Maurice create an engineering school where teaching was in Dutch, and wrote textbooks in the language. He used word frequency analysis and word length to "prove" that it was the best (most efficient) language and the best to do science. Stevin insisted on publishing his own results in Dutch rather than Latin, which may explain why he did not become better known outside his country.

In *Disme*, Stevin expands the notion of numbers from integers and fractions to "that which expresseth the quantitie of each thing" (as an English translation at the time put it). Essentially, Stevin invented the entire concept of real numbers and the number line. Any quantity could go on the number line, including negative numbers, irrational numbers, and what he called "inexplicable" numbers (by which he may have meant transcendental numbers). Of course, Stevin's decimal representations had their own drawbacks, particularly the need to write an infinite number of digits to express a simple value, such as

$$\frac{1}{7} = 0.142857142857142857142857142857\ldots$$

Stevin's representation enabled the solution of previously unsolvable problems. For example, he showed how to compute cube roots, which had given the Greeks so much trouble. His reasoning was similar to what eventually became known as the *Intermediate Value Theorem* (see the "Origins of Binary Search" sidebar in Section 10.8), which says that if a continuous function is negative at one point and positive at another, then there must be an intermediate point where its value is zero. Stevin's idea was to find the interval between two consecutive integers where the function goes from negative to positive, then divide that interval into tenths, and repeat the process with the tenths, hundredths, and so on. He realized that by "zooming in," any such problem could be solved to whatever degree of accuracy was needed, or as he put it, "one may obtain as many decimals of [the true value] as one may wish and come indefinitely near to it."

Although Stevin saw how to represent any number as a point along a line, he did not make the leap to showing pairs of numbers as points on a plane. That invention—what we now call Cartesian coordinates—came from the great French philosopher and mathematician René Descartes (Renatus Cartesius in Latin).

* * *

Stevin's next great achievement was the invention of (univariate[1]) polynomials, also introduced in 1585, in a book called *Arithmétique*. Consider this expression:

$$4x^4 + 7x^3 - x^2 + 27x - 3$$

Prior to Stevin's work, the only way to construct such a number was by performing an algorithm: Take a number, raise it to the 4th power, multiply it by 4, and so on. In, fact, one would need a different algorithm for every polynomial. Stevin realized that a polynomial is simply a finite sequence of numbers: $\{4, 7, -1, 27, -3\}$ for the preceding example. In modern computer science terms, we might say that Stevin was the first to realize that *code could be treated as data*.

With Stevin's insight, we can pass polynomials as data to a generic evaluation function. We'll write one that takes advantage of *Horner's rule*, which uses associativity to ensure that we never have to multiply powers of x higher than 1:

$$4x^4 + 7x^3 - x^2 + 27x - 3 = (((4x + 7)x - 1)x + 27)x - 3$$

For a polynomial of degree n, we need n multiplications and $n - m$ additions, where m is the number of coefficients equal to zero. Usually we will settle for doing n additions, since checking whether each addition is needed is more expensive than just doing the addition. Using this rule, we can implement a polynomial evaluation function like this, where the arguments first and last specify the bounds of a sequence of coefficients of the polynomial:

```
template <InputIterator I, Semiring R>
R polynomial_value(I first, I last, R x) {
    if (first == last) return R(0);
    R sum(*first);
    while (++first != last) {
        sum *= x;
        sum += *first;
    }
    return sum;
}
```

Let's think about the requirements on the types satisfying I and R. I is an iterator, because we want to iterate over the sequence of coefficients.[2] But the value type of the iterator (the type of the coefficients of the polynomial) does not have to be equal to the semiring[3] R (the type of the variable x in the polynomial). For

[1] Univariate polynomials are polynomials with a single variable. For the rest of this chapter, we will assume "polynomial" means univariate polynomial.

[2] We'll explain iterators more formally in Chapter 10, but for now we can think of them as generalized pointers.

[3] A semiring is an algebraic structure whose elements can be added and multiplied and has distributivity. We will give its formal definition in Section 8.5.

example, if we have a polynomial like $ax^2 + b$ where the coefficients are real numbers, that doesn't mean x has to be a real number; in fact, it could be something completely different, like a matrix.

Exercise 8.1. What are the requirements on **R** and the value type of the iterator? In other words, what are the requirements on coefficients of polynomials and on their values?

Stevin's breakthrough allowed polynomials to be treated as numbers and to participate in normal arithmetic operations. To add or subtract polynomials, we simply add or subtract their corresponding coefficients. To multiply, we compute the product of every pair consisting of one coefficient from each polynomial. That is, if a_i and b_i are the ith coefficients of the polynomials being multiplied (starting from the lowest-order term) and c_i is the ith coefficient of the result, then

$$c_0 = a_0 b_0$$
$$c_1 = a_0 b_1 + a_1 b_0$$
$$c_2 = a_0 b_2 + a_1 b_1 + a_2 b_0$$
$$\vdots$$
$$c_k = \sum_{k=i+j} a_i b_j$$
$$\vdots$$

To divide polynomials, we need the notion of *degree*.

Definition 8.1. The **degree** of a polynomial $\deg(p)$ is the index of the highest nonzero coefficient (or equivalently, the highest power of the variable).

For example:

$$\deg(5) = 0$$
$$\deg(x + 3) = 1$$
$$\deg(x^3 + x - 7) = 3$$

Now we can define division with remainder:

Definition 8.2. Polynomial a is divisible by polynomial b with remainder r if there are polynomials q and r such that

$$a = bq + r \ \land \ \deg(r) < \deg(b)$$

(In this equation, q represents the quotient of $a \div b$.)

Doing polynomial division with remainder is just like doing long division of numbers:

$$
\begin{array}{r}
3x^2 +2x\ -2 \\
x-2\ \overline{\big)\ 3x^3 -4x^2 -6x +10} \\
3x^3 -6x^2 \\
\overline{\hphantom{3x^3}\ 2x^2 -6x} \\
2x^2 -4x \\
\overline{\hphantom{2x^2}\ -2x +10} \\
-2x +4 \\
\overline{\hphantom{-2x}\ 6}
\end{array}
$$

Exercise 8.2. Prove that for any two polynomials $p(x)$ and $q(x)$:

1. $p(x) = q(x) \cdot (x - x_0) + r \implies p(x_0) = r$
2. $p(x_0) = 0 \implies p(x) = q(x) \cdot (x - x_0)$

$$\star \quad \star \quad \star$$

Stevin realized that he could use the same Euclidean algorithm (the one we looked at in the end of Section 4.6) to compute the GCD of two polynomials; all we really need to do is change the types:

```
polynomial<real> gcd(polynomial<real> a, polynomial<real> b) {
    while (b != polynomial<real>(0)) {
        a = remainder(a, b);
        std::swap(a, b);
    }
    return a;
}
```

The `remainder` function that we use implements the algorithm for polynomial division, although we do not care about the quotient. The polynomial GCD is used extensively in computer algebra for tasks such as symbolic integration.

Stevin's realization is the essence of generic programming: *an algorithm in one domain can be applied in another similar domain.*

Just as in Section 4.7, we need to show that the algorithm works—specifically, that it terminates and computes the GCD.

To show that the algorithm terminates, we need to show that it computes the GCD in a finite number of steps. Since it repeatedly performs polynomial remainder, we know by Definition 8.2 that

$$\deg(r) < \deg(b)$$

So at every step, the degree of r is reduced. Since degree is a non-negative integer, the decreasing sequence must be finite.

To show the algorithm computes the GCD, we can use the same argument from Section 4.7; it applies to polynomials as well as integers.

Exercise 8.3 (from Chrystal, *Algebra*). Find the GCD of the following polynomials:

1. $16x^4 - 56x^3 - 88x^2 + 278x + 105$,
   $16x^4 - 64x^3 - 44x^2 + 232x + 70$

2. $7x^4 + 6x^3 - 8x^2 - 6x + 1$,
   $11x^4 + 15x^3 - 2x^2 - 5x + 1$

3. $nx^{n+1} - (n+1)x^n + 1$,
   $x^n - nx + (n-1)$

8.2 Göttingen and German Mathematics

In the 18th and 19th centuries, starting long before Germany existed as a unified country, German culture flourished. Composers like Bach, Mozart, and Beethoven, poets like Goethe and Schiller, and philosophers like Kant, Hegel, and Marx were creating timeless works of depth and beauty. German universities created a unique role for German professors as civil servants bound by their commitment to the truth. Eventually this system would produce the greatest mathematicians and physicists of their age, many of them teaching or studying at the University of Götttingen.

The University of Göttingen

The center of German mathematics was a seemingly unlikely place: the University of Göttingen. Unlike many great European universities that had started hundreds of years earlier in medieval times, Göttingen was relatively young, founded in 1734. And the city of Göttingen was not a major population center. Despite this, the University of Göttingen was home to an astonishing series of top mathematicians, including Gauss, Riemann, Dirichlet, Dedekind, Klein, Minkowski, and Hilbert, some of whom we will discuss later in the book. By the early 20th century its community of physicists was equally impressive, including quantum theorists Max Born and Werner Heisenberg.

Göttingen's greatness was destroyed in 1933 by the Nazis, who expelled all Jews from the faculty and student body—including many of the top physicists and mathematicians. Some years later, the Nazi Minister of Education asked the great German mathematician David Hilbert, "How is mathematics in Göttingen now that it has been freed of Jewish influence?" Hilbert replied, "Mathematics in Göttingen? There is none any more."

Perhaps the most important mathematician to come out of Göttingen was Carl Friedrich Gauss, who was the founder of German mathematics in the modern sense. Among his many accomplishments was his seminal work on number theory, described in his 1801 book *Disquisitiones Arithmeticae* ("Investigations of Arithmetic"). Gauss's book is to number theory what Euclid's *Elements* is to geometry—the foundation on which all later work in the field is based. Among other results, it includes the *Fundamental Theorem of Arithmetic*, which states that every integer has a unique prime factorization.

Carl Friedrich Gauss (1777–1855)

Carl Friedrich Gauss grew up in Brunswick, Germany, and was recognized as a child prodigy early in his life. According to a famous story, his elementary school teacher tried to keep the class occupied by asking them to add all the integers from 1 to 100. Nine-year-old Gauss came up with the answer in seconds; he had observed that the first and last numbers added to 101, as did the second and second to last, and so on, so he simply multiplied 101 by 50.

Gauss's talents came to the attention of the Duke of Brunswick, who paid for the young student's education starting at age 14, first at a school in his hometown and later at the University of Göttingen. Initially, Gauss considered a career in classics, which, unlike mathematics, was one of the strengths of the university at the time. However, he continued to do mathematics on his own, and in 1796 he made a discovery that had eluded mathematicians since Euclid: how to construct a 17-sided regular polygon using a ruler and a compass. In fact, Gauss went further, proving that construction of a regular p-gon was possible for prime p only if p is a Fermat prime—that is, a number of the form $2^{2^k} + 1$. This breakthrough convinced him to pursue a career in mathematics. In fact, he was so proud of the discovery that he planned to have the 17-gon engraved on his tomb.

In his Ph.D. dissertation, Gauss proved what became known as the Fundamental Theorem of Algebra, which states that every nonconstant polynomial with complex coefficients has a complex root.

Gauss wrote his great number theory treatise, *Disquisitiones Arithmeticae*, while he was still a student, and had it published in 1801 when he was just 24. While great mathematicians throughout history, such as Euclid, Fermat, and Euler, had worked on number theory, Gauss was the first to codify the field and place it on a formal foundation by introducing modular arithmetic. *Disquisitiones* is still studied today, and, in fact, some important developments in 20th-century mathematics were the result of careful study of Gauss's work.

Gauss became world famous in 1801 when he predicted the location of the asteroid Ceres using his method of least squares. Because of this result, he was later appointed director of the astronomical observatory at Göttingen. This pattern of practical problems inspiring his mathematical results continued throughout his career. His work on geodesy (the science of measuring the Earth) led to his invention of the new field of differential geometry. His observations of errors in data led to the idea of the Gaussian distribution in statistics.

Throughout Gauss's career, he chose his work very carefully, and published only what he considered to be his best results—a small fraction of his potential output. Often he would delay publication, sometimes by years, until he found the perfect way to prove a particular result. His motto was "Few, but ripe."

Because of the breadth and depth of his contributions, Gauss was known as *Princeps Mathematicorum*, the Prince of Mathematicians.

Another of Gauss's innovations was the notion of *complex numbers*. Mathematicians had used imaginary numbers (xi where $i^2 = -1$) for over 200 years, but these numbers were not well understood and were usually avoided. The same was true for the first 30 years of Gauss's career; we have evidence from his notebooks that he used imaginary numbers to derive some of his results, but then he reconstructed the proofs so the published versions would not mention i. ("The metaphysics of i is very complicated," he wrote in a letter.)

But in 1831, Gauss had a profound insight: he realized that numbers of the form $z = x + yi$ could be viewed as points (x, y) on a Cartesian plane. These *complex numbers*, he saw, were just as legitimate and self-consistent as any other numbers.

Here are a few definitions and properties we'll use for complex numbers:

complex number:	$z = x + yi$
complex conjugate:	$\bar{z} = x - yi$
real part:	$\text{Re}(z) = \frac{1}{2}(z + \bar{z}) = x$
imaginary part:	$\text{Im}(z) = \frac{1}{2i}(z - \bar{z}) = y$
norm:	$\|z\| = z\bar{z} = x^2 + y^2$
absolute value:	$|z| = \sqrt{\|z\|} = \sqrt{x^2 + y^2}$
argument:	$\arg(z) = \phi$ such that
	$0 \le \phi < 2\pi$ and $\frac{z}{|z|} = \cos(\phi) + i\sin(\phi)$

The absolute value of a complex number z is the length of the vector z on the complex plane, while the argument is the angle between the real axis and the vector z. For example, $|i| = 1$ and $\arg(i) = 90°$.

Just as Stevin did for polynomials, Gauss demonstrated that complex numbers were in fact full-fledged numbers capable of supporting ordinary arithmetic operations:

addition:	$z_1 + z_2 = (x_1 + x_2) + (y_1 + y_2)i$
subtraction:	$z_1 - z_2 = (x_1 - x_2) + (y_1 - y_2)i$
multiplication:	$z_1 z_2 = (x_1 x_2 - y_1 y_2) + (x_2 y_1 + x_1 y_2)i$
reciprocal:	$\frac{1}{z} = \frac{\bar{z}}{\|z\|} = \frac{x}{x^2 + y^2} - \frac{y}{x^2 + y^2}i$

Multiplying two complex numbers can also be done by adding the arguments and multiplying the absolute values. For example, if we want to find $\sqrt{i}$, we know it will also have an absolute value of 1 and an argument of 45° (since $1 \cdot 1 = 1$ and $45 + 45 = 90$).

*   *   *

Gauss also discovered what are now called *Gaussian integers*, which are complex numbers with integer coefficients. Gaussian integers have some interesting properties. For example, the Gaussian integer 2 is not prime, since it can be expressed as the product of two other Gaussian integers, $1 + i$ and $1 - i$.

We can't do full division with Gaussian integers, but we can do division with remainder. To compute the remainder of z_1 and z_2, Gauss proposed the following procedure:

1. Construct a grid on the complex plane generated by $z_2, iz_2, -iz_2,$ and $-z_2$.

2. Find a square in the grid containing z_1.

3. Find a vertex w of the grid square closest to z_1.

4. $z_1 - w$ is the remainder.

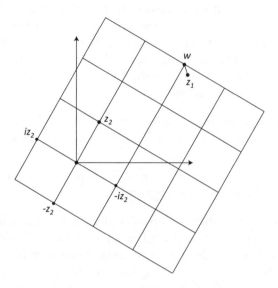

   Gauss realized that with this remainder function, he could apply Euclid's GCD algorithm to complex integers, as we've done here:

```
complex<integer> gcd(complex<integer> a, complex<integer> b) {
    while (b != complex<integer>(0)) {
        a = remainder(a, b);
        std::swap(a, b);
    }
    return a;
}
```

The only thing we've changed are the types.

*   *   *

Gauss's work was extended by another Göttingen professor, Peter Gustav Lejeune-Dirichlet. While Gauss's complex numbers were of the form (in Dirichlet's terminology) $t + n\sqrt{-1}$, Dirichlet realized that this was a special case of $t + n\sqrt{-a}$ where a did not have to be 1, and that different properties followed from the use of different values. For example, the standard GCD algorithm works on numbers of this form when $a = 1$, but it fails when $a = 5$ since there end up being numbers that don't have a unique factorization. For example:

$$21 = 3 \cdot 7 = (1 + 2\sqrt{-5}) \cdot (1 - 2\sqrt{-5})$$

It turns out that if Euclid's algorithm works, then there is a unique factorization. Since we have no unique factorization here, then Euclid's algorithm doesn't work in this case.

Dirichlet's greatest result was his proof that if a and b are coprime (that is, if $\gcd(a, b) = 1$), then there are infinitely many primes of the form $ak + b$.

Most of Dirichlet's results were described in the second great book on number theory, appropriately called *Vorlesungen über Zahlentheorie* ("Lectures on Number Theory"). The book contains the following important insight, which we used in our epigraph for Chapter 4:

> [T]he whole structure of number theory rests on a single foundation, namely the algorithm for finding the greatest common divisor of two numbers.
>
> All the subsequent theorems ... are still only simple consequences of the result of this initial investigation....

The book was actually written and published after Dirichlet's death by his younger Göttingen colleague, Richard Dedekind, based on Dedekind's notes from Dirichlet's lectures. Dedekind was so modest that he published the book under Dirichlet's name, even after adding many additional results of his own in later editions. Unfortunately, Dedekind's modesty hurt his career; he failed to get tenure at Göttingen and ended up on the faculty of a minor technical university.

Dedekind observed that Gaussian integers and Dirichlet's extensions of them were special cases of a more general concept of *algebraic integers*, which are linear integral combinations of roots of *monic* polynomials (polynomials where the coefficient of the highest-order term is 1) with integer coefficients. We say that these polynomials *generate* these sets of algebraic integers. For example:

$x^2 + 1$ generates Gaussian integers $a + b\sqrt{-1}$
$x^3 - 1$ generates *Eisenstein integers* $a + b\frac{-1+i\sqrt{3}}{2}$
$x^2 + 5$ generates integers $a + b\sqrt{-5}$

Dedekind's work on algebraic integers contained almost all the fundamental building blocks of modern abstract algebra. But it would take another great Göttingen mathematician, Emmy Noether, to make the breakthrough to full abstraction.

8.3 Noether and the Birth of Abstract Algebra

Emmy Noether's revolutionary insight was that *it is possible to derive results about certain kinds of mathematical entities without knowing anything about the entities themselves.* In programming terms, we would say that Noether realized that we could use *concepts* in our algorithms and data structures, without knowing anything about which specific *types* would be used. In a very real sense, Noether provided the theory for what we now call generic programming. Noether taught mathematicians to always look for the most general setting of any theorem. In a similar way, generic programming defines algorithms in terms of the most general concepts.

Emmy Noether (1882–1935)

Emmy Noether (pronounced almost like "Nerter," but without finishing the first "r" sound) was born into an academic German-Jewish family. Her father was a distinguished professor of mathematics at the University of Erlangen. Although it was very unusual for women at the time, Noether was able to study at the university and got a doctorate in mathematics in 1907. She then stayed on for several years at Erlangen, assisting her father and teaching without a position or salary.

Women had been excluded from academic careers for centuries. With the single exception of Sofia Kovalevskaya, a Russian mathematician who became a professor in Stockholm in 1884, there were no women in faculty positions in mathematics at universities at the time.

Two of the greatest mathematicians of the day, Felix Klein and David Hilbert, recognized Noether's talent, and felt that she deserved an academic position. They also believed as a matter of principle that women should not be excluded from mathematics. They arranged for Noether to come to Göttingen in 1915.

Unfortunately, she still was not officially allowed to teach; the faculty resisted her appointment. For the next four years, all of Noether's courses were listed under Hilbert's name; she was treated as a kind of unofficial substitute teacher. Even in 1919, when she was finally given the right to teach under her own name, it was an unpaid position as a *Privatdozent*, a kind of adjunct professor.

During her time at Göttingen, Noether made enormous contributions in two fields, physics and mathematics. In physics, she is responsible for

Noether's theorem, which fundamentally connected certain symmetries and physical conservation laws (e.g., conservation of angular momentum). Albert Einstein was impressed by Noether's theorem, which is one of the most profound results in theoretical physics. Her result underlies much of modern physics, from quantum mechanics to the theory of black holes.

In mathematics, Noether created the field of abstract algebra. Although earlier mathematicians such as Cauchy and Galois had worked with groups, rings, and other algebraic objects, they always used specific instances. Noether's breakthrough was to realize that these algebraic stuctures could be studied abstractly, without looking at particular implementations.

Noether was known as an outstanding teacher, and attracted students from all over the world. Under her leadership, these young researchers (often called "Noether's Boys") were creating a new kind of mathematics.

In 1933, when the Nazis expelled Jews from universities, Noether fled to the United States. Despite being one of the greatest mathematicians in the world, no major research university would hire her, primarily because she was a woman. She ended up with a visiting appointment at Bryn Mawr, a small undergraduate women's college.

Tragically, Emmy Noether died in 1935 at age 53, a few days after surgery to remove an ovarian cyst. Since then, her contributions to mathematics have increasingly been recognized as fundamental and revolutionary.

Noether was well known for her willingness to help students and give them her ideas to publish, but she published relatively little herself. Fortunately, a young Dutch mathematician, Bartel van der Waerden, audited her course and wrote a book based on her lectures (which he credits on the title page). Called *Modern Algebra*, it was the first book to describe the abstract approach she had developed.

This book, *Modern Algebra*, led to a fundamental rethinking of the way modern mathematics is presented. Its revolutionary approach—the idea that you express your theorems in the most abstract terms—is Noether's creation. Most of mathematics—not just algebra—changed as a result of her work; she taught people to think differently.

8.4   Rings

One of Noether's most important contributions was the development of the theory of an algebraic structure called a *ring*.[4]

---

[4]The term "ring," coined by Hilbert, was intended to use the metaphor of a bunch of people involved in a common enterprise, like a criminal ring. It has nothing to do with jewelry rings.

Definition 8.3. A **ring** is a set on which the following are defined:

$$\text{operations}: \quad x+y, -x, xy$$
$$\text{constants}: \quad 0_R, 1_R$$

and on which the following axioms hold:

$$x + (y + z) = (x + y) + z$$
$$x + 0 = 0 + x = x$$
$$x + -x = -x + x = 0$$
$$x + y = y + x$$
$$x(yz) = (xy)z$$
$$1 \neq 0$$
$$1x = x1 = x$$
$$0x = x0 = 0$$
$$x(y + z) = xy + xz \qquad (y + z)x = yx + zx$$

Rings[5] have the properties we associate with integer arithmetic—operators that act like addition and multiplication, where addition is commutative and multiplication distributes over addition. Indeed, rings may be thought of as an abstraction of integers, and the canonical example of a ring is the set of integers, $\mathbb{Z}$. Also observe that every ring is an additive group and therefore an abelian group. The "addition" operator is required to have an inverse, but the "multiplication" operator is not.

In practice, mathematicians write the zeroes without their subscripts, just as we've done in the axioms. For example, in discussing a ring of matrices, "0" refers not to the single integer zero but to the additive identity matrix.

Besides integers, other examples of rings include the following sets:

- $n \times n$ matrices with real coefficients

- Gaussian integers

- Polynomials with integer coefficients

We say that a ring is commutative if $xy = yx$. Noncommutative rings usually come from the realm of linear algebra where matrix multiplication does not commute. In contrast, polynomial rings and rings of algebraic integers do commute. These two types of rings lead to two branches of abstract algebra, known as *commutative algebra* and *noncommutative algebra*. Rings are often not explicitly

---

[5]Some mathematicians define rings without the multiplicative identity 1 and its axioms, and call rings that include them *unitary rings*; we do not make that distinction here.

labeled as "commutative" or "noncommutative"; instead, one type of ring or the other is assumed from the branch of algebra. With the exception of Sections 8.5 and 8.6, the rest of this book will deal with commutative algebra—the kind that Dedekind, Hilbert, and Noether worked on—so from then on we will assume our rings are commutative.

Definition 8.4. An element x of a ring is called **invertible** if there is an element x^{-1} such that

$$xx^{-1} = x^{-1}x = 1$$

Every ring contains at least one invertible element: 1. There may be more than one; for example, in the ring of integers $\mathbb{Z}$, both 1 and -1 are invertible.

Definition 8.5. An invertible element of a ring is called a **unit** of that ring.

Exercise 8.4 (very easy). Which ring contains exactly one invertible element? What are units in the ring $\mathbb{Z}[\sqrt{-1}]$ of Gaussian integers?

Theorem 8.1: *Units are closed under multiplication (i.e., a product of units is a unit).*

Proof. Suppose a is a unit and b is a unit. Then (by definition of units) $aa^{-1} = 1$ and $bb^{-1} = 1$. So

$$1 = aa^{-1} = a \cdot 1 \cdot a^{-1} = a(bb^{-1})a^{-1} = (ab)(b^{-1}a^{-1})$$

Similarly, $a^{-1}a = 1$ and $b^{-1}b = 1$, so

$$1 = b^{-1}b = b^{-1} \cdot 1 \cdot b = b^{-1}(a^{-1}a)b = (b^{-1}a^{-1})(ab)$$

We now have a term that, when multiplied by ab from either side, gives 1; that term is the inverse of ab:

$$(ab)^{-1} = b^{-1}a^{-1}$$

So ab is a unit.   □

Exercise 8.5. Prove that:

- 1 is a unit.

- The inverse of a unit is a unit.

Definition 8.6. An element x of a ring is called a **zero divisor** if:

1. $x \neq 0$
2. There exists a $y \neq 0$, $xy = 0$

For example, in the ring $\mathbb{Z}_6$ of remainders modulo 6, 2 and 3 are zero divisors.

Definition 8.7. A commutative ring is called an **integral domain** if it has no zero divisors.

It's called "integral" because its elements act like integers—you don't get zero when you multiply two nonzero things. Here are some examples of integral domains:

- Integers

- Gaussian integers

- Polynomials over integers

- Rational functions over integers, such as $\frac{x^2+1}{x^3-1}$ (A rational function is the ratio of two polynomials.)

The ring of remainders modulo 6 is not an integral domain. (Whether a ring of remainders is integral depends on whether the modulus is prime.)

Exercise 8.6 (very easy). Prove that a zero divisor is not a unit.

8.5   Matrix Multiplication and Semirings

Note: This section and the next assume some basic knowledge of linear algebra. The rest of the book does not depend on the material covered here, and these sections may be skipped without impacting the reader's understanding.

In the previous chapter, we combined power with matrix multiplication to compute linear recurrences. It turns out that we can use this technique for many other algorithms if we use a more general notion of matrix multiplication.

Linear Algebra Review

Let's quickly review how some basic vector and matrix operations are defined.

Inner product of two vectors:

$$\vec{x} \cdot \vec{y} = \sum_{i=1}^{n} x_i y_i$$

In other words, the inner product is the sum of the products of all the corresponding elements. The result of inner product is always a scalar (a single number).

Matrix-vector product:

$$\vec{w} = \left[x_{ij} \right] \vec{v}$$

$$w_i = \sum_{j=1}^{n} x_{ij} v_j$$

Multiplying an $n \times m$ matrix with an m-length vector results in an n-length vector. One way to think of the process is that the ith element of the result is the inner product of the ith row of the matrix with the original vector.

Matrix-matrix product:

$$\left[z_{ij} \right] = \left[x_{ij} \right] \left[y_{ij} \right]$$

$$z_{ij} = \sum_{k=1}^{n} x_{ik} y_{kj}$$

In the matrix product $AB = C$, if A is a $k \times m$ matrix and B is an $m \times n$ matrix, then C will be a $k \times n$ matrix. The element in row i and column j of C is the inner product of the ith row of A and the jth column of B. Note that matrix multiplication is not commutative: there is no guarantee that $AB = BA$. Indeed, it's often the case that only one of AB and BA will be well defined, since the number of columns of the first term has to match the number of rows of the second. Even when both products are defined, they are almost always different.

Just as we generalized our power function to work with any operation, we can now generalize the notion of matrix multiplication. Normally we think of matrix multiplication as consisting of a series of sums of products, as shown in the earlier formula. But what's mathematically essential is actually that there be two operations, a "plus-like" one that is associative and commutative (denoted by $\oplus$) and a "times-like" one that is associative (denoted by $\otimes$), where the latter operation distributes over the first:

$$a \otimes (b \oplus c) = a \otimes b \oplus a \otimes c$$
$$(b \oplus c) \otimes a = b \otimes a \oplus c \otimes a$$

We've just seen an algebraic structure that has operations like this, a *ring*. However, rings have a few requirements we don't need, specifically those involving the additive inverse operation. Instead, what we want is a *semiring*, a ring without minus $(-)$.

Definition 8.8. A **semiring** is a set on which the following are defined:

$$\text{operations}: \quad x+y, xy$$
$$\text{constants}: \quad 0_R, 1_R$$

and on which the following axioms hold:

$$x + (y + z) = (x + y) + z$$
$$x + 0 = 0 + x = x$$
$$x + y = y + x$$
$$x(yz) = (xy)z$$
$$1 \neq 0$$
$$1x = x1 = x$$
$$0x = x0 = 0$$
$$x(y + z) = xy + xz \qquad (y + z)x = yx + zx$$

Our definition follows the mathematical convention of referring to the operations as $+$ and $\times$ rather than $\oplus$ and $\otimes$. But as with all the algebraic structures we've been discussing, the symbols refer to *any* two operations that behave in the manner specified by the axioms.

The canonical example of a semiring is the set of natural numbers $\mathbb{N}$. While natural numbers do not have additive inverses, you can easily perform matrix multiplication on matrices with non-negative integer coefficients. (In fact, we could relax the requirements further by removing the additive identity 0 and the multiplicative identity 1, as well as their corresponding axioms; matrix multiplication[6] would still work. We might refer to a semiring without 0 and 1 as a *weak semiring*.)

8.6 Application: Social Networks and Shortest Paths

We can use semirings to solve a variety of problems. For example, suppose we have a graph of friendships, as in a social network, and we want to find all the people you are connected to through any path. In other words, we want to know who your friends are, the friends of your friends, the friends of the friends of your friends, and so on.

---

[6]Here we are assuming the straightforward algorithm for matrix multiplication; faster algorithms require stronger theories.

Finding all such paths is known as finding the *transitive closure* of the graph. To compute the transitive closure, we take an $n \times n$ Boolean matrix where entry x_{ij} is 1 if the relation holds between i and j (in this case, if person i is friends with person j), and 0 otherwise; we'll also assume people are friends with themselves. Here's a small example:

	Ari	Bev	Cal	Don	Eva	Fay	Gia
Ari	1	1	0	1	0	0	0
Bev	1	1	0	0	0	1	0
Cal	0	0	1	1	0	0	0
Don	1	0	1	1	0	1	0
Eva	0	0	0	0	1	0	1
Fay	0	1	0	1	0	1	0
Gia	0	0	0	0	1	0	1

The matrix tells us who each person's friends are. We can apply generalized matrix multiplication where we replace $\oplus$ by Boolean OR ($\vee$) and $\otimes$ by Boolean AND ($\wedge$). We say this is the matrix multiplication generated by a *Boolean* or $\{\vee, \wedge\}$-*semiring*. Multiplying the matrix by itself using these operations tells us who the friends of our friends are. Doing this multiplication $n - 1$ times will eventually find all the people in each network of friends. Since multiplying the matrix by itself several times is just raising it to a power, we can use our existing power algorithm to do the computation efficiently. Of course, we can use this idea to compute the transitive closure of any relation.

Exercise 8.7. Using the power algorithm from Chapter 7 with matrix multiplication on Boolean semirings, write a program for finding transitive closure of a graph. Apply this function to find the social networks of each person in the preceding table.

Another example of a classic problem we can solve this way is finding the shortest path between any two nodes in a directed graph like this one:

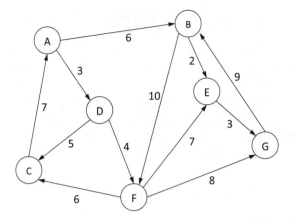

As before, we can represent the graph as an $n \times n$ matrix—this time one whose values a_{ij} represent the distance from node i to node j. If there is no edge from one node to another, we'll initially list the distance as infinity.

	A	B	C	D	E	F	G
A	0	6	∞	3	∞	∞	∞
B	∞	0	∞	∞	2	10	∞
C	7	∞	0	∞	∞	∞	∞
D	∞	∞	5	0	∞	4	∞
E	∞	∞	∞	∞	0	∞	3
F	∞	∞	6	∞	7	0	8
G	∞	9	∞	∞	∞	∞	0

This time, we use matrix multiplication generated by a *tropical* or $\{\min, +\}$-*semiring*:

$$b_{ij} = \min_{k=1}^{n}(a_{ik} + a_{kj})$$

That is, the $\oplus$ operation is min, and the $\otimes$ operation is $+$. Again, we raise the resulting matrix to the $n - 1$ power. The result tells us the shortest path of any length up to $n - 1$ steps.

Exercise 8.8. Using the power algorithm from Chapter 7 with matrix multiplication on tropical semirings, write a program for finding the length of the shortest path in a graph.

Exercise 8.9. Modify the program from Exercise 8.8 to return not just the shortest distance but the shortest path (a sequence of edges).

8.7 Euclidean Domains

We began this chapter by seeing how Euclid's GCD algorithm could be generalized beyond integers, first to polynomials, then to complex numbers, and so on. How far could this generalization go? In other words, what are the most general mathematical entities that the GCD algorithm works on (the *domain* or *setting* for the algorithm)? With the abstractions Noether had developed, she was finally able answer this question: the domain of the GCD algorithm is what Noether called the *Euclidean domain*; it is also sometimes known as a *Euclidean ring*.

Definition 8.9. E is a **Euclidean domain** if:

- E is an integral domain

- E has operations *quotient* and *remainder* such that

$$b \neq 0 \implies a = \text{quotient}(a, b) \cdot b + \text{remainder}(a, b)$$

- E has a non-negative norm $\|x\| : E \to \mathbb{N}$ satisfying

$$\|a\| = 0 \iff a = 0$$
$$b \neq 0 \implies \|ab\| \geq \|a\|$$
$$\|\text{remainder}(a, b)\| < \|b\|$$

The term "norm" here is a measure of magnitude, but it should not be confused with the Euclidean norm you may be familiar with from linear algebra. For integers, the norm is their absolute value; for polynomials, it is the degree of the polynomial; for Gaussian integers, it is the complex norm. The important idea is that when you compute the remainder, the norm decreases and eventually goes to zero, since it maps into natural numbers. We need this property to guarantee that Euclid's algorithm terminates.

*   *   *

Now we can write the fully generic version of the GCD algorithm:

```
template <EuclideanDomain E>
E gcd(E a, E b) {
    while (b != E(0)) {
        a = remainder(a, b);
        std::swap(a, b);
    }
    return a;
}
```

The process we've gone through in transforming the GCD algorithm from something that works only on line segments to something that works on very different types illustrates the following important principle:

> *To make something generic, you don't add extra mechanisms.*
> *Rather, you remove constraints and strip down the algorithm to its essentials.*

8.8   Fields and Other Algebraic Structures

Another important abstraction is the *field*.[7]

Definition 8.10.   An integral domain where every nonzero element is invertible is called a **field**.

Just as integers are the canonical example of rings, so rational numbers ($\mathbb{Q}$) are the canonical example of fields. Other important examples of fields are as follows:

- Real numbers $\mathbb{R}$

- Prime remainder fields $\mathbb{Z}_p$

- Complex numbers $\mathbb{C}$

A *prime field* is a field that does not have a proper subfield (a subfield different from itself). It turns out that every field has one of two kinds of prime subfields: $\mathbb{Q}$ or $\mathbb{Z}_p$. The *characteristic* of a field is p if its prime subfield is $\mathbb{Z}_p$ (the field of integer remainders modulo p), and 0 if its prime subfield is $\mathbb{Q}$.

*   *   *

All fields can be obtained by starting with a prime field and adding elements that still satisfy the field properties. This is called *extending* the field.

In particular, we can extend a field *algebraically* by adding an extra element that is a root of a polynomial. For example, we can extend $\mathbb{Q}$ with $\sqrt{2}$, which is not a rational number, since it is the root of the polynomial $x^2 - 2$.

We can also extend a field *topologically* by "filling in the holes." Rational numbers leave gaps in the number line, but real numbers have no gaps, so the field of real numbers is a topological extension of the field of rational numbers. We can also extend the field to two dimensions with complex numbers. Surprisingly, there are no other finite dimensional fields containing reals.[8]

---

[7]The term "field" relies on the metaphor of a field of study, not a field of wheat.

[8]There are four- and eight-dimensional field-like structures called *quaternions* and *octonions*. These are not quite fields, because they are missing certain axioms; both quaternions and octonions lack commutativity of multiplication, and octonions also lack associativity of multiplication. There are no other finite-dimensional extensions of real numbers.

Up to now, every algebraic structure we've introduced in this book has operated on a single set of values. But there are also structures that are defined in terms of more than one set. For example, an important structure called a *module* contains a primary set (an additive group G) and a secondary set (a ring of coefficients R), with an additional multiplication operation $R \times G \to G$ that obeys the following axioms:

$$a, b \in R \land x, y \in G :$$
$$(a + b)x = ax + bx$$
$$a(x + y) = ax + ay$$

If ring R is also a field, then the structure is called a *vector space*.

A good example of a vector space is two-dimensional Euclidean space, where the vectors are the additive group and the real coefficients are the field.

8.9   Thoughts on the Chapter

In this chapter, we followed the historical development of generalizing the idea of "numbers" and the corresponding generalization of the GCD algorithm. This led to the development of several new algebraic structures, some of which we used to generalize matrix multiplication and apply it to some important graph problems in computer science.

Let's extend our table from Section 6.8 to include the new structures we introduced in this chapter. Note that every row of the table includes all the axioms from earlier rows. (In the case of semirings and rings, the "times" operation inherits all the axioms from monoids, while the "plus" operation inherits the axioms from abelian groups.) To illustrate this, we've grayed out operations, elements, and axioms that appeared previously in the table.

STRUCTURE	OPERATIONS	ELEMENTS	AXIOMS
semigroup	$x \circ y$		$x \circ (y \circ z) = (x \circ y) \circ z$
Example: positive integers under addition			
monoid	$x \circ y$	e	$x \circ (y \circ z) = (x \circ y) \circ z$
			$x \circ e = e \circ x = x$
Example: strings under concatenation			
group	$x \circ y$	e	$x \circ (y \circ z) = (x \circ y) \circ z$
	x^{-1}		$x \circ e = e \circ x = x$
			$x \circ x^{-1} = x^{-1} \circ x = e$
Example: invertible matrices under multiplication			

STRUCTURE	OPERATIONS	ELEMENTS	AXIOMS
abelian group	$x \circ y$ x^{-1}	e	$x \circ (y \circ z) = (x \circ y) \circ z$ $x \circ e = e \circ x = x$ $x \circ x^{-1} = x^{-1} \circ x = e$ $x \circ y = y \circ x$
Example: two-dimensional vectors under addition			
semiring	$x + y$ xy	0_R 1_R	$x + (y + z) = (x + y) + z$ $x + 0 = 0 + x = x$ $x + y = y + x$ $x(yz) = (xy)z$ $1 \neq 0$ $1x = x1 = x$ $0x = x0 = 0$ $x(y + z) = xy + xz$ $(y + z)x = yx + zx$
Example: natural numbers			
ring	$x + y$ $-x$ xy	0_R 1_R	$x + (y + z) = (x + y) + z$ $x + 0 = 0 + x = x$ $x + -x = -x + x = 0$ $x + y = y + x$ $x(yz) = (xy)z$ $1 \neq 0$ $1x = x1 = x$ $0x = x0 = 0$ $x(y + z) = xy + xz$ $(y + z)x = yx + zx$
Example: integers			

As we did before, we can also define some other structures more concisely in terms of others:

STRUCTURE	DEFINITION
integral domain	A commutative ring that has no zero divisors (elements other than 0 whose product is 0)
Euclidean domain	An integral domain that has quotient and remainder operations and a norm that decreases when remainder is computed
field	An integral domain where every nonzero element is invertible (Example: rational numbers)

(Continues)

STRUCTURE	DEFINITION
prime field	A field that does not have a proper subfield
module	Consists of a primary set that is an additive group G and a secondary set of coefficients that is a ring R, with distributive multiplication of coefficients over elements of G
vector space	A module where the ring R is also a field

This diagram shows the relationships between some of the most important structures discussed in this chapter:

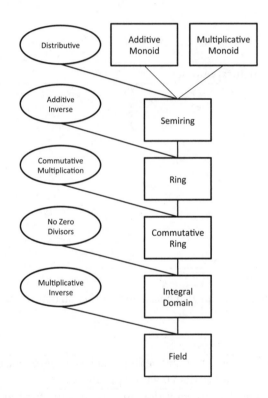

The first time you encounter algebraic structures, it might seem as if there are so many varieties that it's hard to keep track of their properties. However, they fit into a manageable taxonomy that makes their relationships clear—a taxonomy that has enabled great progress in mathematics over the last hundred years.

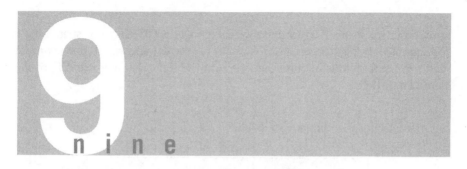

Organizing Mathematical Knowledge

Now we're going to look at some of the building blocks for organizing knowledge, particularly mathematical knowledge. We'll start by exploring the notion of proofs and the introduction of the idea of theorems. Then we'll examine some important examples of attempts to build up bodies of knowledge from axioms.

Mathematicians have been thinking about how to organize knowledge for thousands of years. As programmers, we will use their organizational principles in our domain of algorithms and data structures.

9.1 Proofs

People had been discovering and using mathematical results long before they started proving them. Yet mathematical proofs are also a surprisingly old invention. For centuries mathematicians relied on *visual* proofs. The ancient Greeks realized that they could use our innate spatial reasoning to prove algebraic facts.

Here are some examples of visual proofs.

Commutativity of addition: $a + b = b + a$

If we have two strips of paper and tape them together to make one strip, we get the same length regardless of which one is on the left and which one is on the right. We can see this because the figure on the right is a mirror image of the figure on the left.

Associativity of addition: $(a + b) + c = a + (b + c)$

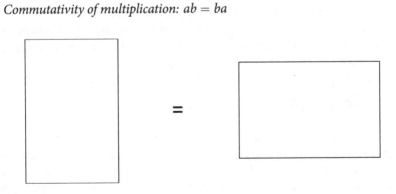

If we have three strips of paper and we tape the pieces together to make one long strip, it doesn't matter if we tape the first two pieces together and then tape the third one to the result, or if instead we tape the last two and then the first. Either way we'll end up with a strip of the same length in the end.

Commutativity of multiplication: $ab = ba$

A rectangle has a certain length and a certain width. If you turn it sideways, you've reversed length and width, but you obviously still have the same rectangle. In fact, this essential argument appears in a 19th-century book by Dirichlet, who says that whether you arrange soldiers in rows or columns, you still have the same number.

Associativity of multiplication: $(ab)c = a(bc)$

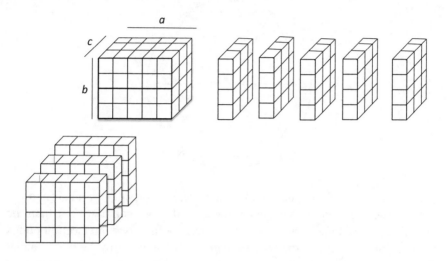

Whether you slice this rectangular prism along one axis or along another, when you put the slices back together, you still have the same volume.

$(a + b)^2 = a^2 + 2ab + b^2$:

It's clear just by looking that the rectangle on the lower left is the same area as the rectangle on the upper right: not only do both have area ab, but you could literally cut one out, turn it sideways, and lay it on the other.

$\pi > 3$:

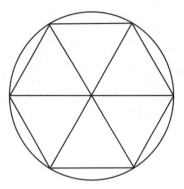

Here we've inscribed a regular unit hexagon (one whose sides are all of length 1) in the circle. It's evident that the perimeter of the hexagon is shorter than the circumference of the circle, because whenever we have two intersection points between the two figures, the shortest path from one point to the next is along the hexagon, not the circle. Since the triangles that make up the hexagon are equilateral, all their sides are length 1, so the diameter of the circle is length 2. So the ratio of the circle's circumference to its diameter (i.e., π) must be greater than the ratio of the hexagon's perimeter (6) to its diameter (2).

Exercise 9.1. Design visual proofs for the following:

$$(a - b)^2 = a^2 - 2ab + b^2$$
$$a^2 - b^2 = (a + b)(a - b)$$
$$(a + b)^3 = a^3 + 3a^2b + 3ab^2 + b^3$$
$$(a - b)^3 = a^3 - 3a^2b + 3ab^2 - b^3$$

Exercise 9.2. Using a visual proof, find an upper bound for π.

*   *   *

As useful as visual proofs are, this technique isn't sufficient to prove every type of proposition in mathematics, and some of the proofs are no longer considered rigorous enough. Modern mathematicians have a variety of proof techniques available to them, some of which we've used throughout this book, and which are summarized in Appendix B. Proofs show connections between different truths. But what exactly constitutes a proof? Today, we use the following definition:

Definition 9.1. A **proof** of a proposition is

- An argument
- Accepted by the mathematical community

- To establish the proposition as valid

The second point is often overlooked: proof is fundamentally a social process, and one that changes over time. Our confidence in a proof increases as more people understand and agree with it. At the same time, what is considered a valid proof today might not be considered a valid proof 300 years from now, just as some proofs that were viewed as valid by Euler—the greatest 18th-century mathematician—are frowned upon today.

Now we'll turn to another building block of mathematical knowledge, theorems.

9.2   The First Theorem

As we discussed in Chapter 2, ancient Mediterranean civilizations believed that the Egyptians were the source of mathematical knowledge. When Greek civilization was just starting, Egyptian civilization had already existed for thousands of years, so it is not surprising that the leading thinkers of ancient Greece would travel to Egypt to study with their priests and learn their wisdom. The first such person known to us is Thales of Miletus. Thales learned geometry from the Egyptians, but he went beyond their work. While the Egyptians had algorithms, Thales had a theorem—in fact, he invented the very notion of a theorem, which is a proposition derivable from other propositions. Today Thales is regarded as the founder of Western philosophy, and might also be considered the first mathematician.

Thales of Miletus (flourished early 6th century BC)

Some time around the year 750 BC a new society started to appear in different coastal regions of the Mediterranean and even as far north as the Black Sea. They called themselves Hellenes; we call them Greeks. They came from a small mountainous country where the geography prevented the emergence of a large unified kingdom as was common elsewhere. Greeks lived in small, independent city-states unified not by a central government, but by a common language and culture. Whenever a city's population exceeded its resources, it would send some of its citizens to settle a colony, a new practically independent city on some conveniently located bay with a river. Within 200 years Greeks settled around the Mediterranean, as Plato put it, "like frogs around a pond."

By somewhere around 600 BC, the Greek colonies in Asia Minor (what is now Turkey) were getting wealthy. Instead of spending all the extra money on luxuries, some of them started supporting intellectual pursuits. For the first time in history they looked beyond mythology for the answers to eternal questions such as what things were made of. The first person to do this in a fundamental way was Thales of Miletus. Thales was the originator of what ancient Greeks would eventually call philosophy and what we now call science. He wanted to find the natural, non-mythological explanation of reality. He proposed that all visible reality is made out of one single substance: water. Therefore, visible reality exists in one of three states—gas, liquid, or solid—and there are transitions between the states.

While in Egypt, Thales collected many geometric algorithms and, probably, some Babylonian astronomical knowledge. Herodotus reports that Thales was able to predict a total solar eclipse a year in advance. Aristotle—usually a reliable source—tells us that Thales was able to predict an exceptionally large harvest of olives by studying weather patterns and, by buying options on the use of all the olive presses in the region, made a fortune. There are many other stories about his accomplishments, such as his discovery of static electricity. While we do not know exactly which stories are true, Thales clearly amassed a large body of scientific knowledge and was able to apply it to practical problems. His knowledge did not perish with him; his students carried the program forward. But more important than any of his specific discoveries was his approach to understanding the world, which is still the basis of all science.

Theorem 9.1 (Thales' Theorem): *For any triangle ABC formed by connecting the two ends of a circle's diameter (AC) with any other point B on the circle, $\angle ABC = 90°$.*

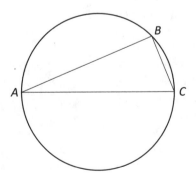

Proof. Consider the triangles formed by joining point B with the center of the circle, D:

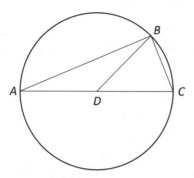

Since DA and DB are both radii of the circle, they are equal and triangle ADB is isosceles. The same is true for DB, DC, and triangle BDC. Therefore

$$\angle DAB = \angle DBA$$
$$\angle DCB = \angle DBC$$
$$\angle DAB + \angle DCB = \angle DBA + \angle DBC$$

where we get the third equation by adding the previous two. It was also known that the angles of a triangle add up to $180°$, and we can see that $\angle CBA$ is the sum of $\angle DBA$ and $\angle DBC$, so

$$\angle DAB + \angle DCB + \angle DBA + \angle DBC = 180°$$

By substituting using the equality we established, we can write this as follows:

$$(\angle DBA + \angle DBC) + (\angle DBA + \angle DBC) = 180°$$
$$2 \cdot (\angle DBA + \angle DBC) = 180°$$
$$\angle DBA + \angle DBC = 90°$$
$$\angle CBA = 90° \qquad \square$$

Why was Thales' discovery so important? What he realized is that truths are connected. He saw that if you have one piece of knowledge, you can use it to find another. Furthermore, theorems are essential to the idea of abstraction, for the value of a theorem is that it applies to *all* entities that have certain properties.

9.3 Euclid and the Axiomatic Method

If we want to build up a system of knowledge, proofs and theorems are essential tools. But we also need to have a set of starting assumptions, or *axioms*, as a foundation for our system.

The first appearance of the *axiomatic method*, in which an entire mathematical system was built on the basis of a few formal principles, is in Euclid's *Elements*. In fact, for centuries Euclid's were the only known examples of axioms, and they applied only to geometry.

Euclid divided his principles into three groups: definitions, postulates, and common notions. He starts with his 23 definitions, which relate to geometric figures. Here are a few of them:[1]

1. A point is that which has no parts.

2. A line is a breadthless length.

$$\vdots$$

23. Parallel straight lines are straight lines which, being in the same plane and being produced indefinitely in both directions, do not meet one another in either direction.

Next, he gave the following five "common notions":

1. Things which are equal to the same thing are also equal to one another.

2. If equals be added to equals, the whole are equal.

3. If equals be subtracted from equals, the remainders are equal.

4. Things which coincide with one another are equal to one another.

5. The whole is greater than the part.

Today we would express these notions as follows:

1. $a = c \land b = c \implies a = b$

2. $a = b \land c = d \implies a + c = b + d$

3. $a = b \land c = d \implies a - c = b - d$

4. $a \cong b \implies a = b$

5. $a < a + b$

What's interesting about these common notions is that, unlike the 23 definitions, the notions are not limited to geometry; they also apply to positive integers. In fact, these common notions, such as transitivity of equality, are essential to programming.[2]

---

[1] As before, we use Sir Thomas Heath's translation of Euclid's *Elements*.
[2] The definition of regular types in Chapter 7 is derived from these Euclidean notions.

Finally, Euclid introduced his famous five postulates. These are stated in terms of allowable operations in the "computational machinery" of his geometric system. You can read the first three as being prefixed with a statement like "There is a procedure...":

1. To draw a straight line from any point to any point.
2. To produce a finite straight line continuously in a straight line.
3. To describe a circle with any center and distance.
4. That all right angles are equal to one another.
5. That, if a straight line falling on two straight lines makes the interior angles on the same side less than two right angles, the two straight lines, if produced indefinitely, meet on that side on which are the angles less than the two right angles.

If we were writing Euclid's system today, we would consider both "common notions" and "postulates" to be *axioms*—unprovable assumptions on which the rest of the system is built.

Euclid's fifth postulate, which provides the basis for reasoning about parallel lines, is the most important axiom in the history of mathematics. Also known as the *parallel postulate*, it expresses the relation shown in the following diagram:

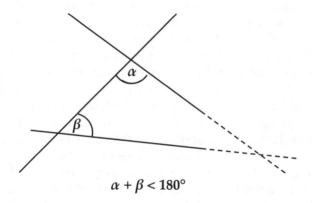

$$\alpha + \beta < 180°$$

However, there are many equivalent ways to express the same notion:

- Given a line and a point not on it, at most one parallel to the given line can be drawn through the point.[3]

- There exists a triangle whose angles add up to 180°.

- There exist two similar triangles that are not congruent.

[3] This formulation, which is often taught as "the parallel postulate" in secondary school geometry, was actually published by Scottish mathematician John Playfair in 1795, and is properly known as *Playfair's Axiom*.

9.4   Alternatives to Euclidean Geometry

Almost from the time Euclid stated his five postulates, mathematicians felt that there was something different about the fifth one. Intuitively, they felt that the first four postulates were somehow more fundamental; perhaps the fifth postulate could be derived from the others, and therefore was not a true axiom. Thus began a 2000-year search for a proof of the fifth postulate, one pursued by such luminaries as the astronomer (and mathematician) Ptolemy (90–168), the poet (and mathematician) Omar Khayyam (1050–1153), and the Italian priest (and mathematician) Giovanni Girolamo Saccheri, S.J. (1667–1733). Saccheri wrote a book called *Euclidus Vindicatus* ("Euclid Vindicated") in which he constructed a whole geometrical system based on the assumption that the fifth postulate is false, then claimed that the consequences would be so bizarre that the postulate must be true.

While most 18th-century mathematicians didn't care about axioms, the mood shifted in the 19th century. Mathematicians started to focus on the foundations of their work. They revisited geometry, no longer taking Euclid for granted, but examining his assumptions.

Around 1824, Russian mathematician Nikolai Lobachevsky was working on the problem. At some point, he realized that the parallel postulate was just one possible assumption, and that the contrary assumption is equally valid. Instead of saying "there is at most one line through a point parallel to a given line," Lobachevsky essentially explored the idea that "there are many lines...." Unlike Saccheri, Lobachevsky realized that the resulting system of geometry was entirely consistent. In other words, he invented an entirely new non-Euclidean geometry, sometimes called *hyperbolic* geometry.

In Lobachevsky's geometry, there are no similar triangles except for congruent ones. By way of analogy, think of triangles on the surface of a sphere. For small triangles, the surface is almost planar, so the sum of the angles is close to 180°. But as the triangles get bigger, the angles need to get bigger because of the curvature of the surface. Lobachevsky's model was similar, but with space curved in the opposite way, so that bigger triangles corresponded to smaller angles.

Lobachevsky's results, first published in 1826, were met with dismissal and scorn from the Russian mathematical community, and Lobachevsky himself was marginalized. One person who did recognize the validity of Lobachevsky's work was Gauss, who learned Russian to read Lobachevsky's book. But in general, it would take many years before his work became an accepted part of mathematics. Today, Lobachevsky's discovery is considered to be a monumental turning point in the history of mathematics.

Nikolai Ivanovich Lobachevsky (1792–1856)

In the early 19th century, Russia was not a major center for mathematics (despite Euler spending much of his career in St. Petersburg). There were no great Russian mathematicians. Yet by the middle of the 20th century, Russia was a mathematical superpower. This transformation began with the first great Russian mathematician, Nikolai Ivanovich Lobachevsky.

Lobachevsky did not come from a major city, nor did he attend one of the two great universities (Moscow and St. Petersburg); he was not sent abroad to learn from the leading thinkers

of Europe. He did not come from the aristocracy or even the upper middle class; he and his brother were charity students at their local school. He grew up in Kazan, a provincial city on the Volga river that did not even have a university until 1805. Lobachevsky entered the recently founded university in 1807. (Interestingly, Tolstoy and Lenin attended the same school decades later.)

When Lobachevsky started at the University of Kazan, there was no one to teach mathematics—students studied on their own. Fortunately, Martin Bartels, one of Gauss's former professors, soon joined the faculty. After receiving a master's degree and continuing to study privately with Bartels, Lobachevsky was appointed as an adjunct professor in 1814. He would go on to spend most of his career at the university, eventually being elected its rector (similar to president) in 1827.

Despite his humble origins, Lobachevsky was never afraid to challenge conventional opinions. His groundbreaking work on non-Euclidean geometry was submitted in 1826, but was not widely known until it was published as a book in 1832. The book was publicly ridiculed in a review by Ostrogradsky, an important Russian mathematician who studied with Cauchy.

Lobachevsky continued his work on non-Euclidean geometry for the rest of his life, refining it and publishing books about it in various languages. By the 1840s, Gauss recognized the importance of the work, even reading some of Lobachevsky's books in the original Russian. Gauss nominated him for membership in the Göttingen Academy of Sciences, a great honor at the time. Yet Lobachevsky was still ostracized by the Russian mathematical establishment until the end of his career.

In his later years, Lobachevsky's life took a tragic turn. He lost his job at the university, his house, and most of his property, suffered the deaths of two of his children, and then became blind. Even under these circumstances, he persisted in his work, dictating a major new book, *Pangeometry*, just before his death in 1856.

Often when a new idea emerges in math or science, it is discovered independently by multiple people at roughly the same time. This was the case with non-Euclidean geometry. At about the same time Lobachevsky was working in Kazan, a young Hungarian mathematician named János Bolyai made a similar discovery. A few years later, Bolyai's father Farkas Bolyai, a well-known math professor and friend of Gauss, included the son's results as an appendix to one of his own books. Farkas sent Gauss the book. Although Gauss privately remarked that young Bolyai was a genius, the letter he sent Farkas had a discouraging message:

> If I commenced by saying that I am unable to praise this work, you would certainly be surprised for a moment. But I cannot say otherwise. To praise it would be to praise myself. Indeed the whole contents of the work, the path taken by your son, the results to which he is led, coincide almost entirely with my meditations, which have occupied my mind partly for the last thirty or thirty-five years.

The letter is typical of Gauss, both in his refusal to give credit to others and in his insistence that his own unpublished thoughts gave him priority. (We now know that Gauss had indeed discovered many of the same ideas, but had decided not to publish them because he was afraid of the reaction.) Why he acknowledged Lobachevsky's work but dismissed Bolyai's we will never know. But whatever the reason, the results were tragic. Bolyai was devastated by Gauss's response and never attempted to publish in mathematics again. Even sadder, he became mentally unstable. When he came across Lobachevsky's book sometime later, he was convinced that "Lobachevsky" was actually a pseudonym for Gauss, whom he believed had stolen his ideas.

*   *   *

Once non-Euclidean geometry was discovered, many mathematicians wrestled with what they considered to be an important question: which geometry is actually correct, Euclid's or Lobachevsky's? Gauss took the question quite seriously, and proposed an ingenious experiment to test the theory.

First, find three mountains forming a triangle that are some distance apart, but close enough so that a person standing on top of each with a telescope can see the others. Then set up surveying equipment on each peak to accurately measure the angles of the triangle. If the angles add up to 180°, then Euclid is right; if their sum is less than 180°, then Lobachevsky is.

The actual experiment was never conducted. But over time, the question became moot. Other mathematicians would ultimately prove the independence of the fifth postulate, showing that if Euclidean geometry is consistent, then so is Lobachevskian geometry. Meanwhile, mathematicians began to treat questions of reality as irrelevant. While math was originally invented to understand aspects of the world we live in, by the end of the 19th century, it began to be seen as a purely formal exercise.

9.5   Hilbert's Formalist Approach

One must be able to say "tables, chairs, beer-mugs" each time in place of "points, lines, planes."

—David Hilbert

David Hilbert, perhaps the greatest mathematician of the early 20th century, was the leader of this formalist approach. In a view that eventually became standard throughout mathematics, he said that if a theory was consistent, it was true.

While all of Euclid's theorems and proofs are correct, by modern standards the axioms are somewhat shaky. It took 2400 years before anyone tried to come up with a better foundation for geometry. Hilbert spent 10 years rethinking Euclid and constructing his own axiomatic system for geometry. As the quotation suggests, Hilbert believed that the validity of his axiomatic system should not rely on any intuitions about geometry. Hilbert's system contained many more axioms than Euclid's, making explicit many things that Euclid took for granted. Hilbert had:

- 7 axioms of connection (e.g., if two points lie on a plane, then all points on the line going through these points are on this plane)

- 4 axioms of order (e.g., there is a point between any two points on a line)

- 1 axiom of parallels

- 6 axioms of congruence (e.g., two triangles are congruent if side-angle-side...)

- 1 Archimedes' axiom

- 1 completeness axiom

Hilbert's geometric system is quite complex, and was the subject of several of his courses. Unfortunately, by the time he was done constructing the axioms, he had no energy left to prove many geometric theorems. Hilbert's work on the axioms of Euclidean geometry was the last major work done on that subject.

David Hilbert 1862–1943

David Hilbert was born in the German city of Königsberg (now Kaliningrad, Russia). He studied mathematics at the University of Königsberg, continued for a Ph.D., and eventually joined the faculty.

At age 33, he accepted an offer to become a professor at the University of Göttingen. He would stay there for the rest of his career. As we saw earlier (Section 8.2), Göttingen was the center of the mathematical universe, and Hilbert eventually became the leader of the mathematical community there during the pinnacle of the department's fame.

It is difficult to convey the astounding variety of fundamental work done by Hilbert and the profound effect he had on all of mathematics.

In his initial work on invariant theory, Hilbert championed the use of nonconstructive proofs, which was a radical idea at the time. In fact, he initially became famous as much for the approach as for the actual result. Today, nonconstructive proofs are common.

When asked to summarize work on algebraic number theory (the area Dedekind had been working on), Hilbert wrote a 600-page volume called *Zahlbericht* ("Report on Numbers"). This book captured and explained all the major developments in the field. While he mostly summarized (and credited) the work of others, Hilbert's unification drove the field forward, eventually leading to Noether's work on abstract algebra.

For the next 10 years, while working on geometry, Hilbert went beyond Lobachevsky and examined the validity of *all* of Euclid's axioms. His book *Foundations of Geometry* not only introduced his new axioms, but also taught people for the first time how to think about and rigorously analyze any axiomatic system.

Hilbert also worked on physics, co-inventing general relativity theory, largely independently and at roughly the same time as Einstein. His invention of *Hilbert spaces*—an extension of vector spaces to infinite dimensions—

became an important building block in the mathematical foundation of quantum mechanics.

In 1900, Hilbert gave a lecture at the Sorbonne in Paris where he listed 10 important unsolved problems in mathematics and challenged the community to work on them. The list was later expanded to 23 problems in a published paper. Work on these problems, which became known as *Hilbert's problems*, defined much of mathematics in the 20th century. He also spent much of the last 25 years of his career working on mechanizing the foundations of mathematics, an effort known as "Hilbert's program." Although Hilbert's program was shown to be flawed by the work of Kurt Gödel and Alan Turing, that same work led to the development of the modern theory of computation.

Hilbert was not only a great mathematician, but also a great mentor and supporter of younger colleagues. When his best friend Hermann Minkowski died, Hilbert spent several years editing and publishing Minkowski's work. He championed the career of Emmy Noether (Section 8.3). He also collaborated with many researchers in several fields; his lectures on physics became the basis of a classic text co-authored by Richard Courant.

Hilbert's one blind spot was his pride in German culture. With good reason, he saw mathematics in Germany as the culmination of 200 years of advances. He welcomed people from all over the world to join the German mathematical community. But he also believed that *only* the research in Germany was worthy of attention. Perhaps the most egregious example was his unwillingness to cite the work of Giuseppe Peano in Italy or recognize its seminal importance to the foundations of mathematics. At the same time, Hilbert was completely opposed to the views of the Nazis (who came to power a few years after his retirement in 1930), having spent much of his career promoting the work of many colleagues who happened to be Jewish, including his best friend Minkowski and his protegé Noether.

Sadly, Hilbert lived to see everything he cared about destroyed. His friends were driven into exile, his once-great department was reduced to mediocrity, and his beloved country embraced beliefs he despised. But his mathematical legacy was carried around the world by his many students and collaborators, and lives on today.

9.6   Peano and His Axioms

Certainly it is permitted to anyone to put forward whatever hypotheses he wishes, and to develop the logical consequences contained in those hypotheses. But in order that this work merit the name of

> Geometry, it is necessary that these hypotheses or postulates express
> the result of the more simple and elementary observations of physi-
> cal figures.
>
> —Giuseppe Peano

Even before Hilbert announced his program on formalizing mathematics, others had been working on similar ideas about formalizing mathematical systems.
One of these was Italian mathematician Giuseppe Peano. As the quotation shows,
Peano was still interested in the connections between mathematics and reality.
In 1891, he began writing *Formulario Mathematico* ("Mathematical Formulas"),
which would become a comprehensive work containing all essential theorems in
mathematics expressed in a symbolic notation Peano invented. Much of his notation, such as the symbols for quantifiers and set operations, is still used today.

In 1889, Peano published a set of axioms that provided a formal basis for
arithmetic. There were five, just like Euclid's:

There is a set $\mathbb{N}$ called the *natural numbers*:

1. $\exists 0 \in \mathbb{N}$
2. $\forall n \in \mathbb{N} : \exists n' \in \mathbb{N}$ – called its *successor*
3. $\forall \mathbb{S} \subset \mathbb{N} : (0 \in \mathbb{S} \wedge \forall n : n \in \mathbb{S} \implies n' \in \mathbb{S}) \implies \mathbb{S} = \mathbb{N}$
4. $\forall n, m \in \mathbb{N} : n' = m' \implies n = m$
5. $\forall n \in \mathbb{N} : n' \neq 0$

In English, we might write them like this:

1. Zero is a natural number.

2. Every natural number has a successor.

3. If a subset of natural numbers contains zero, and every element in the subset
   has a successor in the subset, then the subset contains all natural numbers.

4. If two natural numbers have the same successor, then they are equal.

5. Zero is not the successor of any natural number.

The third axiom, known as the *axiom of induction*, is the most important. It says
that if we take any subset S of $\mathbb{N}$ that contains zero and obeys the rule that the
successor of every element is also in S, then S is the same as $\mathbb{N}$. Another way to
put this is "there are no unreachable natural numbers"; if you start with zero and
keep taking the successor, you'll eventually get to every natural number. Many
modern texts put this axiom last, but we use Peano's order.[4]

---

[4]Modern texts often also start natural numbers with 1 rather than 0.

Peano's axioms transformed arithmetic. In fact, he was building on earlier work by Richard Dedekind and Hermann Grassman, both of whom showed how to derive some basic principles of arithmetic. But Peano went further, and his contributions were so important that mathematicians since then talk about *Peano arithmetic*, not just arithmetic.

Giuseppe Peano (1858–1932)

Giuseppe Peano was born into a peasant family near Turin in the north of Italy, right around the time Italy became a unified country. He attended the University of Turin and eventually joined the faculty there. Later, he also began teaching at the Royal Military Academy. Among his best-known achievements was the discovery of the space-filling curve, known as a Peano curve, which provided a continuous mapping from a one-dimensional segment to every point on a two-dimensional square.

For most of the 1890s, Peano worked on the foundations of mathematics and his great book *Formulario Mathematico*. *Formulario* was meant to be a compendium of all mathematical results, written formally. It was a masterpiece, not only providing a foundation for mathematics but also covering a variety of topics, together with references to the sources in their original languages. Peano gave a copy of the book to the British philosopher Bertrand Russell, and it strongly influenced Russell's work with Whitehead, *Principia Mathematica*, which would come to play an important role in early theories of computation.

Initially, Peano published *Formulario Mathematico* in French, but he was frustrated by the ambiguity inherent in any natural language. Eventually, around 1900, he decided that the only solution was to invent an unambiguous universal language for science and mathematics, and to then use this for his writing.

The language Peano designed was called *Latine sine Flexione* ("Latin without Inflection"), later renamed "Interlingua." His idea was to start with Latin, but to replace all its confusing declensions, conjugations, and irregular words with a simple, logical set of rules.

Peano rewrote *Formulario* in his new language, and this edition was published in 1908. Here's what his famous axioms looked like in Interlingua:

0. N_0 es classe, vel "numero" es nomen commune.
1. Zero es numero.
2. Si *a* es numero, tunc suo successivo es numero.
3. N_0 es classe minimo, que satisfac ad conditione 0, 1, 2; [...]
4. Duo numero, que habe successivo aequale, es aequale inter se.
5. 0 non seque ullo numero.

Peano also started using his formal notation in his teaching, which probably did not endear him to his students. In addition, he turned every course he was supposed to be teaching into a discussion of the foundations of mathematics, which eventually caused him to lose his position at the military academy.

Peano's dream was that other scientists would start publishing their work in Interlingua, but this did not happen. In fact, few people even attempted to read Peano's book, and his work was largely ignored. Toward the end of his life, Peano spent much of his time trying to promote Interlingua, and he was mostly forgotten by the mathematical community; they were more interested in the work of Hilbert and others at Göttingen.

Even today, despite embracing Peano's foundational axioms of arithmetic, most mathematicians have never read more than the first page of his monumental work. It has been out of print for years, and has never been translated into English.

To prove that every axiom is needed, we need to remove each one from the set and demonstrate that the remaining set has consequences that do not meet our intent—in this case, that they do not correspond to what we mean by natural numbers.

Removing existence of 0 axiom. If we remove this axiom, we are forced to drop all axioms that refer to zero. Since we have no elements to start with, the other axioms never apply and can be satisfied by the empty set, which is clearly not a model of natural numbers.

Removing totality of successor axiom. If we remove the requirement that every value have a successor, then we end up allowing finite sets like {0} or {0, 1, 2}. Clearly, no finite set satisfies our notion of natural numbers. (However, on computers, we give up this axiom, since all of our data types are finite; for example, a `uint64` can express only the first 2^{64} integers.)

Removing induction axiom. If we remove the induction axiom, then we end up with the situation where we have more integer-like things than there are integers. These "unreachable" numbers are called *transfinite ordinals* and are designated by ω. So we could end up with sets like $\{0, 1, 2, 3, \ldots, \omega, \omega + 1, \omega + 2, \ldots\}$, $\{0, 1, 2, 3, \ldots, \omega_1, \omega_1 + 1, \omega_1 + 2, \ldots, \omega_2, \omega_2 + 1, \omega_2 + 2, \ldots\}$, and so on.

Removing invertibility of successor axiom. If we remove the requirement that equal successors have equal predecessors, then we're allowing "ρ-shaped" structures where an item can have multiple predecessors, some earlier in the sequence and some later, such as $\{0, 1, 1, 1, \ldots\}$, $\{0, 1, 2, 1, 2, \ldots\}$, or $\{0, 1, 2, 3, 4, 5, 3, 4, 5, \ldots\}$. Since all of these structures are finite, they clearly do not include all natural numbers.

Removing "nothing has 0 as its successor" axiom. If we remove this axiom, then we'd allow structures that loop back to zero, like $\{0, 0, \ldots\}$ and $\{0, 1, 0, 1, \ldots\}$. Again, these structures are finite, so they do not capture our notion of natural numbers.

9.7   Building Arithmetic

Now that we have established that all of Peano's axioms are independent, and therefore necessary for our notion of natural numbers, we can build up arithmetic from first principles. We'll do this now by defining exactly what it means to add and multiply two natural numbers.

Definition of Addition:

$$a + 0 = a \tag{9.1}$$

$$a + b' = (a + b)' \tag{9.2}$$

We are not *proving* these statements; we are defining addition to *be* these statements. All properties of adding natural numbers follow from this definition. For example, here's how we prove that 0 is the left additive identity:

$$0 + a = a \tag{9.3}$$

basis: $0 + 0 = 0$

inductive step: $0 + a = a \implies 0 + a' = (0 + a)' = a'$

In the basis step, we assert that it's true when a is zero. We know this because of Equation 9.1 in the definition of addition. In the inductive step, we assume it's true for any a. By Equation 9.2, we know that $0 + a' = (0 + a)'$. But by the assumption of the inductive step, we can substitute a for $0 + a$, so our result is a', and therefore $0 + a' = a'$.

Definition of Multiplication:

$$a \cdot 0 = 0 \tag{9.4}$$

$$a \cdot b' = (a \cdot b) + a \tag{9.5}$$

We can now prove that $0 \cdot a = 0$, much as we did for addition:

basis: $0 \cdot 0 = 0$

inductive step: $0 \cdot a = 0 \implies 0 \cdot a' = 0 \cdot a + 0 = 0$

Definition of 1. We also define 1 as the successor of 0:

$$1 = 0' \tag{9.6}$$

Now we know how to add 1:

$$a + 1 = a + 0' = (a + 0)' = a' \tag{9.7}$$

We also know how to multiply by 1:

$$a \cdot 1 = a \cdot 0' = a \cdot 0 + a = 0 + a = a$$

We can derive fundamental properties of addition as well; they follow from the axioms.

Associativity of Addition: $(a + b) + c = a + (b + c)$

basis:	$(a + b) + 0 = a + b$	by 9.1
	$= a + (b + 0)$	by 9.1

inductive step:

$(a + b) + c = a + (b + c) \implies$

$(a + b) + c' = ((a + b) + c)'$	by 9.2
$= (a + (b + c))'$	by induction hypothesis
$= a + (b + c)'$	by 9.2
$= a + (b + c')$	by 9.2

To get commutativity, we'll start by proving it for the special case:

$$a + 1 = 1 + a \tag{9.8}$$

basis:	$0 + 1 = 1$	by 9.3
	$= 1 + 0$	by 9.1

inductive step:

$a + 1 = 1 + a \implies$

$a' + 1 = a' + 0'$	by 9.6
$= (a' + 0)'$	by 9.2
$= ((a + 1) + 0)'$	by 9.7
$= (a + 1)'$	by 9.1
$= (1 + a)'$	by induction hypothesis
$= 1 + a'$	by 9.2

Commutativity of Addition: $a + b = b + a$

basis:	$a + 0 = a$	by 9.1
	$= 0 + a$	by 9.3

inductive step:

$a + b = b + a \implies$

$a + b' = a + (b + 1)$		by 9.7
$= (a + b) + 1$	by associativity of addition	
$= (b + a) + 1$	by induction hypothesis	
$= b + (a + 1)$	by associativity of addition	
$= b + (1 + a)$		by 9.8
$= (b + 1) + a$	by associativity of addition	
$= b' + a$		by 9.7

Exercise 9.3. Using induction, prove:

- Associativity and commutativity of multiplication

- Distributivity of multiplication over addition

Exercise 9.4. Using induction, define total ordering between natural numbers.

Exercise 9.5. Using induction, define the partial function *predecessor* on natural numbers.

*   *   *

Do Peano axioms define natural numbers? No; as Peano put it, "number (positive integer) cannot be defined (seeing that the ideas of order, succession, aggregate, etc., are as complex as that of number)." In other words, if you don't already know what they are, Peano's definitions won't tell you. Instead, they *describe* our existing idea of numbers, formalizing our notions of arithmetic, which helps provide a way to structure proofs.

In general, we can say that axioms explain, not define. The explanation may not be constructive; that is, it might not say how the result is achieved. Even if it does suggest an algorithm, the algorithm could be computationally very inefficient. No sane person would do addition by repeated application of the successor function. But these axioms still serve a useful purpose; they get us to think about which properties of natural numbers are essential and which are not.

This approach is a good attitude to take when studying the documentation for a programming interface. Why is that requirement imposed? What would the consequences be if it were not there?

9.8   Thoughts on the Chapter

We began the chapter by looking at the notion of proof, a formal—yet social—process for demonstrating the truth of a proposition. We saw how proofs show connections between truths; proof systems are a way to organize knowledge. We also looked at the discovery of theorems, and the important abstraction they provide.

Next we looked at a richer formalism for organizing knowledge, the axiomatic system, and saw how geometry and arithmetic could be built up from first principles. The critical role of axiomatic systems is their ability to reduce the complexity of knowledge. You don't need to memorize all the true propositions, because you can derive them from a few axioms and inference rules.

However, it's important to remember that historically, mathematicians did not really start with axioms and derive theorems from them. The axioms were proposed only after the interrelationships between the theorems were well understood and the assumptions underlying them identified. The same process holds for programming: designing good abstractions requires examining a large number of real algorithms and understanding their interrelationships.

While axiomatic systems allow us to organize knowledge, they presuppose that we already have some knowledge to organize. Discovery of a theorem is a more important thing than proving it—you cannot attempt to prove something unless you have reason to believe it is a truth.

Sometimes modern mathematicians forget the empirical origins of knowledge. In his book *The Method*, the great Greek mathematician Archimedes discussed how any means for acquiring mathematical knowledge was valid, including measurement and experimentation. Only after discovering mathematical truths should one attempt to derive a rigorous proof. The same principle applies to programming: before trying to prove a program correct, we should try to write correct programs—even if our attempts involve trial and error.

10

ten

Fundamental Programming Concepts

All humans naturally desire to know.

Aristotle, *Metaphysics* I, 1

In this chapter we will introduce some of the important ideas associated with generic programming, including concepts and iterators. We'll also consider some common programming tasks that rely on them. But we'll start by looking at the origins of the notion of abstraction.

10.1 Aristotle and Abstraction

The School of Athens, a famous painting by Italian Renaissance painter Raphael, depicts many ancient Greek philosophers (see detail of painting on the next page). At the center are Plato and Aristotle, the two most important philosophers of the ancient world. Plato is pointing upward, while his student Aristotle holds his hand out over the ground. According to popular interpretation, Plato is pointing to the heavens, indicating that we should contemplate the eternal, while Aristotle is indicating that we need to study the world. In fact, it could be said that Plato invented mathematics and Aristotle invented the study of everything else, especially science. Aristotle's works cover everything from aesthetics to zoology.

Aristotle (384 BC–322 BC)

Aristotle came from Stageira, a city in the far north of Greece. We know very little about his early life, but we know that at some point he decided to move to Athens in search of wisdom. He studied (and at some point, probably taught) at Plato's Academy for about 20 years. Around the time of Plato's death—perhaps disappointed because he was not appointed Plato's successor—he left Athens.

In 343 BC, King Philip of Macedon appointed Aristotle to be a tutor for his son Alexander and Alexander's companions. We don't know much about Aristotle's relationship with the prince, but in later years when Alexander became king and began the Asian conquests that earned him the nickname "the Great," he sent Aristotle exotic plant and animal specimens for the philosopher's collection.

Around 335 BC, Aristotle returned to Athens and created his own great school, the Lyceum. During the next 12 years, he produced the most astonishing collection of knowledge ever assembled. While his teacher Plato had focused on studying eternal truths, Aristotle wanted to understand the world as it really was. For example, when Plato wanted to write about politics, he described what the ideal society would be. When Aristotle wrote about politics, he asked his students to visit each of the important Greek city-states and then report on their constitutions. Aristotle's approach was to observe everything, describe it, and come up with explanations for what he saw.

Aristotle taught, and wrote about, nearly every subject imaginable. According to several important writers of the period, Aristotle wrote beautifully; unfortunately the books he intended for publication, such as his dialogues, have all been lost. What we have instead are terse treatises that were probably lecture notes. Nevertheless, many of his works, such as *Nicomachean Ethics*, *Politics*, and *Metaphysics* are still essential reading today. And regardless of their style, his collected works constitute the first encyclopedic treatment of knowledge.

Although Aristotle's scientific descriptions include factual errors, he was the first person to systematically describe the scientific world, with observations on topics as detailed as how the octopus reproduces.

Aristotle left Athens around 322 BC and died soon afterward. While other philosophical traditions (e.g., Stoicism, Platonism) persisted in ancient times long after their founders' deaths, Aristotle's did not. Greek philosophy became increasingly introspective and lost interest in Aristotle's idea of studying observable reality. The Lyceum rapidly declined in importance, and few scholars in later Greek and Roman times considered themselves Aristotelians. Even when his work was rediscovered in the Middle Ages, medieval scholars slavishly studied his writings rather than following his methodology of going out and observing the world. Aristotle's great legacy is his empirical approach, which is the foundational principle of all modern science. Furthermore, the organization of knowledge reflected in the departments of modern universities is a direct descendent of the taxonomy that Aristotle proposed.

Aristotle's writings were preserved toward the end of the first millennium AD by Arab philosophers. In the 12th century, when Christian kingdoms recaptured much of Spain from the Islamic state known as Al-Andalus, they found a library in the Spanish city of Toledo containing a great number of books in Arabic, including translations of Aristotle's works. Eventually the books were translated from the original Greek into Latin, and an Aristotelian renaissance spread through Europe. Aristotle became known as simply "the Philosopher," and his works became a part of generally accepted knowledge. The great Andalusian philosopher Ibn Rushd (known as Averroes to Europeans) wrote widely read commentaries on Aristotle, reconciling his philosophy with the teachings of Islam; he became known simply as "the Commentator." In the 13th century, Christian scholars such as Thomas Aquinas and Duns Scotus similarly showed that Aristotelianism was compatible with Christianity; this was often described as "baptizing" Aristotle. As a result, Aristotle's works were part of the required study at European universities for literally hundreds of years.

Among Aristotle's most important works is the *Organon*, a collection of six treatises on various aspects of logic that would define the field for the next 2600 years.[1] In *Categories*, the first part of the *Organon*, Aristotle introduced the notion of *abstraction*. He wrote about the distinction between an *individual*, a *species*, and a *genus*. While today most people think of these as biological distinctions, for Aristotle they applied to everything. A species incorporates all the "essential" properties of a type of thing. A genus may contain many species, each identified by its *differentia* —the things that differentiate it from other species in the genus.

It is Aristotle's idea of genus that inspired the term *generic programming*—a way to think about programming that focuses on the level of *genera* (the plural of genus) rather than species.

10.2   Values and Types

Now we will see how some of the ideas we've been discussing fit in computer programming. First, we need a few definitions:

Definition 10.1. A **datum** is a sequence of bits.

01000001 is an example of a datum.

Definition 10.2. A **value** is a datum together with its interpretation.

A datum without an interpretation has no meaning. The datum 01000001 might have the interpretation of the integer 65, or the character "A," or something else altogether. Every value must be associated with a datum in memory; there is no way to refer to disembodied values in a language like C++ or Java.

Definition 10.3. A **value type** is a set of values sharing a common interpretation.

Definition 10.4. An **object** is a collection of bits in memory that contain a value of a given value type.

---

[1] Unlike Aristotle's other works, a Latin version of the *Organon* was available to Europeans much earlier; Boethius provided the translation in the early 6th century.

There is nothing in the definition that says that all the bits of an object must be contiguous. In fact, it's quite common for parts of an object to be located at different places in memory; these are called *remote parts*.

An object is *immutable* if the value never changes, and *mutable* otherwise. An object is *unrestricted* if it can contain any value of its value type.

Definition 10.5. An **object type** is a uniform method of storing and retrieving values of a given value type from a particular object when given its **address**.

What we call "types" in programming languages are object types. C++, Java, and other programming languages do not provide mechanisms for defining value types.[2] Every type resides in memory and is an object type.

10.3 Concepts

The essence of generic programming lies in the idea of *concepts*. A concept is a way of describing a family of related object types. The relationship between concept and type is exactly the relationship between theory and model in mathematics, and between genus and species in the scientific taxonomy introduced by Aristotle.

Natural Science	Mathematics	Programming	Programming Examples
genus	theory	concept	**Integral, Character**
species	model	type or class	`uint8_t, char`
individual	element	instance	01000001 (65, `'A'`)

Here are some examples of concepts and some of their types in C++:

- **Integral:**[3] `int8_t, uint8_t, int16_t, …`

- **UnsignedIntegral:** `uint8_t, uint16_t, …`

- **SignedIntegral:** `int8_t, int16_t, …`

While concepts exist in many languages implicitly, very few languages provide an explicit way to talk about them.[4]

---

[2] The iterator trait `value_type` in C++, despite its name, does not actually return a value type in the sense described here. Rather, it returns the object type of the value pointed to by the iterator.

[3] This refers specifically to the list of built-in C++ integral types. There is a broader concept **Integer** that includes all of these plus other representations of integers such as infinite-precision integers.

[4] There have been proposals to include concepts in C++; the work is still in progress. There are also concept-like features in some functional programming languages such as Haskell.

Many programming languages provide a mechanism to specify the interface of a type to be implemented later: abstract classes in C++, interfaces in Java, and so on. However, these mechanisms completely specify the interface, including strict requirements on the types of arguments and return values. In contrast, concepts allow interfaces to be specified in terms of families of related types. For example, in both Java and C++, you can specify an interface containing a function size() returning a value of type int32. In the world of concepts, you can have an interface with a function size() that returns a value of any integral type—uint8, int16, int64, etc.

A concept can be viewed as a set of requirements on types, or as a predicate[5] that tests whether types meet those requirements. The requirements concern

- The *operations* the types must provide

- Their *semantics*

- Their *time/space complexity*

A type is said to *satisfy* a concept if it meets these requirements.

When first encountering concepts, programmers often wonder why the third requirement, for space/time complexity, is included. Isn't complexity just an implementation detail? To answer this question, consider a real-world example. Suppose you defined the abstract data type *stack*, but you implemented it as an array, in such a way that every time you pushed something onto the array, you had to move every existing element to the next position to make room. Instead of pushing on the stack being a fast operation (constant time), it's now a slow operation (linear time). This violates a programmer's assumption of how stacks should behave. In a sense, a stack that doesn't have fast push and pop is *not really a stack*. Therefore these very basic complexity constraints are part of what it means to satisfy a concept.

*   *   *

Two useful ideas related to concepts are *type functions* and *type attributes*. A type function is a function that, given a type, returns an affiliated type. For example, it would be nice to have type functions like this:

- value_type(Sequence)

- coefficient_type(Polynomial)

- ith_element_type(Tuple, size_t)

Unfortunately, mainstream programming languages do not contain type functions, even though they would be easy to implement. (After all, the compiler already knows things like the type of elements in a sequence.)

---

[5]A predicate is a function that returns true or false.

A type attribute is a function that, given a type, returns a value representing one of its attributes. For example:

- `sizeof`

- `alignment_of`

- Number of members in a struct

- Name of the type

Some languages provide some type attributes, like `sizeof()` in C and C++.

*   *   *

Let's look at some very general concepts. The first one is **Regular**,[6] which we introduced back in Chapter 7. Roughly speaking, a type is regular if it supports these operations:

- Copy construction

- Assignment

- Equality

- Destruction

Having a copy constructor implies having a default constructor, since `T a(b)` should be equivalent to `T a; a = b;`. To describe the semantics of **Regular**, we'll express the requirements as axioms:

$$\forall a \, \forall b \, \forall c \; : T \, a(b) \implies (b = c \implies a = c)$$
$$\forall a \, \forall b \, \forall c \; : a \leftarrow b \implies (b = c \implies a = c)$$
$$\forall f \in \text{RegularFunction} \; : a = b \implies f(a) = f(b)$$

The first axiom says that if you copy construct a from b, then anything that was equal to b will now also be equal to a. The second axiom says that if you assign b to a, then anything that was equal to b will now also be equal to a. The third axiom uses the notion of a *regular function* (not to be confused with a regular type), which is one that produces equal results given equal inputs. It's the responsibility of the programmer to specify which functions are supposed to be regular; only then can other programmers (or, in the future, the compiler) rely on the fact that these functions will preserve equality.

The complexity requirements on **Regular** are that each operation is no worse than linear in the area of the object, where area is defined as all space occupied by the object, both its header and its remote parts, both its data and its connectors.[7]

---

[6]By convention, we write concept names with initial capitals, and display them with a **Sans Serif** typeface.

[7]For a more formal treatment of the concept **Regular**, see *Elements of Programming* Section 1.5.

The concept **Regular** is universal—it's not specific to any programming language. A type in any language is regular if it satisfies the requirements.

A related concept is **Semiregular**, which is just like **Regular** except that equality is not explicitly defined. This is needed in a few situations where it is very difficult to implement an equality predicate. Even in these situations, equality is assumed to be implicitly defined, so that axioms that control copying and assignment are still valid. After all, as we saw earlier, the meaning of assigning a to b is that b's value will be *equal* to a's value afterward.

10.4   Iterators

An *iterator* is a concept used to express where we are in a sequence. In fact, iterators were originally going to be called "coordinates" or "positions"; they may be viewed as a generalization of pointers. In some programming languages, what they call iterators are heavyweight bundles of functionality, but the *concept* of an iterator just expresses this very simple notion of position.

To be an iterator, a type must support three operations:

• Regular type operations

• Successor

• Dereference

One way to think of an iterator is "something that lets you do linear search in linear time." The essence of an iterator is the notion of *successor*. Indeed, iterators come to us directly from Peano's axioms; essentially, the concept **Iterator** is "a theory with successor." However, our iterator concepts will be less strict, because we don't require all of Peano's axioms. For example, in Peano arithmetic, every number has a successor, while with iterators, this is not always the case—sometimes we get to the end of our data. Peano also tells us that if successors are equal, the predecessors must be equal, and that we can't have loops. These requirements are also not the case for programmers; we're allowed to have data structures that link back to earlier elements and form loops. In fact, this is sometimes exactly what we need to do a computational task efficiently.

The second iterator operation, *dereferencing*, is a way to get from an iterator to its value. Dereferencing has a time complexity requirement; it's assumed to be "fast," which means that there is not a faster way of getting to data than through the iterator. Iterators are sometimes bigger than traditional pointers, in situations where they need to store some additional state to enable fast navigation. Iterators may also support special values indicating that we are past the end of the object, as well as singular values like the null pointer that cannot be dereferenced. It's okay that dereferencing is a partial function (i.e., that it isn't defined for all values); after all, mathematicians have no trouble saying what division is, even though division by zero is not defined.

Dereferencing and successor are closely connected,[8] and this relationship imposes the following restrictions:

- Dereferencing is defined on an iterator if and only if successor is defined.

- If you are not at the end of the range, you can dereference.

Why do we need equality as a requirement for iterators? In other words, why do we need iterators to be regular rather than semiregular? Because we need to be able to see when one iterator reaches another.

10.5   Iterator Categories, Operations, and Traits

There are several kinds of iterators, which we call *iterator categories*. Here are the most important:

- *Input iterators* support one-directional traversal, but only once, as is found in single-pass algorithms. The canonical model of an input iterator is the position in an *input stream*. Bytes are coming over the wire and we can process them one at a time, but once they are processed, they are gone. In particular, with input iterators i == j does not imply ++i == ++j; for example, if you've already consumed a character from an input stream, you can't consume the same character again with a different iterator. Keep in mind that just because an algorithm only *requires* input iterators does not mean it is limited to operating on input streams.

- *Forward iterators* also support only one-directional traversal, but this traversal can be repeated as needed, as in multi-pass algorithms. The canonical model of a forward iterator is the position in a *singly linked list*.[9]

- *Bidirectional iterators* support bidirectional traversal, repeated as needed (i.e., they also can be used in multi-pass algorithms). The canonical model of a bidirectional iterator is the position in a *doubly linked list*. Bidirectional iterators have an invertible successor function: if an element x has a successor y, then y has a predecessor x.

- *Random-access iterators* support random-access algorithms; that is, they allow access to any element in constant time (both *far* and *fast*). The canonical model is the position in an *array*.

---

[8]See Chapter 6 of *Elements of Programming* for more about the relationship between dereferencing and successor.

[9]We assume that link structure of the list is not modified as it is traversed.

In addition, there is another common iterator category that behaves differently from the others:

- *Output iterators* support alternating successor (++) and dereference (*) operations, but the results of dereferencing an output iterator can appear only on the left-hand side of an assignment operator, and they provide no equality function. The canonical model of an output iterator is the position in an *output stream*. We can't define equality because we can't even get to the elements once they've been output.

While the iterators described so far are the only ones included in C++, other useful iterator concepts also exist:

- *Linked iterators* work in situations where the successor function is mutable (for example, a linked list where the link structure is modified).

- *Segmented iterators* are for cases where the data is stored in noncontiguous *segments*, each containing contiguous sequences. `std::deque`, a data structure that is implemented as a segmented array, would immediately benefit; instead of needing each successor operation to check whether the end of the segment has been reached, a "top level" iterator could find the next segment and know its bounds, while the "bottom level" iterator could iterate through that segment.

Iterators like these can easily be implemented. Just because a concept is not built into the language does not mean it's not useful. In general, STL should be viewed as a set of well-chosen examples, not an exhaustive collection of all useful concepts, data structures and algorithms.

∗   ∗   ∗

A simple but important thing we may want to do is find the distance between two iterators. For an input iterator, we might write our `distance()` function like this:

```
template <InputIterator I>
DifferenceType<I> distance(I f, I l, std::input_iterator_tag) {
    // precondition: valid_range(f, l)
    DifferenceType<I> n(0);
    while (f != l) {
        ++f;
        ++n;
    }
    return n;
}
```

There are three notable things about this code: the use of the type function `DifferenceType`, the use of the iterator tag argument, and the precondition. We'll discuss all of these soon, but before we do, let's compare this to a different implementation—one that's optimized for random access iterators:

```
template <RandomAccessIterator I>
DifferenceType<I> distance(I f, I l,
                           std::random_access_iterator_tag) {
    // precondition: valid_range(f, l)
    return l - f;
}
```

Since we have random access, we don't have to repeatedly increment (and count) from one iterator to the other; we can just use a constant time operation—subtraction—to find the distance.

The *difference type* of an iterator is an integral type that is large enough to encode the largest possible range. For example, if our iterators were pointers, the difference type in C++ could be `ptrdiff_t`. But in general we don't know in advance which type the iterator will be, so we need a type function to get the difference type. Although C++ does not have a general mechanism for type functions, STL iterators have a special set of attributes known as *iterator traits*, one of which gives us the difference type. The complete set of iterator traits is

- `value_type`

- `reference`

- `pointer`

- `difference_type`

- `iterator_category`

We've mentioned `value_type` before; it returns the type of the values pointed to by the iterator. The `reference` and `pointer` traits are rarely used in current architectures,[10] but the others are very important.

Since the syntax for accessing iterator traits is rather verbose, we'll implement our own type function for accessing `difference_type`, with the `using` construct of C++11. (See Appendix C for more information about `using`.)

```
template <InputIterator I>
using DifferenceType =
        typename std::iterator_traits<I>::difference_type;
```

---

[10]Earlier versions of the Intel processor architecture included different types for shorter and longer pointers, so it was important to know which to use for a given iterator. Today, if the value type of an iterator is T, the `pointer` iterator trait would normally be T*.

This gives us the `DifferenceType` type function used in the earlier code.

The iterator trait `iterator_category` returns a tag type representing the kind of iterator we're dealing with. Objects of these tag types contain no data. As we did for `DifferenceType`, we define the following type function:

```
template <InputIterator I>
using IteratorCategory =
          typename std::iterator_traits<I>::iterator_category;
```

Now we can return to the use of the iterator tag argument in the `distance` functions. The iterator tags shown in the examples (`input_iterator_tag` and `random_access_iterator_tag`) are possible values of the iterator category trait, so by including them as arguments, we are distinguishing the type signature of the two function implementations. (We will see more examples of this in Chapter 11.) This allows us to perform *category dispatch* on the `distance` function; that is, we can write a general form of the function for any iterator category, and the fastest one will be invoked:

```
template <InputIterator I>
DifferenceType<I> distance(I f, I l) {
    return distance(f, l, IteratorCategory<I>());
}
```

Note that the third argument is actually a constructor call creating an instance of the appropriate type, because we cannot pass types to functions. When the client calls `distance()`, it uses the two-argument version shown here. That function then invokes the implementation that matches the iterator category. This dispatch happens at compile time and the general function is inline, so there is literally no performance penalty for choosing the right version of the function.

The use of tag types as arguments to distinguish versions of the function may seem redundant, since we already specified different concepts in the templates. However, recall that our use of concepts serves only as documentation for the programmer; current C++ compilers don't know anything about concepts. Once concepts are added to the language, the arcane iterator category tag mechanism will no longer be needed.

10.6 Ranges

A range is a way of specifying a contiguous sequence of elements. Ranges can be either *semi-open* or *closed*;[11] a closed range $[i, j]$ includes items i and j, while a semi-open range $[i, j)$ includes i but ends just before j. It turns out that semi-open ranges are the most convenient for defining interfaces. This is because

---

[11]In mathematics, there are also *open* ranges, but they are less useful in programming, so we do not include them here.

algorithms that operate on sequences of n elements need to be able to refer to $n + 1$ positions. For example, there are $n + 1$ places to insert a new item: before the first element, between any two elements, or after the last element. Also, semi-open ranges, unlike closed ranges, can describe an empty range. Furthermore, a semi-open empty range can be specified at any position; it provides more information than a simple "nil" or empty list.

A range can be specified in one of two ways: a *bounded* range has two iterators (one pointing to the beginning and one pointing just past the end), while a *counted* range has an iterator pointing to the beginning and an integer n indicating how many items are included. This gives us four kinds of ranges altogether:

	semi-open	closed
bounded: two iterators	$[i, j)$	$[i, j]$
counted: iterator and integer	$[i, n)$	$[i, n]$

(A closed counted range must have $n > 0$.) As we shall see, there are different situations where bounded or counted ranges are preferable.

While mathematical texts index sequences from 1, computer scientists start from 0, and we will use the latter convention for our ranges. Interestingly, although 0-based indexing in computer science was initially used as a way to indicate the offset in memory, this convention turns out to be more natural regardless of implementation, since it means that for a sequence with n elements, the indices are in the range $[0, n)$ and any iteration is bounded by the length.

*   *   *

Now we can return to the third notable feature of our `distance` functions: the `valid_range` precondition. It would be nice if we could have a `valid_range` function that returned true if the range specified by the two iterators was valid and false otherwise, but unfortunately, it's not possible to implement such a function. For example, if two iterators each represent cells in a linked list, we have no way of knowing if there's a path from one to the other. But even if we're dealing with simple pointers, we still cannot compute `valid_range`: there is no way in C or C++ to determine if two pointers point to a single contiguous block of memory; there might be gaps in the middle.

So we can't write a `valid_range` function, but we can still use it as a precondition. Instead of guaranteeing the correct behavior in code, we'll use axioms that, if satisfied, ensure that our `distance` function will behave as intended. Specifically, we postulate the following two axioms:

$$\text{container}(c) \implies \text{valid}(\text{begin}(c), \text{end}(c))$$
$$\text{valid}(x, y) \land x \neq y \implies \text{valid}(\text{successor}(x), y)$$

The first axiom says that if it's a container, the range from `begin()` to `end()` is valid. The second axiom says that if $[x, y)$ is a nonempty valid range, then the

range [successor(x), y) is also valid. All STL-style containers, as well as C++
arrays, must obey these axioms. This allows us to prove the algorithms correct.
For example, if you go back to our original distance function for input iterators
in Section 10.5, you'll see that the second axiom ensures that if we start with a
valid range, we'll still have one each time through the loop.

∗   ∗   ∗

In addition to the successor (++) and distance operations, it's useful to have
a way to move an iterator by several positions at once. We call this function
advance. As before, we'll implement two versions, one for input iterators:

```
template <InputIterator I>
void advance(I& x, DifferenceType<I> n, std::input_iterator_tag) {
    while (n) {
        --n;
        ++x;
    }
}
```

and another for random access iterators:

```
template <RandomAccessIterator I>
void advance(I& x, DifferenceType<I> n,
             std::random_access_iterator_tag) {
    x += n;
}
```

We'll also provide with a top-level function for doing the dispatch:

```
template <InputIterator I>
void advance(I& x, DifferenceType<I> n) {
    advance(x, n, IteratorCategory<I>());
}
```

10.7 Linear Search

Linear search is a fundamental programming task that all programmers should
understand. The simplest idea of linear search is to scan a linear list until we
find a specific element. But we will generalize that to a function that scans the
list until it finds an element that satisfies a given predicate. So in addition to
being able to search for a specific value, we could find, for example, the first odd
element, or the first element that has no vowels, or whatever else we like. Of
course, there might not be such an element, so we need some way to indicate
that no item is found. We'll call our function find_if—"find it if it's there":[12]

---

[12]This name originated in the programming language Common Lisp.

```
template <InputIterator I, Predicate P>
I find_if(I f, I l, P p) {
    while (f != l && !p(*f)) ++f;
    return f;
}
```

This function relies on equality, dereference, and successor. If no item that satisfies the predicate exists, the returned value of f will be the same as l, the iterator that points past the end of the range. The calling function uses this comparison to determine whether a matching item has been found. C and C++ guarantee that a pointer is valid one position past the end of an array. However, such a pointer should never be dereferenced. All STL containers provide similar guarantees for their iterators.

This function has an implicit semantic precondition: the value type of the iterator and the argument type of the predicate must be the same; otherwise, there is no way to apply the predicate to the items in the range.

Here's a variation of our linear search function for the input iterator case. Although we could have overloaded the name, we've deliberately added _n to emphasize that this version uses a counted range:

```
template <InputIterator I, Predicate P>
std::pair<I, DifferenceType<I>>
find_if_n(I f, DifferenceType<I> n, P p) {
    while (n && !p(*f)) { ++f; --n; }
    return {f, n};
}
```

Why do we return a pair? Wouldn't it be sufficient to return the iterator that points to the found element, as we did in the previous version? No. In the previous version, the caller had the "last" iterator to compare to; here, it does not. So the second returned value tells the caller whether we're at the end, in which case the item was not found and the returned iterator cannot be dereferenced. But just as importantly, if we do find a matching item, this allows us to *restart the search where we left off*. Without this, there would be no way to search a range for anything but the first occurrence of a desired item.

This illustrates an important point: just as there can be bugs in code, so there can also be bugs in the interface. We'll see an example of one in the next section.

10.8   Binary Search

If we have a sorted sequence, we can search it much more efficiently by using another essential algorithm, *binary search*. This function is easy to describe, but hard to implement correctly and even harder to specify (design an interface for) correctly.

Origins of Binary Search

The idea of binary search originated in the *Intermediate Value Theorem* (IVT), also known as the *Bolzano-Cauchy Theorem*:

> If f is a continuous function in an interval $[a, b]$ such that $f(a) < f(b)$, then $\forall u \in [f(a), f(b)]$ there is $c \in [a, b]$ such that $u = f(c)$.

The proof of the theorem consists of doing binary search. Suppose, as an example, we have a continuous function such that $f(a)$ is -3 and $f(b)$ is 5. The IVT tells us that for a particular point in the image of the function— let's say, 0—there is a point c in the domain such that $f(c) = 0$. How can we find that point? We can start by finding the point x_1 that is half the distance between a and b, and computing $f(x_1)$. If it equals 0, we're done; we've found c. If it's greater than 0, we repeat with a point x_2 that's half the distance from a to x_1. If it's less, we take half the distance from x_1 to b. As we keep repeating the process, we asymptotically converge to c.

Simon Stevin had a similar idea in 1594, when he devised a version of the IVT for polynomials. But since Stevin was interested in doing everything with decimals, he actually divided the interval into tenths rather than halves, and examined all of them until he found the tenth that contained the desired value. It was Lagrange who first described the binary approach for polynomials in 1795. Bolzano and Cauchy generalized the IVT in the early 19th century, and it is their version used by mathematicians today.

Binary search was first discussed as a programming technique in 1946 by physicist and computing pioneer John Mauchly, co-creator of the ENIAC (the first electronic general-purpose computer). However, many details were left unspecified. The first "correct" algorithm for performing binary search was published in 1960 by D. H. Lehmer, a mathematician who had worked on the ENIAC years earlier. However, Lehmer's version did not use the correct interface, and this error was repeated for several decades afterward.

An example of the erroneous interface remains today in the UNIX `bsearch()` function. According to the POSIX[13] standard:

> The `bsearch()` function shall return a pointer to a matching member of the array, or a null pointer if no match is found. If two or more members compare equal, which member is returned is unspecified.[14]

---

[13] POSIX is the set of standards for UNIX-like operating systems. Linux, for example, is a POSIX-compliant OS.

[14] http://www.unix.com/man-page/POSIX/3posix/bsearch/

There are two fundamental flaws with this interface. The first concerns the return of a null pointer to indicate that the item is not found. Often you are doing the search because you want to insert an item if it isn't there, *at the place it would have been if it were there.* With this interface, you have to start from scratch to find your insert position, this time using linear search! Furthermore, there are many applications where you actually want to find the closest or next value to where the missing item would be; the item you're searching for may simply be a prefix of the kinds of items you hope to find.

The second flaw concerns the situation where there are multiple matches. The matches may be keys of items that you need to retrieve. So how do you obtain the entire range of equal items, if you don't know which one you're on? You have to do linear search both backward and forward to find the ends of the matching sequence.

*   *   *

The right way to implement binary search begins with the idea of a *partition point*. Assume that we have a sequence of items $[f, l)$ that is arranged such that a certain predicate is true of the items in the range $[f, m)$ and false for $[m, l)$.[15] Then the partition point is the position m. Formally, if we have a function that computes the partition point, then its precondition is

$$\exists m \in [f, l) \; : \; \Big(\forall i \in [f, m) \; : \; p(i)\Big) \; \wedge \; \Big(\forall i \in [m, l) \; : \; \neg p(i)\Big)$$

(i.e., the elements are already partitioned as described earlier). Its postcondition is that it returns the value m from the precondition. Note that f in this expression refers to the first element in the range, not to a function.

For a counted range, the partition point algorithm looks like this:

```
template <ForwardIterator I, Predicate P>
I partition_point_n(I f, DifferenceType<I> n, P p) {
    while (n) {
        I middle(f);
        DifferenceType<I> half(n >> 1);
        advance(middle, half);
        if (!p(*middle)) {
            n = half;
        } else {
            f = ++middle;
            n = n - (half + 1);
```

---

[15]In retrospect, it would have been better to have the false items first, since the Boolean value false sorts before true; unfortunately, the "wrong" order is now part of the C++ language standard.

```
        }
    }
    return f;
}
```

This is an extremely important algorithm, and it's worth spending some time to make sure you understand it. It uses a binary-search-style strategy just like the Intermediate Value Theorem. Recall that the goal is to return the first "bad" element—that is, the first element for which the predicate is false. The outer loop continues until n is zero. Inside the loop, we position the iterator middle to a point halfway between f and f + n. If our predicate is false for the element at that position, we set n to half of its previous value and repeat. Otherwise, we know the predicate is true, so we set our starting point f to the next value after the middle, adjust n to reflect the number of items left, and repeat. When we are done, the return value is the partition point: the point after the last true value.

Notice that our function uses advance to move the iterator. Since we don't know the iterator type, we can't assume that addition is allowed. However, if we have a random access iterator, the advance function we wrote earlier will call the fast implementation. (If we don't have a random access iterator, we might have to make as many as n moves, but in either case we'll never have to do more than $\log n$ comparisons.)

If we are given a bounded range instead, we simply compute the distance and invoke the counted range version:

```
template <ForwardIterator I, Predicate P>
I partition_point(I f, I l, P p) {
    return partition_point_n(f, distance(f, l), p);
}
```

Now let's return to the general binary search problem. To solve it, we're going to make use of the following lemma:

Lemma 10.1 (Binary Search Lemma): *For any sorted range $[i, j)$ and a value a (the item you're searching for), there are two iterators, lower bound b_l and upper bound b_u such that*

$$1.\ \forall k \in [i, b_l)\ :\ v_k < a$$
$$2.\ \forall k \in [b_l, b_u)\ :\ v_k = a$$
$$3.\ \forall k \in [b_u, j)\ :\ v_k > a$$

where v_k is the value at position k.

These bounds always exist, though in the special case where there is no matching item, $b_l = b_u$. It may help to picture the data in the range:

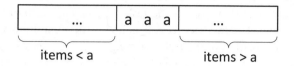

Exercise 10.1. Prove the Binary Search Lemma.

Now we can use our partition point function to perform binary search. If we have total ordering, any sorted range is partitioned for any value *a* according to the predicate $x < a$. STL actually provides a few functions that perform binary search, depending on our task. If we want to find the *first* position where the item is found, we use the `lower_bound` function. Using the features in C++11, we can write `lower_bound` like this:

```
template <ForwardIterator I>
I lower_bound(I f, I l, ValueType<I> a) {
    return partition_point(f, l,
                         [=](ValueType<I> x) { return x < a; });
}
```

The last line defines a new anonymous function (also known as a *lambda expression*[16]) that returns true if its argument is less than *a*, then passes that function as the predicate used by `partition_point`. The `lower_bound` function returns the position of the item *a*, or the position it would be in if it were there. `ValueType` is just a shorthand type function for accessing the appropriate iterator trait, like the one we wrote earlier for `DifferenceType`:

```
template <InputIterator I>
using ValueType = typename std::iterator_traits<I>::value_type;
```

In the case where the returned position is not l, we still need to know whether we found the item. To do this, the caller needs to check whether the dereferenced return value is equal to *a*.

If instead we want to find the *last* position where the item is found, we use `upper_bound`. The code is almost the same, except that we define the predicate to check if the value is less than or equal to *a*, rather than strictly less than *a*:

```
template <ForwardIterator I>
I upper_bound(I f, I l, ValueType<I> a) {
    return partition_point(f, l,
                         [=](ValueType<I> x) {return x <= a;});
}
```

---

[16]See Appendix C for details on how to use lambda expressions.

Some readers may be wondering which function is the "real" binary search. The answer is that it depends on the task. If you want to find the position of the first matching element, then `lower_bound` is the "real" binary search. If you want to find the position of the last matching element, then it's `upper_bound`. If you want to know the entire range of matching elements, STL provides a third function, `equal_range`. And if all you care about is whether there was a match, there is a function `binary_search`—but keep in mind that all it's doing is calling `lower_bound` and testing whether the dereferenced return value is equal to the item.

The additional functionality of `equal_range` clearly benefits from the STL convention of using semi-open ranges. Even when the element is not present, the function returns an empty range at the position where it could be inserted.

10.9   Thoughts on the Chapter

We began this chapter by seeing how Aristotle's levels of abstraction (individual, species, genus) correspond to the programming notions of instance, type, and concept. It is the notion of concept that allows a generic program to work in a variety of settings.

One of your central goals as a programmer should be to identify existing concepts in your application. You will often develop new algorithms, occasionally develop a new data structure, and only rarely define a new concept. In that rare situation, a lot of work is needed to ensure that it is a true concept and not just a collection of unrelated requirements. To restate Occam's Razor, one should not introduce new concepts without necessity.

We then introduced the concept of iterators, and saw the role they play in some fundamental algorithms. By using compile-time type dispatch on different kinds of iterators, we can ensure that the most efficient implementation gets executed in a given situation.

Finally, we saw the importance of writing not only correct code, but also correct interfaces. An incorrect interface can severely limit the utility of a function; a correct interface allows it to be used in a variety of situations without loss of efficiency.

11

eleven

Permutation Algorithms

An algorithm must be seen to be believed.

Donald Knuth

Complex computer programs are built up from smaller pieces that perform commonly used fundamental tasks. In the previous chapter, we looked at some tasks involving searching for data. In this chapter, we'll look at tasks that involve shifting data into new positions, and show how to implement them in a generic way. We'll see how these tasks also end up using two ideas discussed earlier in the book: groups from abstract algebra and the greatest common divisor (GCD) from number theory.

The tasks we will focus on—rotate and reverse—allow us to introduce algorithms that do the same task differently depending on the concept of the iterator to which they apply. In addition to illustrating some generic programming techniques, these algorithms are of great practical importance. The `rotate` algorithm in particular is probably the most used algorithm inside the implementation of STL components from `vector` to `stable_sort`.

11.1 Permutations and Transpositions

Our exploration of the GCD algorithm led us to learn about groups and other algebraic structures. Using this knowledge, we're going to start investigating the mathematical operations *permutation* and *transposition*, which play an important role in some fundamental algorithms.

Definition 11.1. A **permutation** is a function from a sequence of n objects onto itself.

The formal notation for permutations[1] looks like this:

$$\begin{pmatrix} 1 & 2 & 3 & 4 \\ 2 & 4 & 1 & 3 \end{pmatrix}$$

The first row represents the indexes (positions) of a sequence of objects; mathematicians start numbering from 1. The second row represents where the items in those positions end up after applying the permutation. In this example, the item that used to be at position 1 will end up in position 2, the item that was in position 2 will end up in position 4, and so on.

In practice, permutations are usually written using a shorthand format that omits the first row:

$$\begin{pmatrix} 2 & 4 & 1 & 3 \end{pmatrix}$$

In other words, at position i, you write where the ith original element will end up. An example of applying a permutation is

$$(2\,4\,1\,3) : \{a, b, c, d\} = \{c, a, d, b\}$$

We can use the notion of permutation to define a *symmetric group*:

Definition 11.2. The set of all permutations on n elements constitutes a group called the **symmetric group** S_n.

A symmetric group has the following group properties:

binary operation:	composition (associative)
inverse operation:	inverse permutation
identity element:	identity permutation

This is the first example we've seen where the elements of a group are themselves functions, and the group operation is an operation on functions. If we have a permutation x that shifts items two positions to the right, and another permutation y that shifts items three positions to the right, then the composition $x \circ y$ shifts items five positions to the right.

This is perhaps the most important group to know about, since every finite group is a subgroup of a symmetric group. It is known as *Cayley's Theorem*.

Exercise 11.1. Prove Cayley's Theorem.

Exercise 11.2. What is the order of S_n?

---

[1] This is the same notation mathematicians use for matrices; hopefully the context will make it clear which interpretation is intended.

Now let's look at a special case of permutation, *transposition*.

Definition 11.3. A **transposition**(i, j) is a permutation that exchanges the ith and jth elements $(i \neq j)$, leaving the rest in place.

The notation for transpositions indicates which two positions should get exchanged:

$$(2\ 3) : \{a, b, c, d\} = \{a, c, b, d\}$$

In programming, we have a simpler name for transposition: we call it swap. In C++, we might implement it like this:

```cpp
template <Semiregular T>
void swap(T& x, T& y) {
    T tmp(x);
    x = y;
    y = tmp;
}
```

The *swap* operation requires only that the types of its arguments satisfy the concept **Semiregular**.[2] We can see that swap requires the ability to copy-construct, assign, and destruct its data, since those operations are used in the code. It does not need to explicitly test for equality, so we do not need the types to be **Regular**. When we design an algorithm, we'll want to know which concepts the types need to satisfy, but we'll also want to make sure not to impose extra requirements we don't need.

* * *

The *transposition lemma* demonstrates how fundamental the swap operation is:

Lemma 11.1 (Transposition Lemma): *Any permutation is a product of transpositions.*

Proof. One transposition can put at least one element into its final destination. Therefore, at most $n - 1$ transpositions will put all n elements into their final destinations. □

Why do we need only $n - 1$ transpositions? Because once $n - 1$ items are in the right place, the nth item must also be in the right place; there's no place else for it to go.

Exercise 11.3. Prove that if $n > 2$, S_n is not abelian.

---

[2] A discussion of C++ move semantics is beyond the scope of this book.

Every permutation defines a directed graph of n elements. After applying the permutation enough times, a given element will eventually be put back in its original position, representing a *cycle* in the graph. Every permutation can be decomposed into cycles. For example, consider the permutation (2 3 5 6 1 4). The element in position 4 moves to position 6, and the element in position 6 moves to position 4, so after applying the permutation twice, both of those elements will end up where they started. We see a similar pattern for the elements at positions 1, 2, 3, and 5, although this time it takes four operations before they get back to the beginning. We say that the permutation (2 3 5 6 1 4) can be decomposed into two cycles, and we show them graphically like this:

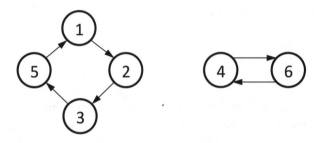

We write this decomposition as (2 3 5 6 1 4) = (1 2 3 5)(4 6).

The cycle notation, used on the right, may be thought of as an extension of the transposition notation. Although the notation is ambiguous (is this a cycle or a permutation?), it is usually clear from the context. Also, permutations always contain all the integers from 1 to n, while cycles might not.

Cycles are disjoint. If you are at a position in a cycle, you can get to all other positions in that cycle. Therefore, if two cycles share one position, they share all positions; that is, they are the same cycle. So the only way to have separate cycles is if they don't share any positions.

Definition 11.4. A cycle containing one element is called a *trivial cycle*.

Exercise 11.4. How many nontrivial cycles could a permutation of n elements contain?

Theorem 11.1 (Number of Assignments): *The number of assignments needed to perform an arbitrary permutation in place is $n - u + v$, where n is the number of elements, u is the number of trivial cycles, and v is the number of nontrivial cycles.*

Proof. Every nontrivial cycle of length k requires $k + 1$ assignments, since each element needs to be moved, plus we need to save the first value being overwritten; since every nontrivial cycle requires one extra move, moving all v cycles requires

v extra moves. Elements in trivial cycles don't need to be moved at all, and there are u of those. So we need to move $n - u$ elements, plus v additional moves for the cycles.   □

A common permutation that has exactly $n/2$ cycles is *reverse*. In some sense this is the "hardest" permutation because it requires the largest number of assignments. We'll look at reverse in greater detail in Section 11.5.

Exercise 11.5. Design an in-place[3] reverse algorithm for forward iterators; that is, the algorithm should work for singly linked lists without modifying the links.

11.2   Swapping Ranges

Sometimes we want to swap more than one item at a time. In fact, a common operation in programming is to swap all the values in one range of data with the corresponding values in another (possibly overlapping) range. We do it in a loop, one swap at a time:

```
while (condition) std::swap(*iter0++, *iter1++);
```

where `iter0` and `iter1` are iterators pointing to the respective values in each range. Recall from Chapter 10 that we prefer to use semi-open ranges—those where the range includes all elements from the first bound up to but not including the second bound.

When we swap two ranges, often only one of them needs to be specified explicitly. Here, `first0` and `last0` specify the bounds of the first range, while `first1` refers to the start of the second range:

```
template <ForwardIterator I0, ForwardIterator I1>
// ValueType<I0> == ValueType<I1>
I1 swap_ranges(I0 first0, I0 last0, I1 first1) {
    while (first0 != last0) swap(*first0++, *first1++);
    return first1;
}
```

There's no point in specifying the end of the second range, since for the swap to work, it must contain (at least) the same number of elements as the first range. Why do we return `first1`? Because it might be useful to the caller. For example, if the second range is longer, we might want to know where the unmodified part of the second range begins. It's information that the caller doesn't have, and it costs us almost nothing to return.

This is a good time to review the *law of useful return*, which we introduced in Section 4.6.

---

[3]We'll discuss the notion of in-place algorithms more in Section 11.6; see Definition 11.6.

The Law of Useful Return, Revisited

When writing code, it's often the case that you end up computing a value that the calling function doesn't currently need. Later, however, this value may be important when the code is called in a different situation. In this situation, you should obey the *law of useful return*:

> *A procedure should return all the potentially useful information it computed.*

The quotient-remainder function that we saw in Chapter 4 is a good example: when we first wrote it, we needed only the remainder, but we had already done all the work to find the quotient. Later, we saw other applications that use both values.

The law does *not* imply doing unneeded extra computations, nor does it imply that useless information should be returned. For example, in the code given earlier, it's not useful to return `first0`, because the algorithm guarantees that at the end it's equal to `last0`, which the caller already has. It's useless to give me information I already have.

The Law of Separating Types

The `swap_ranges` code illustrates another important programming principle, the *law of separating types*:

> *Do not assume that two types are the same when they may be different.*

Our function was declared with two iterator types, like this:

```
template <ForwardIterator I0, ForwardIterator I1>
// ValueType<I0> == ValueType<I1>
I1 swap_ranges(I0 first0, I0 last0, I1 first1);
```

rather than assuming that they're the same type, like this:

```
template <ForwardIterator I>
I swap_ranges(I first0, I last0, I first1);
```

The first way gives us more generality and allows us to use the function in situations we wouldn't otherwise be able to, without incurring any additional computation cost. For example, we could swap a range of elements in a linked list with a range of elements in an array and it would just work.

However, just because two types are distinct does not mean there is no relationship between them. In the case of `swap_ranges`, for the implementation to be able to call swap on the data, we need to ensure that the value type of I0 is the same as the value type of I1. While the compiler cannot check this condition today, we can indicate it with a comment in the code.

In situations where we're not sure if the second range is long enough to perform all the needed swaps, we can make both ranges explicit and have our `while` test check to make sure neither iterator has run off the end of the range:

```
template <ForwardIterator I0, ForwardIterator I1>
std::pair<I0, I1> swap_ranges(I0 first0, I0 last0,
                              I1 first1, I1 last1) {
    while (first0 != last0 && first1 != last1) {
        swap(*first0++, *first1++);
    }
    return {first0, first1};
}
```

This time we do return both `first0` and `first1`, because one range may be exhausted before the other, so we won't necessarily have reached `last0` and `last1`.

Swapping counted ranges is almost the same, except that instead of checking to see if we reached the end of the range, we count down from n to 0:

```
template <ForwardIterator I0, ForwardIterator I1, Integer N>
std::pair<I0, I1> swap_ranges_n(I0 first0, I1 first1, N n) {
    while (n != N(0)) {
        swap(*first0++, *first1++);
        --n;
    }
    return {first0, first1};
}
```

The Law of Completeness

Observe that we created both `swap_ranges` and `swap_ranges_n`. Even though in a particular situation the programmer might need only one of these versions, later on a client might need the other version.

This follows the *law of completeness:*

When designing an interface, consider providing all the related procedures.

If there are different ways of invoking an algorithm, provide interfaces for those related functions. In our swap example, we've already provided two related interfaces for bounded ranges, and we'll also provide interfaces for counted ranges.

This rule is not saying that you need to have a *single* interface to handle multiple cases. It's perfectly fine to have one function for counted ranges and another for bounded ranges. You especially should not have a single interface for disparate operations. For example, just because containers need to provide both "insert element" and "erase element" functionality doesn't mean your interface should have a single "insert_or_erase" function.

Counted ranges are easier for the compiler, because it knows the number of iterations, called the *trip count*, in advance. This allows the compiler to make certain optimizations, such as loop unrolling or software pipelining.

Exercise 11.6. Why don't we provide the following interface?

```
pair<I0, I1> swap_ranges_n(I0 first0, I1 first1, N0 n0, N1 n1)
```

11.3 Rotation

One of the most important algorithms you've probably never heard of is `rotate`. It's a fundamental tool used behind the scenes in many common computing applications, such as buffer manipulation in text editors. It implements the mathematical operation *rotation*.

Definition 11.5. A permutation of n elements by k where $k \geq 0$:

$$(k \bmod n, k + 1 \bmod n, ..., k + n - 2 \bmod n, k + n - 1 \bmod n)$$

is called an n **by** k **rotation**.

If you imagine all n elements laid out in a circle, we're shifting each one "clockwise" by k.

At first glance, it might seem that rotation could be implemented with a modular shift, taking the beginning and end of the range, together with the amount to shift, as arguments. However, doing modular arithmetic on every operation is quite expensive. Also, it turns out that rotation is equivalent to exchanging different length blocks, a task that is extremely useful for many applications. Viewed this way, it is convenient to present rotation with three iterators: f, m, and l, where $[f, m)$ and $[m, l)$ are valid ranges.[4] Rotation then interchanges ranges $[f, m)$ and $[m, l)$. If the client wants to rotate k positions in a range $[f, l)$, then it should pass a value of m equal to $l - k$. As an example, if we want to do a rotation with $k = 5$ on a sequence specified by the range $[0, 7)$, we choose $m = l - k = 7 - 5 = 2$:

---

[4]The names f, m, and l are meant to be mnemonics for *first*, *middle*, and *last*.

```
0 1 2 3 4 5 6
f   m         l
```

which produces this result:

```
2 3 4 5 6 0 1
```

Essentially, we're moving each item 5 spaces to the right (and wrapping around when we run off the end).

Exercise 11.7. Prove that if we do `rotate(f, m, l)`, it performs distance(f, l) by distance(m, l) rotation.

An important `rotate` algorithm was developed by David Gries, a professor at Cornell University, together with IBM scientist Harlan Mills:

```
template <ForwardIterator I>
void gries_mills_rotate(I f, I m, I l) {
    // u = distance(f, m) && v = distance(m, l)
    if (f == m || m == l) return;          // u == 0 || v == 0
    pair<I, I> p = swap_ranges(f, m, m, l);
    while(p.first != m || p.second != l) {
        if (p.first == m) {                // u < v
            f = m; m = p.second;           // v = v - u
        } else {                           // v < u
            f = p.first;                   // u = u - v
        }
        p = swap_ranges(f, m, m, l);
    }
    return;                                // u == v
}
```

The algorithm first uses the regular `swap_ranges` function to swap as many elements as we can—as many elements as there are in the shorter range. The `if` test checks whether we've exhausted the first range or the second range. Depending on the result, we reset the start positions of f and m. Then we do another swap, and repeat the process until neither range has remaining elements.

This is easier to follow with an example. Let's look at how a range is transformed, and how the iterators move, as the algorithm runs:

Start:

```
0 1 2 3 4 5 6
f   m         l
```

Swap [0, 1] and [2, 3]. Have we exhausted both ranges? No, only the first one, so we set `f = m` and `m = p.second`, which points to the first element in the sequence that hasn't yet been moved:

```
2 3 0 1 4 5 6
  f   m     l
```

Swap [0, 1] and [4, 5]. Have we exhausted both ranges? No, only the first one, so again we set f = m and m = p.second:

```
2 3 4 5 0 1 6
      f   m l
```

Swap [0] with [6]. Have we exhausted both ranges? No, only the second one this time, so we set f = p.first:

```
2 3 4 5 6 1 0
          f m l
```

Swap [1] with [0]. Have we exhausted both ranges? Yes, so we're done.

```
2 3 4 5 6 0 1
            f m
              l
```

Now look at the comments in the gries_mills_rotate code (shown in bold-face). We call u the length of the first range $[f, m)$, and v the length of the second range $[m, l)$. We can observe something remarkable: the annotations are performing our familiar subtractive GCD! At the end of the algorithm, $u = v =$ GCD of the lengths of the initial two ranges.

Exercise 11.8. If you examine swap_ranges, you will see that the algorithm does unnecessary iterator comparisons. Rewrite the algorithm so that no unnecessary iterator comparisons are done.

It turns out that many applications benefit if the rotate algorithm returns a new middle: a position where the first element moved. If rotate returns this new middle, then rotate(f, rotate(f, m, l), l) is an identity permutation. First, we need the following "auxiliary rotate" algorithm:

```
template <ForwardIterator I>
void rotate_unguarded(I f, I m, I l) {
    // assert(f != m && m != l)
    pair<I, I> p = swap_ranges(f, m, m, l);
    while (p.first != m || p.second != l) {
        f = p.first;
        if (m == f) m = p.second;
        p = swap_ranges(f, m, m, l);
    }
}
```

The central loop is the same as in the Gries-Mills algorithm, just written differently. (We could have written it this way before but wanted to make the *u* and *v* computations clearer.)

We need to find *m'*—the element whose distance to the last is the same as *m*'s distance from the first. It's the value returned by the first call to swap_ranges. To get it back, we can embed a call to rotate_unguarded in our final version of rotate, which works as long as we have forward iterators. As we'll explain shortly, the forward_iterator_tag type in the argument list will help us invoke this function only in this case:

```
template <ForwardIterator I>
I rotate(I f, I m, I l, std::forward_iterator_tag) {
    if (f == m) return l;
    if (m == l) return f;
    pair<I, I> p = swap_ranges(f, m, m, l);
    while (p.first != m || p.second != l) {
        if (p.second == l) {
            rotate_unguarded(p.first, m, l);
            return p.first;
        }
        f = m;
        m = p.second;
        p = swap_ranges(f, m, m, l);
    }
    return m;
}
```

How much work does this algorithm do? Until the last iteration of the main loop, every swap puts one element in the right place and moves another element out of the way. But in the final call to swap_ranges, the two ranges are the same length, so every swap puts both elements it is swapping into their final positions. In essence, we get an extra move for free on every swap. The total number of swaps is the total number of elements n, minus the number of free swaps we saved in the last step. How many swaps did we save in the last step? The length of the ranges at the end, as we saw earlier, is $\gcd(n-k,k) = \gcd(n,k)$, where $n = $ distance(f, l) and $k = $ distance(m, l). So the total number of swaps is $n-\gcd(n,k)$. Also, since each swap takes three assignments (tmp = a; a = b; b = tmp), the total number of assignments is $3(n - \gcd(n,k))$.

11.4 Using Cycles

Can we find a faster rotate algorithm? We can if we exploit the fact that rotations, like any permutations, have cycles. Consider a rotation of $k = 2$ for $n = 6$ elements:

```
0 1 2 3 4 5
⇓
4 5 0 1 2 3
```

The item in position 0 ends up in position 2, 2 ends up in position 4, and 4 ends up back in position 0. These three elements form a cycle. Similarly, item 1 ends up in 3, 3 in 5, and 5 back in 1, forming another cycle. So this rotation has two cycles. Recall from Section 11.1 that we can perform any permutation in $n - u + v$ assignments, where n is the number of elements, u is the number of trivial cycles, and v is the number of nontrivial cycles. Since we normally don't have any trivial cycles, we need $n + v$ assignments.

Exercise 11.9. Prove that if a rotation of n elements has a trivial cycle, then it has n trivial cycles. (In other words, a rotation either moves all elements or no elements.)

It turns out that the number of cycles is $\gcd(k, n)$, so we should be able to do the rotation in $n + \gcd(k, n)$ assignments,[5] instead of the $3(n - \gcd(n, k))$ we needed for the Gries-Mills algorithm. Furthermore, in practice GCD is very small; in fact, it is 1 (that is, there is only one cycle) about 60% of the time. So a rotate algorithm that exploits cycles always does fewer assignments.

There is one catch: Gries-Mills only required moving one step forward; it works even for singly linked lists. But if we want to take advantage of cycles, we need to be able to do long jumps. Such an algorithm requires stronger requirements on the iterators—namely, the ability to do random access.

To create our new rotate function, we'll first write a helper function that moves every element in a cycle to its next position. But instead of saying "which position does the item in position x move to," we'll say "in which position do we find the item that's going to move to position x." Even though these two operations are symmetric mathematically, it turns out that the latter is more efficient, since it needs only one saved temporary variable per cycle, instead of one for every item that needs to be moved (except the last).

Here's our helper function:

```
template <ForwardIterator I, Transformation F>
void rotate_cycle_from(I i, F from) {
    ValueType<I> tmp = *i;
    I start = i;
    for (I j = from(i); j != start; j = from(j)) {
        *i = *j;
        i = j;
    }
    *i = tmp;
}
```

---
[5]See *Elements of Programming*, Section 10.4, for the proof.

Note that we're using the ValueType type function we defined near the end of Section 10.8.

How does rotate_cycle_from know which position an item comes from? That information will be encapsulated in a function object from that we pass in as an argument. You can think of from(i) as "compute where the element moving into position *i* comes from."

The function object we're going to pass to rotate_cycle_from will be an instance of rotate_transform:

```
template <RandomAccessIterator I>
struct rotate_transform {
    DifferenceType<I> plus;
    DifferenceType<I> minus;
    I m1;

    rotate_transform(I f, I m, I l) :
        plus(m - f), minus(m - l), m1(f + (l - m)) {}
        // m1 separates items moving forward and backward

    I operator()(I i) const {
        return i + ((i < m1) ?  plus : minus);
    }
};
```

The idea is that even though we are conceptually "rotating" elements, in practice some items move forward and some move backward (because the rotation caused them to wrap around the end of our range). When rotate_transform is instantiated for a given set of ranges, it precomputes (1) how much to move forward for items that should move forward, (2) how much to move backward for things that move backward, and (3) what the crossover point is for deciding when to move forward and when to move backward.

Now we can write the cycle-exploiting version of algorithm for rotation, which is a variation of the algorithm discovered by Fletcher and Silver in 1965:

```
template <RandomAccessIterator I>
I rotate(I f, I m, I l, std::random_access_iterator_tag) {
    if (f == m) return l;
    if (m == l) return f;
    DifferenceType<I> cycles = gcd(m - f, l - m);
    rotate_transform<I> rotator(f, m, l);
    while (cycles-- > 0) rotate_cycle_from(f + cycles, rotator);
    return rotator.m1;
}
```

After handling some trivial boundary cases, the algorithm first computes the number of cycles (the GCD) and constructs a `rotate_transform` object. Then it calls `rotate_cycle_from` to shift all the elements along each cycle, and repeats this for every cycle.

Let's look at an example. Consider the rotation $k = 2$ for $n = 6$ elements that we used at the beginning of this section. For simplicity, we'll assume that our values are integers stored in an array:

```
0 1 2 3 4 5
```

We also assume our iterators are integer offsets in an array, starting at 0. (Be careful to distinguish between the values at a position and the position itself.) To perform a $k = 2$ rotation, we'll need to pass the three iterators $f = 0$, $m = 4$, and $l = 6$:

```
0 1 2 3 4 5
f       m   l
```

The boundary cases of our new `rotate` algorithm don't apply, so the first thing it does is compute the number of cycles, which is equal to $\gcd(m - f, l - m) = \gcd(4, 2) = 2$. Then it constructs the `rotator` object, initializing its state variables as follows:

$$plus \leftarrow m - f = 4 - 0 = 4$$
$$minus \leftarrow m - l = 4 - 6 = -2$$
$$m1 \leftarrow f + (l - m) = 0 + (6 - 4) = 2$$

The main loop of the function rotates all elements of a cycle, then moves on to the next cycle. Let us see what happens when `rotate_cycle_from` is called.

Initially, we pass $f + d = 0 + 2 = 2$ as the first argument. So inside the function, $i = 2$. We save the value at position 2, which is also 2, to our `tmp` variable and set `start` to our starting position of 2.

Now we go through a loop as long as a new variable, `j`, is not equal to `start`. Each time through the loop, we are going to set `j` by using the rotator function object that we passed in through the variable `from`. Basically, all that object does is add the stored values `plus` or `minus` to its argument, depending on whether the argument is less than the stored value `m1`. For example, if we call `from(0)`, it will return $0 + 4$, or 4, since 0 is less than 2. If we call `from(4)`, it will return $4 + (-2)$, or 2, since 4 is not less than 2.

Here's how the values in our array change as we go through the loop in `rotate_cycle_from`:

$i \leftarrow 2$, $j \leftarrow from(2) = 0$

```
0 1 2 3 4 5
j   i
```

$*i \leftarrow *j$

```
0  1  0  3  4  5
j     i
```

$i \leftarrow j = 0, \ \ j \leftarrow from(0) = 4$

```
0  1  0  3  4  5
i        j
```

$*i \leftarrow *j$

```
4  1  0  3  4  5
i        j
```

$i \leftarrow j = 4, \ \ j \leftarrow from(4) = 2$ which is *start*, so loop ends

```
4  1  0  3  4  5
   j     i
```

$*i \leftarrow tmp$

```
4  1  0  3  2  5
   j     i
```

This completes the first call to `rotate_cycle_from` in the `while` loop of our rotate function.

Exercise 11.10. Continue to trace the preceding example until the `rotate` function finishes.

Notice that the signatures of this `rotate` function and the previous one differ by the type of the last argument. In the next section, we'll write the wrapper that lets the fastest implementation for a given situation be automatically invoked.

When Is an Algorithm Faster in Practice?

We have seen an example where one algorithm does fewer assignments than another algorithm. Does that mean it will run faster? Not necessarily. In practice, the ability to fit relevant data in cache can make a dramatic difference in this speed. An algorithm that involves large jumps in memory—that is, one that has poor locality of reference—may end up being slower than one that requires more assignments but has better locality of reference.

11.5   Reverse

Another fundamental algorithm is *reverse*, which (obviously) reverses the order
of the elements of a sequence. More formally, reverse permutes a k-element list
such that item 0 and item $k - 1$ are swapped, item 1 and item $k - 2$ are swapped,
and so on.

If we have `reverse`, we can implement `rotate` in just three lines of code:

```
template <BidirectionalIterator I>
void three_reverse_rotate(I f, I m, I l) {
    reverse(f, m);
    reverse(m, l);
    reverse(f, l);
}
```

For example, suppose we want to perform our $k = 2$ rotation on the sequence
`0 1 2 3 4 5`. The algorithm would perform the following operations:

```
                       f         m   l
    start              0 1 2 3 4 5
    reverse(f, m)      3 2 1 0 4 5
    reverse(m, l)      3 2 1 0 5 4
    reverse(f, l)      4 5 0 1 2 3
```

Exercise 11.11. How many assignments does 3-reverse rotate perform?

This elegant algorithm, whose inventor is unknown, works for bidirectional
iterators. However, it has one problem: it doesn't return the new middle position.
To solve this, we're going to break the final `reverse` call into two parts. We'll need
a new function that reverses elements until one of the two iterators reaches the
end:

```
template <BidirectionalIterator I>
pair<I, I> reverse_until(I f, I m, I l) {
    while (f != m && m != l) swap(*f++, *--l);
    return {f, l};
}
```

At the end of this function, the iterator that didn't hit the end will be pointing to
the new middle.

Now we can write a general `rotate` function for bidirectional iterators. When
it gets to what would have been the third `reverse` call, it does `reverse_until`
instead, saves the new middle position, and then finishes reversing the rest of
the range:

```
template <BidirectionalIterator I>
I rotate(I f, I m, I l, bidirectional_iterator_tag) {
    reverse(f, m);
    reverse(m, l);
    pair<I, I> p = reverse_until(f, m, l);
    reverse(p.first, p.second);
    if (m == p.first) return p.second;
    return p.first;
}
```

We have seen three different implementations of `rotate`, each optimized for different types of iterators. However, we'd like to hide this complexity from the programmer who's going to be using these functions. So, just as we did with the `distance` functions in Section 10.5, we're going to write a simpler version that works for any type of iterator, and use category dispatch to let the compiler decide which implementation will get executed:

```
template <ForwardIterator I>
I rotate(I f, I m, I l) {
    return rotate(f, m, l, IteratorCategory<I>());
}
```

The programmer just needs to call a single `rotate` function; the compiler will extract the type of the iterator being used and invoke the appropriate implementation.

*   *   *

We've been using a `reverse` function, but how might we implement it? For bidirectional iterators, the code is fairly straightforward; we have a pointer to the beginning that moves forward, and a pointer to the end that moves backward, and we keep swapping the elements they point to until they run into each other:

```
template <BidirectionalIterator I>
void reverse(I f, I l, std::bidirectional_iterator_tag) {
    while (f != l && f != --l) std::swap(*f++, *l);
}
```

Exercise 11.12. Explain why we need two tests per iteration in the preceding `while` loop.

It might appear that according to the law of useful return we should return `pair<I, I>(f, l)`. However, there is no evidence that this information is actually useful; therefore the law does not apply.

Of course, if we already knew in advance how many times we had to execute the loop (the *trip count*), we wouldn't need two comparisons. If we pass the trip count n to our function, we can implement it with only $n/2$ tests:

```
template <BidirectionalIterator I, Integer N>
void reverse_n(I f, I l, N n) {
    n >>= 1;
    while (n-- > N(0)) {
        swap(*f++, *--l);
    }
}
```

In particular, if we have a random access iterator, we can compute the trip count in constant time, and implement reverse using reverse_n, like this:

```
template <RandomAccessIterator I>
void reverse(I f, I l, std::random_access_iterator_tag) {
    reverse_n(f, l, l - f);
}
```

What if we have only forward iterators and we still want to reverse? We'll use a recursive auxiliary function that keeps partitioning the range in half (the h in the code). The argument n keeps track of the length of the sequence being reversed:

```
template <ForwardIterator I, Integer N>
I reverse_recursive(I f, N n) {
    if (n == 0) return f;
    if (n == 1) return ++f;
    N h = n >> 1;
    I m = reverse_recursive(f, h);
    if (odd(n)) ++m;
    I l = reverse_recursive(m, h);
    swap_ranges_n(f, m, h);
    return l;
}
```

Exercise 11.13. Using the sequence {0, 1, 2, 3, 4, 5, 6, 7, 8} as an example, trace the operation of the reverse_recursive algorithm.

The function returns the end of the range, so the first recursive call returns the midpoint. Then we advance the midpoint by 1 or 0 depending on whether the length is even or odd.

Now we can write our reverse function for forward iterators:

```
template <ForwardIterator I>
void reverse(I f, I l, std::forward_iterator_tag) {
    reverse_recursive(f, distance(f, l));
}
```

Finally, we can write the generic version of reverse that works for any iterator type, just as we did for rotate earlier:

```
template <ForwardIterator I>
void reverse(I f, I l) {
    reverse(f, l, IteratorCategory<I>());
}
```

The Law of Interface Refinement

What is the correct interface for rotate? Originally, std::rotate returned void. After several years of usage, it became clear that returning the new middle (the position where the first element moved) made implementation of several other STL algorithms, such as in_place_merge and stable_partition, simpler.

Unfortunately, it was not immediately obvious how to return this value without doing any extra work. Only after this implementation problem was solved was it possible to redesign the interface to return the required value. It then took more than 10 years to change the C++ language standard.

This is a good illustration of the *law of interface refinement*:

> *Designing interfaces, like designing programs, is a multi-pass activity.*

We can't really design an ideal interface until we have seen how the algorithm will be used, and not all the uses are immediately apparent. Furthermore, we can't design an ideal interface until we know which implementations are feasible.

11.6   Space Complexity

When talking about concrete algorithms, programmers need to think about where they fall in terms of time and space complexity. There are many levels of time complexity (e.g., constant, logarithmic, quadratic). However, the traditional view of space complexity put algorithms into just two categories: those that perform their computations *in place* and those that do not.

Definition 11.6. An algorithm is **in-place** (also called **polylog space**) if for an input of length n it uses $O((\log n)^k)$ additional space, where k is a constant.

Initially, in-place algorithms were often defined as using constant space, but this was too narrow a restriction. The idea of being "in place" was supposed to capture algorithms that didn't need to make a copy of their data. But many of these non-data-copying algorithms, like quicksort, use a divide-and-conquer technique that requires logarithmic extra space. So the definition was formalized in a way that included these algorithms.

Algorithms that are not in-place use more space—usually, enough to create a copy of their data.

*   *   *

Let's use our `reverse` problem to see how a non-in-place algorithm can be faster than an in-place algorithm. First, we need this helper function, which copies elements in reverse order, starting at the end of a range:

```
template <BidirectionalIterator I, OutputIterator O>
O reverse_copy(I f, I l, O result) {
    while (f != l) *result++ = *--l;
    return result;
}
```

Now we can write a non-in-place `reverse` algorithm. It copies all the data to a buffer, then copies it back in reverse order:

```
template <ForwardIterator I, Integer N, BidirectionalIterator B>
I reverse_n_with_buffer(I f, N n, B buffer) {
    B buffer_end = copy_n(f, n, buffer);
    return reverse_copy(buffer, buffer_end, f);
}
```

This function takes only $2n$ assignments, instead of the $3n$ we needed for the swap-based implementations.

11.7   Memory-Adaptive Algorithms

In practice, the dichotomy of in-place and non-in-place algorithms is not very useful. While the assumption of unlimited memory is not realistic, neither is the assumption of only polylog extra memory. Usually 25%, 10%, 5%, or at least 1% of extra memory is available and can be exploited to get significant performance gains. Algorithms need to adapt to however much memory is available; they need to be *memory adaptive*.

Let's create a memory-adaptive algorithm for `reverse`. It takes a `buffer` that we can use as temporary space, and an argument `bufsize` indicating how big the buffer is. The algorithm is recursive—in fact, it's almost identical to the `reverse_recursive` function in the previous section. But the recursion happens only on large chunks, so the overhead is acceptable. The idea is that for a given invocation of the function, if the length of the sequence being reversed fits in the buffer, we do the fast reverse with buffer. If not, we recurse, splitting the sequence in half:

```
template <ForwardIterator I, Integer N, BidirectionalIterator B>
I reverse_n_adaptive(I f, N n, B buffer, N bufsize) {
    if (n == N(0)) return f;
    if (n == N(1)) return ++f;
    if (n <= bufsize) return reverse_n_with_buffer(f, n, buffer);
    N h = n >> 1;
    I m = reverse_n_adaptive(f, h, buffer, bufsize);
    advance(m, n & 1);
    I l = reverse_n_adaptive(m, h, buffer, bufsize);
    swap_ranges_n(f, m, h);
    return l;
}
```

The caller of this function should ask the system how much memory is available, and pass that value as bufsize. Unfortunately, such a call is not provided in most operating systems.

A Sad Story about get_temporary_buffer

When the C++ STL library was designed by the first author of this book, he realized that it would be helpful to have a function get_temporary_buffer that takes a size *n* and returns the largest available temporary buffer up to size *n* that fits into physical memory. As a placeholder (since the correct version needs to have knowledge that only the operating system has), he wrote a simplistic and impractical implementation, which repeatedly calls malloc asking for initially huge and gradually smaller chunks of memory until it returns a valid pointer. He put in a prominent comment in the code saying something like, "This is a bogus implementation, replace it!" To his surprise, he discovered years later that all the major vendors that provide STL implementations are still using this terrible implementation—but they removed his comment.

11.8   Thoughts on the Chapter

One of the things we've seen in both this chapter and the previous one is how simple computational tasks offer rich opportunities to explore different algorithms and learn from them. The programming principles that arise from these examples—the laws of useful return, separating types, completeness, and interface refinement—carry over into nearly every programming situation.

This chapter has also presented some good examples of how theory and practice come together in programming. Our knowledge of the theory of permutations—itself based on group theory—allowed us to come up with a more efficient algorithm for rotation, one that exploited the properties that our theory guaranteed. At the same time, the example of memory-adaptive algorithms demonstrated how practical considerations such as the amount of available memory can have a profound impact on the choice of algorithm and its performance. Theory and practice are two sides of the same coin; good programmers rely on knowledge of both.

twelve

Extensions of GCD

I swear by the even and the odd.
Quran, Surah Al-Fajr

Programmers often assume that since a data structure or algorithm is in a text-book or has been used for years, it represents the best solution to a problem. Surprisingly, this is often not the case—even if the algorithm has been used for *thousands* of years and has been worked on by everyone from Euclid to Gauss. In this chapter we'll look at an example of a novel solution to an old problem—computing the GCD. Then we'll see how proving a theorem from number theory resulted in an important variation of the algorithm still used today.

12.1 Hardware Constraints and a More Efficient Algorithm

In 1961, an Israeli Ph.D. student, Josef "Yossi" Stein, was working on something called Racah Algebra for his dissertation. He needed to do rational arithmetic, which required reducing fractions, which uses the GCD. But because he had only limited time on a slow computer, he was motivated to find a better way. As he explains:

> Using "Racah Algebra" meant doing calculations with numbers of the form $a/b \cdot \sqrt{c}$, where, a, b, c were integers. I wrote a program for the only available computer in Israel at that time—the WEIZAC at the Weizmann institute. Addition time was 57 microseconds, division took about 900 microseconds. Shift took less than addition.... We had neither compiler nor assembler, and no floating-point

219

numbers, but used hexadecimal code for the programming, and had only 2 hours of computer-time per week for Racah and his students, and you see that I had the right conditions for finding that algorithm. Fast GCD meant survival.[1]

What Stein observed was that there were certain situations where the GCD could be easily computed, or easily expressed in terms of another GCD expression. He looked at special cases like taking the GCD of an even number and an odd number, or a number and itself. Eventually, he came up with the following exhaustive list of cases:

$$
\begin{aligned}
\text{first zero:}\quad & \gcd(0, n) = n \\
\text{second zero:}\quad & \gcd(n, 0) = n \\
\text{equal values:}\quad & \gcd(n, n) = n \\
\text{even, even:}\quad & \gcd(2n, 2m) = 2 \cdot \gcd(n, m) \\
\text{even, odd:}\quad & \gcd(2n, 2m + 1) = \gcd(n, 2m + 1) \\
\text{odd, even:}\quad & \gcd(2n + 1, 2m) = \gcd(2n + 1, m) \\
\text{small odd, big odd:}\quad & \gcd(2n + 1, 2(n + k) + 1) = \gcd(2n + 1, k) \\
\text{big odd, small odd:}\quad & \gcd(2(n + k) + 1, 2n + 1) = \gcd(2n + 1, k)
\end{aligned}
$$

Using these observations, Stein wrote the following algorithm:

```
template <BinaryInteger N>
N stein_gcd(N m, N n) {
    if (m < N(0)) m = -m;
    if (n < N(0)) n = -n;
    if (m == N(0)) return n;
    if (n == N(0)) return m;

    // m > 0 && n > 0

    int d_m = 0;
    while (even(m)) { m >>= 1; ++d_m;}

    int d_n = 0;
    while (even(n)) { n >>= 1; ++d_n;}

    // odd(m) && odd(n)

    while (m != n) {
        if (n > m) swap(n, m);
```

---

[1] J. Stein, personal communication, 2003.

```
        m -= n;
        do m >>= 1; while (even(m));
    }

    // m == n

    return m << min(d_m, d_n);
}
```

Let's look at what the code is doing. The function takes two **BinaryIntegers**—that is, an integer representation that supports fast shift and even/odd testing, like typical computer integers. First, it eliminates the easy cases where one of the arguments is zero, and inverts the sign if an argument is negative, so that we are dealing with two positive integers.

Next, it takes advantage of the identities with even arguments, removing factors of 2 (by shifting) while keeping track of how many there were. We can use a simple int for the counts, since what we're counting is at most the total number of bits in the original arguments. After this part, we are operating on two odd numbers.

Now comes the main loop. We repeatedly subtract the smaller from the larger each time (since we know the difference of two odd numbers is even), and again use shifts to remove additional powers of 2 from the result.[2] When we're done, our two numbers will be equal. Since we're halving at least once each time through the loop, we know we'll iterate no more than log n times; the algorithm is bounded by the number of 1-bits we encounter.

Finally, we return our result, using a shift to multiply our number by 2 for each of the minimum number of 2s we factored out at the beginning. We don't need to worry about 2s in the main loop, because by that point we've reduced the problem to the GCD of two odd numbers; this GCD does not have 2 as a factor.

Here's an example of the algorithm in operation. Suppose we want to compute GCD(196, 42). The computation looks like this:

	m	n		d_m	d_n
factor out 2s:					
	196	42		0	0
	98	42		1	0
	49	42		2	0
	49	21		2	1

(Continues)

---

[2] We use do-while rather than while because we don't need to run the test the first time; we know we're starting with an even number so we know we have to do at least one shift.

	m n		d_m d_n

main loop iteration:

49	21		2 1
28	21	(by subtracting n from m)	2 1
14	21	(by shifting m)	2 1
7	21	(by shifting m)	2 1
21	7	(by swapping m and n)	2 1
14	7	(by subtracting n from m)	2 1
7	7	(by shifting m)	2 1

result:

$$7 \times 2^{\min(2,1)} = 7 \times 2 = 14$$

As we saw, Stein took some observations about special cases and turned them into a faster algorithm. The special cases had to do with even and odd numbers, and places where we could factor out 2, which is easy on a computer; that's why Stein's algorithm is faster in practice. (Even today, when the remainder function can be computed in hardware, it is still much slower than simple shifts.) But is this just a clever hack, or is there more here than meets the eye? Does it make sense only because computers use binary arithmetic? Does Stein's algorithm work just for integers, or can we generalize it just as we did with Euclid's algorithm?

12.2   Generalizing Stein's Algorithm

To answer these questions, let's review some of the historical milestones for Euclid's GCD:

- Positive integers: Greeks (5th century BC)

- Polynomials: Stevin (ca. 1600)

- Gaussian integers: Gauss (ca. 1830)

- Algebraic integers: Dirichlet, Dedekind (ca. 1860)

- Generic version: Noether, van der Waerden (ca. 1930)

It took more than 2000 years to extend Euclid's algorithm from integers to polynomials. Fortunately, it took much less time for Stein's algorithm. In fact, just 2 years after its publication, Knuth already knew of a version for single-variable polynomials over a field $\mathbb{F}[x]$.

The surprising insight was that we can have x play the role for polynomials that 2 plays for integers. That is, we can factor out powers of x, and so on. Carrying the analogy further, we see that $x^2 + x$ (or anything else divisible by x) is "even," $x^2 + x + 1$ (or anything else with a zero-order coefficient) is "odd," and $x^2 + x$ "shifts" to $x + 1$. Just as division by 2 is easier than general division for binary integers, so division by x is easier than general division for polynomials—in both cases, all we need is a shift. (Remember that a polynomial is really a sequence of coefficients, so division by x is literally a shift of the sequence.)

Stein's "special cases" for polynomials look like this:

$$\gcd(p, 0) = \gcd(0, p) = p \tag{12.1}$$

$$\gcd(p, p) = p \tag{12.2}$$

$$\gcd(xp, xq) = x \cdot \gcd(p, q) \tag{12.3}$$

$$\gcd(xp, xq + c) = \gcd(p, xq + c) \tag{12.4}$$

$$\gcd(xp + c, xq) = \gcd(xp + c, q) \tag{12.5}$$

$$\deg(p) \geq \deg(q) \implies \gcd(xp + c, xq + d) = \gcd\left(p - \frac{c}{d}q, xq + d\right) \tag{12.6}$$

$$\deg(p) < \deg(q) \implies \gcd(xp + c, xq + d) = \gcd\left(xp + c, q - \frac{d}{c}q\right) \tag{12.7}$$

Notice how each of the last two rules cancels one of the zero-order coefficients, so we convert the "odd, odd" case to an "even, odd" case.

To get the equivalence expressed by Equation 12.6, we rely on two facts. First, if you have two polynomials u and v, then $\gcd(u, v) = \gcd(u, av)$, where a is a nonzero coefficient. So we can multiply the second argument by the coefficient $\frac{c}{d}$, and we'll have the same GCD:

$$\gcd(xp + c, xq + d) = \gcd\left(xp + c, \frac{c}{d}(xq + d)\right)$$

Second, $\gcd(u, v) = \gcd(u, v - u)$, which we noted when we introduced GCD early in the book (Equation 3.9). So we can subtract our new second argument from the first, and we'll still have the same GCD:

$$\gcd(xp + c, xq + d) = \gcd\left(xp + c - \frac{c}{d}(xq + d), xq + d\right)$$
$$= \gcd\left(xp + c - \frac{c}{d}xq - c, xq + d\right)$$
$$= \gcd\left(xp - \frac{c}{d}xq, xq + d\right)$$

Finally, we can use the fact that if one of the GCD arguments is divisible by x and the other is not, we can drop x because the GCD will not contain it as a factor. So we "shift" out the x, which gives

$$\gcd(xp + c, xq + d) = \gcd\left(p - \frac{c}{d}q, xq + d\right)$$

which is what we wanted.

We also see that in each transformation, the norm—in this case, the degree of the polynomial—gets reduced. Here's how the algorithm would compute $\gcd(x^3 - 3x - 2, x^2 - 4)$:

m	n	OPERATION
$x^3 - 3x - 2$	$x^2 - 4$	$m - (0.5x^2 - 2)$
$x^3 - 0.5x^2 - 3x$	$x^2 - 4$	shift(m)
$x^2 - 0.5x - 3$	$x^2 - 4$	$m - (0.75x^2 - 3)$
$0.25x^2 - 0.5x$	$x^2 - 4$	normalize(m)
$x^2 - 2x$	$x^2 - 4$	shift(m)
$x - 2$	$x^2 - 4$	$n - (2x - 4)$
$x - 2$	$x^2 - 2x$	shift(n)
$x - 2$	$x - 2$	GCD : $x - 2$

First we see that the ratio of their free coefficients (the c and d in Equations 12.6 and 12.7) is 1/2, so we will multiply n by 1/2 and subtract it from m (shown in the first line of the preceding table), resulting in the new m shown on the second line. Then we "shift" m by factoring out x, resulting in the third line, and so on.

In 2000, Andre Weilert further generalized Stein's algorithm to Gaussian integers. This time, $1 + i$ plays the role of 2; the "shift" operation is division by $1 + i$. In 2003, Damgård and Frandsen extended the algorithm to Eisenstein integers.

In 2004, Agarwal and Frandsen demonstrated that there is a ring that is not a Euclidean domain, but where the Stein algorithm still works. In other words, there are cases where Stein's algorithm works but Euclid's does not. If the domain of the Stein algorithm is not the Euclidean domain, then what is it? As of this writing, this is an unsolved problem.

What we do know is that Stein's algorithm depends on the notion of even and odd; we generalize *even* to be *divisible by a smallest prime*, where p is a smallest prime if any remainder when dividing by it is either zero or an invertible element. (We say "a smallest prime" rather than "the smallest prime" because there could be multiple smallest primes in a ring. For example, for Gaussian integers, $1 + i$, $1 - i$, $-1 + i$, and $-1 - i$ are all smallest primes.)

Why do we factor out 2 when we're computing the GCD of integers? Because when we repeatedly divide by 2, we eventually get 1 as a remainder; that is, we have an odd number. Once we have two odd numbers (two numbers whose remainders modulo 2 are both units), we can use subtraction to keep our GCD algorithm going. This ability to cancel remainders works because 2 is the smallest integer prime. Similarly, x is the smallest prime for polynomials, and $i + 1$ for Gaussian integers.[3] Division by the smallest prime always gives a remainder of zero or a unit, because a unit is the number with the smallest nonzero norm. So 2 works for integers because it's the smallest prime, not because computers use binary arithmetic. The algorithm is possible because of fundamental properties

---

[3]Note that 2 is not prime in the ring of Gaussian integers, since it can be factored into $(1+i)(1-i)$.

of integers, not because of the hardware implementation, although the algorithm is *efficient* because computers use binary arithmetic, making shifts fast.

Exercise 12.1. Compare the performance of the Stein and Euclid algorithms on random integers from the ranges $[0, 2^{16})$, $[0, 2^{32})$, and $[0, 2^{64})$.

12.3   Bézout's Identity

To understand the relationship of GCD and ring structures, we need to introduce *Bézout's identity*, which also leads to an important practical algorithm for computing the multiplicative inverse. The identity says that for any two values a and b in the Euclidean domain, there exist coefficients such that the linear combination gives the GCD of the original values.

Theorem 12.1 (Bézout's Identity):

$$\forall a, b \, \exists x, y \; : \; xa + yb = \gcd(a, b)$$

For example, if $a = 196$ and $b = 42$, then this says there are values x and y such that $196x + 42y = \gcd(196, 42)$. Since $\gcd(196, 42) = 14$, in this case $x = -1$ and $y = 5$. We'll see later in the chapter how to compute x and y in general.

Like many results in mathematics, this one is named after someone other than its discoverer. Although 18th-century French mathematician Étienne Bézout did prove the result for polynomials, it was actually shown first for integers a hundred years earlier, by Claude Bachet.

Claude Gaspar Bachet de Méziriac (1581–1638)

Claude Gaspar Bachet de Méziriac, generally known as Bachet, was a French mathematician during the Renaissance. Although he was a scholar in many fields, he is best known for two things. First, he translated Diophantus' *Arithmetic* from Greek to Latin, the common language of science and philosophy in Europe at the time. It is his 1621 translation that most mathematicians relied on, and it was in a copy of his translation that Fermat famously wrote the marginal note describing his last theorem. Second, Bachet wrote the first book on recreational mathematics, *Problèmes*

Plaisants, originally published in 1612. Through this book, mathematics became a popular topic among educated people in France, something they would discuss and spend time on as a hobby. *Problèmes Plaisants* introduced magic squares, as well as proving what is now known as Bézout's identity.

Bachet was chosen as one of the original members of *Académie Française* (French Academy), the organization created by Cardinal Richelieu to be the ultimate authority on the French language, and tasked with the creation and maintenance of the official French dictionary.

Recall that a ring is an algebraic structure that behaves similar to integers; it has both plus-like and times-like operations, but only an additive inverse. (You can review the definition of a ring in Definition 8.3 in Section 8.4.)

To prove Bézout's identity, we need to show that the coefficients x and y always exist. To do this, we need to introduce a new algebraic structure, the *ideal*.

Definition 12.1. An **ideal** I is a nonempty subset of a ring R such that

$$1. \forall x, y \in I \ : \ x + y \in I$$
$$2. \forall x \in I, \ \forall a \in R \ : \ ax \in I$$

The first property says that the ideal is closed under addition; in other words, if you add any two elements of the ideal, the result is in the ideal. The second property is a bit more subtle; it says that the ideal is closed under multiplication with *any* element of the ring, not necessarily an element of the ideal.

An example of an ideal is the set of even numbers, which are a nonempty subset of the ring of integers. If you add two even numbers, you get an even number. If you multiply an even number by any number (not necessarily even), you still get an even number. Other examples of ideals are univariate polynomials with root 5, and polynomials with x and y and free coefficient 0 (e.g., $x^2 + 3y^2 + xy + x$); we'll see shortly why this last case is important. Note that just because something is a subring doesn't mean it's an ideal. Integers are a subring of Gaussian integers, but they aren't an ideal of Gaussian integers, because multiplying an integer by the imaginary number i does not produce an integer.

Exercise 12.2.

1. Prove that an ideal I is closed under subtraction.

2. Prove that I contains 0.

Lemma 12.1 (Linear Combination Ideal): *In a ring, for any two elements a and b, the set of all elements $\{xa + yb\}$ forms an ideal.*

Proof. First, this set is closed under addition:

$$(x_1 a + y_1 b) + (x_2 a + y_2 b) = (x_1 + x_2)a + (y_1 + y_2)b$$

Next, it is closed under multiplication by an arbitrary element:

$$z(xa + yb) = (zx)a + (zy)b$$

Therefore, it is an ideal. □

Exercise 12.3. Prove that all the elements of a linear combination ideal are divisible by any of the common divisors of a and b.

Lemma 12.2 (Ideals in Euclidean Domains): *Any ideal in a Euclidean domain is closed under the remainder operation and under Euclidean GCD.*

Proof.

1. Closed under remainder: By definition,

$$\text{remainder}(a, b) = a - \text{quotient}(a, b) \cdot b$$

   If b is in the ideal, then by the second axiom of ideals, anything multiplied by b is in the ideal, so quotient$(a, b) \cdot b$ is in the ideal. By Exercise 12.2, the difference of two elements of an ideal is in the ideal.

2. Closed under GCD: Since the GCD algorithm consists of repeatedly applying remainder, this immediately follows from 1. □

Definition 12.2. An ideal I of the ring R is called a **principal ideal** if there is an element $a \in R$ called the **principal element** of I such that

$$x \in I \iff \exists y \in R : x = ay$$

In other words, a principal ideal is an ideal that can be generated from one element. An example of a principal ideal is the set of even numbers (2 is the principal element). Polynomials with root 5 are another principal ideal. In contrast, polynomials with x and y and free coefficient 0 are ideals, but not principal ideals. Remember the polynomial $x^2 + 3y^2 + xy + x$, which we gave as an example of an ideal? There's no way to generate it starting with just x (it would never contain y), and vice versa.

Exercise 12.4. Prove that any element in a principal ideal is divisible by the principal element.

Recall that an integral domain is a ring with no zero divisors (Definition 8.7).

Definition 12.3. An integral domain is called a **principal ideal domain (PID)** if every ideal in it is a principal ideal.

For example, the ring of integers is a PID, while the ring of multivariate polynomials over integers is not.

Theorem 12.2: $ED \implies PID$. *Every Euclidean domain is a principal ideal domain.*

Proof. Any ideal I in a Euclidean domain contains an element m with a minimal positive norm (a "smallest nonzero element"). Consider an arbitrary element $a \in I$; either it is a multiple of m or it has a remainder r:

$$a = qm + r \quad \text{where } 0 < \|r\| < \|m\|$$

But we chose m as the smallest element, so we cannot have a smaller remainder—that would be a contraction. Therefore our element a can't have a remainder; $a = qm$. So we can obtain every element from one element, which is the definition of a PID. □

Now we can prove Bézout's identity. Since it says that there is at least one value of x and one value of y that satisfy the equation $xa + yb = \gcd(a, b)$, we can restate it as saying that the set of all possible linear combinations $xa + yb$ contains the desired value.

Bézout's Identity, Restated: *A linear combination ideal $I = \{xa + yb\}$ of a Euclidean domain contains $\gcd(a, b)$.*

Proof. Consider the linear combination ideal $I = \{xa + yb\}$. a is in I because $a = 1a + 0b$. Similarly, b is in I because $b = 0a + 1b$. By Lemma 12.2, any ideal in a Euclidean domain is closed under the GCD; thus $\gcd(a, b)$ is in I. □

We can also use Bézout's identity to prove the Invertibility Lemma, which we encountered in Chapter 5:

Lemma 5.4 (Invertibility Lemma):

$$\forall a, n \in \mathbb{Z} \; : \; \gcd(a, n) = 1 \implies \exists x \in \mathbb{Z}_n \; : \; ax = xa = 1 \bmod n$$

Proof. By Bézout's identity,

$$\exists x, y \in \mathbb{Z} \; : \; xa + yn = \gcd(a, n)$$

So if $\gcd(a, n) = 1$, then $xa + yn = 1$. Therefore, $xa = -yn + 1$, and

$$xa = 1 \bmod n \qquad\qquad \square$$

Exercise 12.5. Using Bézout's identity, prove that if p is prime, then any $0 < a < p$ has a multiplicative inverse modulo p.

12.4 Extended GCD

The proof of Bézout's identity that we saw in the last section is interesting. It shows why the result must be true, but it doesn't actually tell us how to find the coefficients. This is an example of a *nonconstructive* proof. For a long time, there was a debate in mathematics about whether nonconstructive proofs were as valid as constructive proofs. Those who opposed the use of nonconstructive proofs were known as *constructivists* or *intuitionists*. At the turn of the 20th century, the tide turned against the constructivists, with David Hilbert and the Göttingen school leading the charge. The lone major defender of constructivism, Henri Poincaré, lost the battle, and today nonconstructive proofs are routinely used.

Henri Poincaré (1854–1912)

Jules Henri Poincaré was a French mathematician and physicist. He came from a deeply patriotic family, and his cousin Raymond was a prime minister of France. He published more than 500 papers on a variety of subjects, including several on special relativity developed independently of, and in some cases prior to, Einstein's work on the subject. Although he worked on many practical problems, such as establishing time zones, he mostly valued science as a tool for understanding the universe.

As he wrote:

> The scientist must not dally in realizing practical aims. He no
> doubt will obtain them, but must obtain them in addition. He
> never must forget that the special object he is studying is only
> a part of this big whole, which must be the sole motive of his
> activity. Science has had marvelous applications, but a science
> that would only have applications in mind would not be science
> anymore, it would be only cookery.

Poincaré also wrote several important books about the philosophy of science, and was elected a member of the *Académie Française*.

Poincaré contributed to almost every branch of mathematics, originating several subfields, such as algebraic topology. People at the time debated about whether Poincaré or Hilbert was the greatest mathematician in the world. However, Poincaré's criticism of set theory and the formalist agenda of Hilbert put him on the wrong side of the rivalry between France and a recently unified Germany. The rejection of Poincaré's intuitionist approach by the formalists was a great loss for 20th-century mathematics. Both points of view complement each other.

Whatever the view of formalist mathematicians, from a programming perspective, it is clearly more satisfactory to actually have an algorithm than simply to know that one exists. So in this section, we will derive a constructive proof of Bézout's identity—in other words, an algorithm for finding x and y such that $xa + yb = \gcd(a, b)$.

To understand the process, it's helpful to review what happens in several iterations of Euclid's algorithm to compute the GCD of a and b.

```
template <EuclideanDomain E>
E gcd(E a, E b) {
    while (b != E(0)) {
        a = remainder(a, b);
        std::swap(a, b);
    }
    return a;
}
```

Each time through the main loop, we replace a by the remainder of a and b, then swap a and b; our final remainder will be the GCD. So we are computing this sequence of remainders:

$$r_1 = \text{remainder}(a, b)$$
$$r_2 = \text{remainder}(b, r_1)$$

$$r_3 = \text{remainder}(r_1, r_2)$$

$$\vdots$$

$$r_n = \text{remainder}(r_{n-2}, r_{n-1})$$

Note how the second argument to the remainder function on iteration k shifts over to become the first argument on iteration $k + 1$.

Since the remainder of a and b is what's left over from a after dividing a by b, we can write the sequence like this:

$$r_1 = a - b \cdot q_1 \tag{12.8}$$
$$r_2 = b - r_1 \cdot q_2$$
$$r_3 = r_1 - r_2 \cdot q_3$$

$$\vdots$$

$$r_n = r_{n-2} - r_{n-1} \cdot q_n \tag{12.9}$$

where the q terms are the corresponding quotients. We can solve each equation for the first term on the right—the first argument of the remainder function:

$$a = b \cdot q_1 + r_1$$
$$b = r_1 \cdot q_2 + r_2$$
$$r_1 = r_2 \cdot q_3 + r_3$$

$$\vdots$$

$$r_{n-2} = r_{n-1} \cdot q_n + r_n$$

In Section 4.7, we showed how the last nonzero remainder r_n in the sequence is equal to the GCD of the original arguments. For Bézout's identity, we'd like to show that $r_n = \gcd(a, b) = xa + yb$. If each of the equations in the preceding series could be written as linear combinations of a and b, the next one could as well. The first three are easy:

$$a = 1 \cdot a + 0 \cdot b \tag{12.10}$$
$$b = 0 \cdot a + 1 \cdot b \tag{12.11}$$
$$r_1 = 1 \cdot a + (-q_1) \cdot b$$

The last equation comes from our original definition of r_1 in the first remainder sequence (Equation 12.8). The next one requires substituting the expansion of r_1 and rearranging terms:

$$r_2 = b - r_1 q_2$$
$$= b - (a - q_1 b)q_2$$
$$= b - q_2 a + q_1 q_2 b$$
$$= -q_2 a + (1 + q_1 q_2)b$$

Next, we have an iterative recurrence. Assume that we already figured out how to represent two successive remainders as linear combinations:

$$r_i = x_i a + y_i b$$
$$r_{i+1} = x_{i+1} a + y_{i+1} b$$

Then we can use our previous observation about how to define an arbitrary remainder in the sequence using the two previous ones (Equation 12.9), substituting those previous values and again distributing and rearranging to group all the coefficients with a and all the coefficients with b:

$$r_{i+2} = r_i - r_{i+1} q_{i+2}$$
$$= x_i a + y_i b - (x_{i+1} a + y_{i+1} b)q_{i+2}$$
$$= x_i a + y_i b - x_{i+1} q_{i+2} a - y_{i+1} q_{i+2} b$$
$$= x_i a - x_{i+1} q_{i+2} a + y_i b - y_{i+1} q_{i+2} b$$
$$= (x_i - x_{i+1} q_{i+2})a + (y_i - y_{i+1} q_{i+2})b$$

We have seen how we can express every entry in the sequence as a linear combination of a and b, and our procedure gives us the coefficients x and y at every step. Furthermore, we observe that the coefficients on a are defined in terms of the previous coefficients on a (i.e., the only variables are xs), and the coefficients on b are defined in terms of the previous coefficients on b (i.e., the only variables are ys). In particular, the coefficients on iteration $i + 2$ are

$$x_{i+2} = x_i - x_{i+1} q_{i+2} \qquad (12.12)$$
$$y_{i+2} = y_i - y_{i+1} q_{i+2}$$

When we reach the end, we have coefficients x and y such that $xa + yb = \gcd(a, b)$, which was what we wanted all along.

We've seen that that the ys do not depend on the xs and the xs do not depend on the ys. Since we know $xa + yb = \gcd(a, b)$, then as long as $b \neq 0$, we can rearrange these terms to define y as

$$y = \frac{\gcd(a, b) - ax}{b}$$

This means we don't need to go through the trouble of computing all the intermediate values of y.

Exercise 12.6. What are x and y if $b = 0$?

*   *   *

Now that we know how to compute the coefficient x from Bézout's identity, we can enhance our GCD algorithm to return this value as well. The new algorithm is called *extended GCD* (also known as the *extended Euclid algorithm*). It will still compute the usual series of remainders for GCD, but it will also compute the series of x coefficients from our earlier equations.

As we have seen, we don't need to keep every value in the recurrence; we just need the two previous ones, which we'll call x_0 and x_1. Of course, we need to know the first two values to get the series started, but fortunately we have them — they are the coefficients of a in the first two linear combinations (Equations 12.10 and 12.11), namely 1 and 0. Then we can use the x_{i+2} formula we have just derived (Equation 12.12) to compute the new value each time. Each new x computation requires a quotient, so we'll need a function for that. Meanwhile we're still computing the GCD, so we still need the remainder. Since we need both quotient and remainder, we'll use the generic version of the `quotient_remainder` function we introduced in Section 4.6, which returns a pair whose first element is the quotient and whose second element is the remainder. Here is our extended GCD code:

```
template <EuclideanDomain E>
std::pair<E, E> extended_gcd(E a, E b) {
    E x0(1);
    E x1(0);
    while (b != E(0)) {
        // compute new r and x
        std::pair<E, E> qr = quotient_remainder(a, b);
        E x2 = x0 - qr.first * x1;
        // shift r and x
        x0 = x1;
        x1 = x2;
        a = b;
        b = qr.second;
    }
    return {x0, a};
}
```

At the end, when b is zero, the function returns a pair consisting of the value of x that we wanted for Bézout's identity, and the GCD of a and b.

Exercise 12.7. Develop a version of the extended GCD algorithm based on Stein's algorithm.

12.5   Applications of GCD

To wrap up our discussion of GCD, we consider some important uses of the algorithm.

Cryptography. As we shall see in the next chapter, modern cryptographic algorithms rely on being able to find the multiplicative inverse modulo n for large numbers, and the extended GCD algorithm allows us to do this.

We know from Bézout's identity that

$$xa + yb = \gcd(a, b)$$

so

$$xa = \gcd(a, b) - yb$$

If $\gcd(a, b) = 1$, then

$$xa = 1 - yb$$

Thus multiplying x and a gives 1 plus some multiple of b, or to put it another way,

$$xa = 1 \bmod b$$

As we learned in Chapter 5, two numbers whose product is 1 are multiplicative inverses. Since the `extended_gcd` algorithm returns x and $gcd(a, b)$, if the GCD is 1, then x is the multiplicative inverse of a mod b; we don't even need y.

Rational Arithmetic. Rational arithmetic is very useful in many areas, and it can't be done without reducing fractions to their canonical form, which requires the GCD algorithm.

Symbolic Integration. One of the primary components of symbolic integration is decomposing a rational fraction into primitive fractions, which uses the GCD of polynomials over real numbers.

Rotation Algorithms. We saw in Chapter 11 how the GCD plays a role in rotation algorithm. In fact, the `std::rotate` function in C++ relies on this relationship.

12.6   Thoughts on the Chapter

In this chapter, we saw two examples of how continued exploration of an old algorithm can lead to new insights. Stein's observations about patterns of odd and even numbers when computing the GCD allowed him to come up with a more efficient algorithm, one that exposed some important mathematical relationships. Bachet's proof of a theorem about the GCD gave us the extended GCD algorithm, which has many practical uses.

In particular, the discovery of the Stein algorithm illustrates a few important programming principles:

1. *Every useful algorithm is based on some fundamental mathematical truth.* When Stein noticed some useful patterns in computing the GCD of odd and even numbers, he wasn't thinking about smallest primes. Indeed, it's very common that the discoverer of an algorithm might not see its most general mathematical basis. There is often a long time between the first discovery of the algorithm and its full understanding. Nevertheless, its underlying mathematical truth is there. For this reason, every useful program is a worthy object of study, and behind every optimization there is solid mathematics.

2. *Even a classical problem studied by great mathematicians may have a new solution.* When someone tells you, for example, that sorting can't be done faster than $n \log n$, don't believe them. That statement might not be true for your particular problem.

3. *Performance constraints are good for creativity.* The limitations that Stein faced using the WEIZAC computer in 1961 are what drove him to look for alternatives to the traditional approach. The same is true in many situations; necessity really is the mother of invention.

13

thirteen

A Real-World Application

> *I am fairly familiar with all forms of secret writings, and am*
> *myself the author of a trifling monograph upon the subject,*
> *in which I analyze one hundred and sixty separate ciphers,*
> *but I confess that this is entirely new to me.*
>
> Sherlock Holmes

Throughout this book, we've seen examples of important algorithms that came out of work on number theory. We've also seen how attempts to generalize those mathematical results brought about the development of abstract algebra, and how its ideas about abstraction led directly to the principles of generic programming. Now we're going put it all together. We'll show how our mathematical results and our generalized algorithms can be used to implement a real-world application: a particular kind of system for secure communication, known as a *public-key cryptosystem*.

13.1 Cryptology

Cryptology is the science of secret communication. *Cryptography* is concerned with developing codes and ciphers;[1] *cryptanalysis* with breaking them.

The idea of sending secret messages dates back to ancient times, with examples of cryptography in many societies including Sparta and Persia. Julius Caesar used the technique of replacing letters with those in a "rotated" alphabet (now known as the *Caesar cipher*) to send military messages. In the 19th

---

[1] Technically, a *code* is a system for secret communication where a meaningful concept such as the name of a person, place, or event is replaced with some other text, while a *cipher* is a system for modifying text at the level of its representation (letters or bits). But we'll use the terms interchangeably; in particular, we'll use *encode* and *decode* informally to mean *encipher* and *decipher*.

century, cryptography and "cryptograms," puzzles that use a simple substitution cipher, caught the public's imagination. In an 1839 magazine article, Edgar Allen Poe claimed he could decipher any such messages his readers submitted— and apparently succeeded. A few years later he published a short story called "The Gold Bug," which includes an account of how to break such a code. A substitution cipher also featured prominently, several decades later, in Sir Arthur Conan Doyle's Sherlock Holmes mystery, "The Adventure of the Dancing Men."

But the importance of cryptography went well beyond casual entertainment. Codes and ciphers played an important role in diplomacy, espionage, and warfare. By the early 20th century, creating better cryptographic schemes was a top priority for the military of the world's leading powers. The ability to break these codes could make the difference between success and failure on the battlefield.

Bletchley Park and the Development of Computers

In World War II, the main British cryptanalysis group was based at an estate in the countryside called Bletchley Park. At the time, the German navy was using an enhanced version of a commercial encryption mechanism called the Enigma machine. An earlier version of the Engima had been cracked by Polish cryptographer Marian Rejewski, using an electromechanical device that tested many possible Enigma settings in parallel.

At Bletchley Park, a brilliant young mathematician named Alan Turing, whose previous work provided much of the foundations of what became computer science, designed a much more sophisticated version of Rejewski's device called a "bombe." Through the work of Turing and many others, the Allies were able to decipher the Enigma messages, a great help in winning the war.

Another encryption mechanism used by the Nazis was called the Lorenz machine. To break the Lorenz cipher, the British cryptographers realized that the electromechanical bombes were not fast enough. So an engineer named Tommy Flowers designed a much more powerful electronic device using vacuum tubes, called "Colossus." Although it was not a general-purpose machine and was only partially programmable, Colossus may have been the world's first programmable electronic digital computer.

A *cryptosystem* consists of algorithms for encrypting and decrypting data. The original data is called the *plaintext*, and the encrypted data is called the *ciphertext*. A set of *keys* determine the behavior of the encryption and decryption algorithms:

$$\text{ciphertext} = \text{encryption}(key_0, \text{plaintext})$$
$$\text{plaintext} = \text{decryption}(key_1, \text{ciphertext})$$

The system is *symmetric* if $key_0 = key_1$; otherwise, it is *asymmetric*.

Many early cryptosystems were symmetric and used secret keys. The problem with this is that the sender and the receiver of the message both must have the keys in advance. If the key is compromised and the sender wants to switch to a new one, he has the additional problem of figuring out how to secretly convey the new key to the receiver.

*   *   *

A *public-key cryptosystem* is an encryption scheme that makes use of a pair of keys: a public key *pub* for encrypting, and a private key *prv* for decrypting. If Alice wants to send a message to Bob, she encrypts the message with Bob's public key. The ciphertext is then unreadable to anyone but Bob, who uses his private key to decrypt the message.

To have a public-key cryptosystem, the following requirements must be satisfied:

1. The encryption function needs to be a *one-way* function: easy to compute, with an inverse that is hard to compute. Here, "hard" has its technical computer science meaning of taking exponential time—in this case, exponential in the size of the key.

2. The inverse function has to be easy to compute when you have access to a certain additional piece of information, known as the *trapdoor*.

3. Both encryption and decryption algorithms are publicly known. This ensures the confidence of all parties in the technique being used.

A function meeting the first two requirements is known as a *trapdoor one-way function*.

Perhaps the best-known and most widely used public-key cryptosystem is the RSA algorithm, named after its creators (Rivest, Shamir, and Adleman). As we'll see shortly, RSA depends on some mathematical results about primes.

Who Invented Public-Key Cryptography?

For years, it was believed that Stanford professor Martin Hellman, together with two graduate students, Whitfield Diffie and Ralph Merkle, invented public-key cryptography in 1976. They proposed how such a system would work, and realized it would require a trapdoor one-way function. Unfortunately, they didn't give an example of such a function—it was just a hypothetical construct. In 1977, MIT researchers Ron Rivest, Adi Shamir, and Len Adleman came up with a procedure for creating a trapdoor one-way function, which became known as the *RSA* algorithm after the inventors' initials.

In 1997, the British government disclosed that one of their intelligence researchers, Clifford Cocks, had actually invented a special case of RSA in 1973—but it took 20 years after the publication of the RSA algorithm before they declassified Cocks' memo. After that, Admiral Bobby Ray Inman, the former head of the U.S. National Security Agency, claimed that his agency had invented some sort of public-key cryptographic technique even earlier, in the 1960s, although no evidence was given. Who knows which country's intelligence agency will come forward next with an earlier claim?

13.2 Primality Testing

The problem of distinguishing prime numbers from composite ... is known to be one of the most important and useful in arithmetic.

C. F. Gauss, *Disquisitiones Arithmeticae*

An important problem in modern cryptography is determining whether an integer is prime. Gauss believed that (1) deciding whether a number is prime or composite is a very hard problem, and so is (2) factoring a number. He was wrong about #1, as we shall see. So far, he seems to be right about #2, which is a good thing for us, since modern cryptosystems are based on this assumption.

To find out if a number n is prime, it helps to have a predicate that tells us whether it's divisible by a given number i:

```
template <Integer I>
bool divides(const I& i, const I& n) {
    return n % i == I(0);
}
```

We can call this repeatedly to find the smallest divisor of a given number n. Just as we did with the Sieve of Eratosthenes in Chapter 3, our loop for testing divisors will start at 3, advance by 2, and stop when the square of the current candidate reaches n:

```
template <Integer I>
I smallest_divisor(I n) {
    // precondition: n > 0
    if (even(n)) return I(2);
    for (I i(3); i * i <= n; i += I(2)) {
        if (divides(i, n)) return i;
    }
    return n;
}
```

Now we can create a simple function to determine whether n is prime:

```
template <Integer I>
I is_prime(const I& n) {
    return n > I(1) && smallest_divisor(n) == n;
}
```

This is mathematically correct, but it's not going to be fast enough. Its complexity is $O(\sqrt{n}) = O(2^{(\log n)/2})$. That is, it's exponential in the *number of digits*. If we want to test a 200-digit number, we may be waiting for more time than the life of the universe.

To overcome this problem, we're going to need a different approach, which will rely on the ability to do modular multiplication. We'll use a function object that provides what we need:

```
template <Integer I>
struct modulo_multiply {
    I modulus;
    modulo_multiply(const I& i) : modulus(i) {}

    I operator() (const I& n, const I& m) const {
        return (n * m) % modulus;
    }
};
```

We'll also need an identity element:

```
template <Integer I>
I identity_element(const modulo_multiply<I>&) {
    return I(1);
}
```

Now we can compute a multiplicative inverse modulo prime p. It uses the result we showed in Chapter 5 that, as a consequence of Fermat's Little Theorem, the inverse of an integer a, where $0 < a < p$, is a^{p-2} (see Section 5.4, right after the proof of Fermat's Little Theorem). It also uses the power function we created in Chapter 7:

```
template <Integer I>
I multiplicative_inverse_fermat(I a, I p) {
    // precondition: p is prime & a > 0
    return power_monoid(a, p - 2, modulo_multiply<I>(p));
}
```

With these pieces, we can now use Fermat's Little Theorem to test if a number n is prime. Recall that Fermat's Little Theorem says:

If p is prime, then $a^{p-1} - 1$ is divisible by p for any $0 < a < p$.

Equivalently:

If p is prime, then $a^{p-1} = 1 \bmod p$ for any $0 < a < p$.

We want to know if n is prime. So we take an arbitrary number a smaller than n, raise it to the $n - 1$ power using modular multiplication (mod n), and check if the result is 1. (We call the number a we're using a *witness*.) If the result is *not* equal to 1, we know definitely by the contrapositive of the theorem that n is not prime. If the result *is* equal to 1, we know that there's a good chance that n is prime, and if we do this for lots of random witnesses, there's a very good chance that it is prime:

```
template <Integer I>
bool fermat_test(I n, I witness) {
    // precondition: 0 < witness < n
    I remainder(power_semigroup(witness,
                        n - I(1),
                        modulo_multiply<I>(n)));
    return remainder == I(1);
}
```

This time we use `power_semigroup` instead of `power_monoid`, because we know we're not going to be raising anything to the power 0. The Fermat test is very fast, because we have a fast way to raise a number to a power—our $O(\log n)$ generalized Egyptian multiplication algorithm from Chapter 7.

*   *   *

While the Fermat test works the vast majority of the time, it turns out that there are some pathological cases of numbers that will fool it for all witnesses coprime to n; they produce remainders of 1 even though they're composite. These are called *Carmichael numbers*.

Definition 13.1. A composite number $n > 1$ is a **Carmichael number** if and only if

$$\forall b > 1, \quad \text{coprime}(b, n) \implies b^{n-1} = 1 \bmod n$$

172081 is an example of a Carmichael number. Its prime factorization is $7 \cdot 13 \cdot 31 \cdot 61$.

Exercise 13.1. Implement the function:

```
bool is_carmichael(n)
```

Exercise 13.2. Find the first seven Carmichael numbers using your function from Exercise 13.1.

13.3   The Miller-Rabin Test

To avoid worrying about Carmichael numbers, we're going to use an improved version of our primality tester, called the *Miller-Rabin* test; it will again rely on the speed of our power algorithm.

We know that $n - 1$ is even (it would be awfully silly to run a primality test on an even n), so we can represent $n - 1$ as the product $2^k \cdot q$. The Miller-Rabin test uses a sequence of squares $w^{2^0 q}, w^{2^1 q}, \ldots, w^{2^k q}$, where w is a random number less than the one we are testing. The last exponent in this sequence is $n - 1$, the same value the Fermat test uses; we'll see why this is important shortly.

We're also going to rely on the self-canceling law (Lemma 5.3), except we'll write it with new variable names and assuming modular multiplication:

$$\text{For any } 0 < x < n \ \wedge \ \text{prime}(n), \ \ x^2 = 1 \bmod n \implies x = 1 \ \vee \ x = -1$$

Remember that in modular arithmetic, $-1 \bmod n$ is the same as $(n - 1) \bmod n$, a fact that we rely on in the following code. If we find some $x^2 = 1 \bmod n$ where x is neither 1 nor -1, then n is not prime.

Now we can make two observations: (1) If $x^2 = 1 \bmod n$, then there's no point in squaring x again, because the result won't change; if we reach 1, we're done. (2) If $x^2 = 1 \bmod n$ and x is not -1, then we know n is not prime (since we already ruled out $x = 1$ earlier in the code).

Here's the code, which returns true if n is probably prime, and false if it definitely is not:

```
template <Integer I>
bool miller_rabin_test(I n, I q, I k, I w) {

    // precondition n > 1  ∧  n − 1 = 2^k q  ∧  q is odd

    modulo_multiply<I> mmult(n);
    I x = power_semigroup(w, q, mmult);
    if (x == I(1) || x == n - I(1)) return true;
    for (I i(1); i < k; ++i) {

        // invariant x = w^(2^(i−1) q)

        x = mmult(x, x);
        if (x == n - I(1)) return true;
        if (x == I(1))     return false;
    }
    return false;
}
```

Note that we pass in q and k as arguments. Since we're going to call the function many times with different witnesses, we don't want to refactor $n - 1$ every time.

Why can we return true at the beginning if the `power_semigroup` call returns 1 or -1? Because we know that squaring the result will give 1, and squaring is equivalent to multiplying the exponent in the power calculation by a factor of 2, and doing this k times will make the exponent $n - 1$, the value we need for Fermat's Little Theorem to hold. In other words, if $w^q \bmod n = 1$ or -1, then $w^{2^k q} \bmod n = w^{n-1} \bmod n = 1$.

Let's look at an example. Suppose we want to know if $n = 2793$ is prime. We choose a random witness $w = 150$. We factor $n - 1 = 2792$ into $2^2 \cdot 349$, so $q = 349$ and $k = 2$. We compute

$$x = w^q \bmod n = 150^{349} \bmod 2793 = 2019$$

Since the result is neither 1 nor -1, we start squaring x:

$$i = 1; \quad x^2 = 150^{2^1 \cdot 349} \bmod 2793 = 1374$$

$$i = 2; \quad x^2 = 150^{2^2 \cdot 349} \bmod 2793 = 2601$$

Since we haven't reached 1 or -1 yet, and $i = k$, we can stop and return false; 2793 is not prime.

Like the Fermat test, the Miller-Rabin test is right most of the time. Unlike the Fermat test, the Miller-Rabin test has a provable guarantee: it is right at least 75% of the time[2] for a random witness w. (In practice, it's even more often.) Randomly choosing, say, 100 witnesses makes the probability of error less than 1 in 2^{200}. As Knuth remarked, "It is much more likely that our computer has dropped a bit, due ... to cosmic radiations."

AKS: A New Test for Primality

In 2002, Neeraj Kayal and Nitin Saxena, two undergraduate students at the Indian Institute of Technology at Kanpur, together with their advisor, Manindra Agrawal, came up with a *deterministic* polynomial-time algorithm for primality testing, and published their result. This is a problem that people in number theory had been working on for centuries.

There is a very clear paper by Andrew Granville describing the technique. Although it is a dense mathematical paper, it is understandable to a surprisingly wide audience. This is unusual; most important mathematical results being published in recent decades require years of prior mathematical study to be understood. Determined readers who are willing to put in serious effort are encouraged to read it.

---

[2]In fact, the requirement that q must be odd is needed for this probability guarantee.

> Despite the fact that the AKS algorithm is a great accomplishment, we're not going to use it here, because the probabilistic Miller-Rabin algorithm is still considerably faster.

13.4   The RSA Algorithm: How and Why It Works

The RSA algorithm is one of the most important and widely used cryptosystems in use today. It is often used for authentication—to prove that users, companies, websites, and other entities with an online presence are who they say they are. It is also often used to exchange private keys that are used in a separate, faster symmetric cryptosystem used to encode data being communicated.

Some of the important communication protocols that use RSA are:

IPSec	security for low-level data transport
PPTP	virtual private networks
SET	secure electronic transactions (e.g., credit card transactions)
SSH	secure remote access to another computer
SSL/TLS	secure data transfer layer

We use many of these protocols daily. For example, anytime you visit a "secure" website (one whose URL has an `https` prefix), you're relying on SSL/TLS, which in turn uses RSA or (depending on the implementation) a similar public-key cryptosystem.

RSA relies on the mathematical results we've just shown for primality testing. RSA requires two steps: key generation, which needs to be done only rarely, and encoding/decoding, which is done every time a message is sent or received.

Key generation works as follows. First, the following values are computed:

- Two random large primes, p_1 and p_2 (the Miller-Rabin test makes this feasible)

- Their product, $n = p_1 p_2$

- The Euler function of their product, which we can compute using Equation 5.5 from Chapter 5: $\phi(p_1 p_2) = (p_1 - 1)(p_2 - 1)$

- A random public key pub, coprime with $\phi(p_1 p_2)$

- A private key prv, the multiplicative inverse of pub modulo $\phi(p_1 p_2)$ (To compute this, we'll use the extended GCD function we derived in Chapter 12.)

When these computations are complete, p_1 and p_2 are destroyed; pub and n are published, and prv is kept secret. At this point, there is no feasible way to factor n, since it is such a large number with such large factors.

The encoding and decoding process is simpler. The text is divided into equal-size blocks, say 256 bytes long, which are interpreted as large integers. The message block size s must be chosen so that $n > 2^s$. To encode a plaintext block, we use our familiar power algorithm:

```
power_semigroup(plaintext_block, pub, modulo_multiply<I>(n));
```

Decoding looks like this:

```
power_semigroup(ciphertext_block, prv, modulo_multiply<I>(n));
```

Observe that *we do exactly the same operation to encode and decode.* The only difference is which text and which key we pass in.

*   *   *

How does RSA work? Encryption consists of raising a message m to a power *pub*; decryption consists of raising the result to the power *prv*. We need to show that the result of applying these two operations is the original message m (modulo n):

$$(m^{\text{pub}})^{\text{prv}} = m \bmod n$$

Proof. Recall that we specifically created *prv* to be the multiplicative inverse of *pub* modulo $\phi(p_1 p_2)$, so by definition, the product of *pub* and *prv* is some multiple q of $\phi(p_1 p_2)$ with a remainder of 1. We can make that substitution in the exponent on the right.

$$(m^{\text{pub}})^{\text{prv}} = m^{\text{pub} \times \text{prv}}$$
$$= m^{1 + q\phi(p_1 p_2)}$$
$$= mm^{q\phi(p_1 p_2)}$$
$$= m(m^{\phi(p_1 p_2)})^q$$

Now we can apply Euler's theorem from Chapter 5, which says that $a^{\phi}(n) - 1$ is divisible by n; that is, $a^{\phi}(n) = 1 + vn$. Making that substitution, we have

$$= m(1 + vn)^q$$

When we expand $(1 + vn)^q$, every term will be a multiple of n except 1, so we can collapse all of these and just say we have 1 plus some other multiple of n:

$$= m + wn$$
$$= m \bmod n \qquad \square$$

The Euler theorem step depends on m being coprime with $n = p_1 p_2$. Since the message m could be anything, how do we know that it will be coprime to

$p_1 p_2$? Since p_1 and p_2 are enormous primes, that probability is practically indistinguishable from 1, and people normally do not worry about it. However, if you want to address this, you can add one extra byte to the end of m. The extra byte is not actually part of the message, but is there only to ensure that we have a coprime. When we create m, we check whether it is coprime; if it isn't, we simply add 1 to this extra byte.

*   *   *

Why does RSA work? In other words, why do we believe it's secure? The reason is that factoring is hard, and therefore computing ϕ is not feasible. Perhaps if quantum computers prove to be realizable in the future, it will be possible to run an exponential number of divisor tests in parallel, making factoring a tractable problem. But for now, we can rely on RSA for many secure communications applications.

Project

Exercise 13.3. Implement an RSA key generation library.

Exercise 13.4. Implement an RSA message encoder/decoder that takes a string and the key as its arguments.

Hints:

- If your language does not support arbitrary-precision integers, you'll need to install a package for handling them.

- Remember that two numbers are coprime if their GCD is 1. This will come in handy for one of the key generation steps.

- You'll need the results that we derived in Chapter 12. There are two relevant functions, `extended_gcd` and `multiplicative_inverse`.

  Recall that the `extended_gcd` function from Chapter 12 returns a pair (x, y) such that $ax + ny = \gcd(a, n)$. You can use this function to check for coprimes. It's also part of the implementation of `multiplicative_inverse`, a function that returns the multiplicative inverse of a modulo n if it exists, or 0 if it does not. Unlike the function `multiplicative_inverse_fermat` that we introduced in Section 13.2, this one works for any n, not just primes:

```
template <Integer I>
I multiplicative_inverse(I a, I n) {
    std::pair<I, I> p = extended_gcd(a, n);
    if (p.second != I(1)) return I(0);
    if (p.first < I(0)) return p.first + n;
    return p.first;
}
```

You'll need this to get the private key from the public key.

13.5   Thoughts on the Chapter

Issues of identity, privacy, and security are becoming increasingly important as more of our personal data lives online and more of our personal communication travels over the Internet. As we have seen, many important protocols for keeping data private and secure from tampering rely on RSA or similar public-key cryptosystems for authentication, exchange of keys used for encryption, or other security features.

These important practical capabilities owe their existence to results from one of the most theoretical branches of mathematics, number theory. There is a perception among programmers that mathematicians are people who don't know or care about practical concerns and that mathematics, particularly in its more abstract areas, has little practical value. Looking at the history, we can see that both of these perceptions are false. The greatest mathematicians enthusiastically worked on extremely practical problems—for example, Gauss worked on one of the first electromechanical telegraphs, and Poincaré spent years developing time zones. Perhaps more importantly, it is impossible to know which theoretical ideas are going to have practical applications.

14

fourteen

Conclusions

*The strongest arguments prove nothing so long as
the conclusions are not verified by experience.*
Roger Bacon, *Opus Tertium*

We started this book by characterizing generic programming as an attitude toward programming that focuses on abstracting algorithms to their most general setting without losing efficiency. Throughout the book, we've seen examples of this abstraction process in mathematics and in programming. We saw how mathematicians' attempts to find the most general setting for Euclid's GCD algorithm led to the development of abstract algebra, an entire area of mathematics devoted to abstract structures, which itself provided the basis for generic programming. We also saw how to use those same principles of abstraction to generalize an ancient algorithm for multiplying positive integers to a fast power function on semigroups, enabling a range of applications ranging from computing Fibonacci numbers to finding the shortest path in a graph to encrypting data in Internet communication protocols. This process—starting with a specific efficient solution and, whenever possible, relaxing the requirements—is at the heart of generic programming.

While the idea of abstraction in generic programming comes to us directly from abstract algebra, as programmers we also care about efficiency. A generic algorithm that runs more slowly than its type-specific counterpart will not get used. That's why efficiency is also part of the definition of generic programming. We've shown examples throughout the book of specific techniques for improving efficiency, from rewriting code to use strength reduction, to using memory-adaptive algorithms, to exploiting compile-time type dispatch so the computer can invoke the fastest available implementation for a given situation.

249

More generally, we have found that attempts to find generic versions of algorithms often lead to simpler and more efficient solutions.

We've also seen how the correctness of a programming interface can be just as important as the correctness of the program itself. A correct interface can enable a wider range of applications. It can also bring efficiency benefits—for example, by returning all the relevant computations (the law of useful return) to avoid a duplication of effort. In contrast, an incorrect interface cripples the application by limiting what it can do. For example, we saw how a find function that returns only a Boolean value instead of the position of a found item makes it impossible to see if a second matching item exists. And just as you need to rewrite a program a few times to get it right, so you need to redesign the interface; the correct interface usually won't be clear until you've already implemented an algorithm and explored its use cases.

Another idea that's essential to understanding generic programming is the distinction between type and concept. In much the same way that axioms in a mathematical theory are requirements that tell us what it means to be a certain kind of abstract mathematical entity (such as a group), concepts in programing are requirements on types; they tell us what it means to be a certain kind of computational entity. Choosing the right concepts for an algorithm or data structure is essential to good programming. Choosing a concept with too many requirements places unnecessary limitations on the range of situations in which an algorithm can be used. Choosing a concept with too few requirements makes it impossible to define algorithms that do anything useful.

Next time you set out to write a program, try to adopt the generic programming attitude. Start with specific implementations of your functions, then revise and refine them to be more efficient and more general. As you refine your code, think carefully about how the pieces fit together and how to provide an interface that will still be useful in the future. Choose concepts that provide just the right requirements for your data, without imposing unnecessary assumptions. And remember that you are the inheritor of a long mathematical tradition of algorithmic thought. In following the principles of generic programming, you are already benefiting from the work of those who came before, from Euclid to Stevin to Noether. By designing beautiful, general algorithms, you are adding your own small contribution to their work.

Further Reading

Readers who are interested in learning more about the topics discussed in this book may wish to look at some of the references mentioned here. Complete citations are included in the Bibliography.

Chapter 1

Generic Programming. The language Tecton, which first used generic programming concepts, is described in "Tecton: A Language for Manipulating Generic Objects" by Kapur, Musser, and Stepanov (1981). The Ada library is described in the paper "Generic Programming" by Musser and Stepanov (1988), and C++ STL in "The Standard Template Library" by Stepanov and Lee (1994). All of these materials are available on www.stepanovpapers.com.

Chapter 2

History of Mathematics. A good comprehensive reference, not only for this chapter but also for much of the mathematical history in the book, is Katz's *A History of Mathematics: An Introduction* (2009). This general textbook combines thoroughness and mathematical rigor with accessibility to the layperson. An incisive book that explains the historical development of some major mathematical ideas is *Mathematics and Its History* by John Stillwell (2010).

Rhind Papyrus. To see a reproduction of the Rhind Papyrus, together with its translation, see *The Rhind Mathematical Papyrus: An Ancient Egyptian Text* by Robins and Shute (1987). Van der Waerden includes a discussion of the Rhind Papyrus in *Geometry and Algebra in Ancient Civilizations* (1983).

Chapter 3

Egyptian and Greek Mathematics. In addition to Katz, two excellent resources are Van der Waerden's *Science Awakening* (1963) and the two-volume *History of Greek Mathematics* by Sir Thomas Heath (originally published in 1921 but available in a 1981 reprint). Both are very accessible to the general reader.

Figurate Numbers. The best introduction to Pythagorean arithmetic is the book by Nicomachus of Gerasa, which can easily be found in the 10th volume of the Britannica's *Great Books of the Western World*, edited by Mortimer Adler. This volume also contains the complete works of Euclid and Archimedes.

Basic Number Theory. A good introduction to basic number theory is in Chapter III of George Chrystal's *Algebra: An Elementary Text-Book.*

Chapter 4

Greatest Common Measure. For general history of Greek mathematics, including the topics covered in this chapter, the best reference is still Heath's *A History of Greek Mathematics*, mentioned in the topics for Chapter 3. For a fascinating and mathematically sophisticated account of the mathematical studies in Plato's Academy, including the algorithm for the greatest common measure, see David Fowler's *The Mathematics of Plato's Academy, a New Reconstruction.* For those interested in reading the source, Plato's complete works are available in a one-volume edition, with a clear modern translation, edited by John M. Cooper. A good explanation of the GCD may be found in Chapter III of George Chrystal's *Algebra: An Elementary Text-Book.*

Decline of Greek Science. An important account of the rise and decline of Greek mathematics is presented in the book by Lucio Russo, *The Forgotten Revolution: How Science Was Born in 300 BC and Why It Had to Be Reborn.*

History of Zero. Our account of the history of zero is largely taken from van der Waarden's *Science Awakening*, pp. 56–57.

Leonardo Pisano (Fibonacci). A short autobiography of Leonardo Pisano has been translated by Richard Grimm. His great work *Liber Abaci* is available in an English translation by Laurence Sigler. A brief but thorough description of Leonardo Pisano's number theoretic treatise is given in McClenon's 1919 article "Leonardo of Pisa and His Liber Quadratorum." Readers interested in history of arithmetic algorithms may want to read Leonardo Pisano's original *Liber Quadratorum*, available in a modern English translation by L. E. Sigler (see Fibonacci in the Bibliography).

Remainder and Quotient. The full treatment of the extension of GCD to remainder and quotient is in Chapter 5 of *Elements of Programming* by Stepanov and McJones (2009). Floyd and Knuth's algorithm for remainder appears in their 1990 article "Addition Machines."

Chapter 5

Fermat's and Euler's Number Theory Work. A source for much of the material in this chapter is *Number Theory: An Approach through History from Hammurapi to Legendre* by André Weil. While this book does not assume any advanced math, it is probably too detailed for most casual readers. The classic number theory texts by Gauss (*Disquisitiones Arithmeticae*) and Dirichlet (*Lectures on Number Theory*) are still of great value, but would be of interest to serious scholars only.

Euler's Books. Our biography of Euler also mentions his foundational works on calculus. Although they are not directly related to the topics of this book, they are still worth careful reading. Euler's first book on the subject, *Introduction to Analysis of the Infinite* is available in English. Sadly, only the first half of his second book, *Foundations of Differential Calculus*, has an English translation, and all of his *Integral Calculus* still awaits an English translation. The book *Letters to a German Princess* is available on the Internet.

Chapter 6

Group Theory. A classic book on group theory is Burnside's *Theory of Groups of Finite Order.* Though first published in 1897, it still gives an unparalleled introduction to what group theory is about and includes many more examples than most modern books. It was reprinted by Dover Press in 2004.

Model Theory. Sadly, we are not aware of an introduction to model theory accessible to a layperson. For a more advanced reader, a good introduction is H. Jerome Keisler's "Fundamentals of Model Theory," a chapter in the *Handbook of Mathematical Logic.*

Chapter 7

Requirements on Types. Many topics in this chapter are discussed more formally in *Elements of Programming* by Stepanov and McJones.

Reduction. Iverson discusses reduction in his paper "Notation as a Tool of Thought" (1980). The idea is also discussed in Backus' "Can Programming Be Liberated from the Von Neumann Style?" (1978). Using reduction for parallel computation was discussed in "Operators and Algebraic Structures" by Kapur, Musser, and Stepanov (1981). Dean's use of reduction is described in "Map-Reduce: Simplified Data Processing on Large Clusters" (2004).

Chapter 8

Simon Stevin. Despite Stevin's great contributions to science and mathematics, very little has been published about his work. A good overview is Sarton's "Simon Stevin of Bruges."

Polynomial Division and GCD. For a refresher on polynomial division and polynomial GCD, see Chapters 5 and 6 of Chrystal's *Algebra.*

Origins of Abstract Algebra. A good introduction to Gaussian integers is Chapter 6 of Stillwell's *Elements of Number Theory.* The classic text that introduced the general notion of algebraic integers is Richard Dedekind's *Theory of Algebraic Integers.* Stillwell's translation includes an excellent introduction that explains many of the ideas. Leo Corry's *Modern Algebra and the Rise of Mathematical Structures* is an exhaustive scholarly treatment of the emergence of abstract algebra from Dedekind to Noether and later developments.

Abstract Algebra. For the reader who wants to take the next step in understanding abstract algebra, a serious but accessible (and historically informed) text is Stillwell's *Elements of Algebra*.

Rings. Stillwell's *Elements of Number Theory* covers these topics thoroughly and is quite accessible. (While its title might suggest that this topic is covered in Stillwell's *Elements of Algebra*, that book focuses on Galois's work and therefore does not cover rings.)

Chapter 9

Social Nature of Proof. The idea that proof is a social process is discussed in "Social Processes and Proofs of Theorems and Programs," by De Millo, Lipton, and Perlis (1979).

Euclid. Sir Thomas Heath's translation of Euclid, *The Thirteen Books of the Elements*, is widely available. This edition includes very extensive commentary by the translator. In addition, there is new reproduction of Oliver Byrne's 1847 unique edition, which demonstrates all the proofs through visual illustrations. Robin Hartshorne's *Geometry: Euclid and Beyond* is a textbook aimed at university math majors, but the first chapter (describing Euclid's geometry) is quite accessible.

Axioms of Geometry. Chapters 1 and 2 of Hartshorne's *Geometry: Euclid and Beyond* provide a good introduction to Euclid's axiomatic method and Hilbert's modern version of Euclidean axioms. Hilbert's *Foundations of Geometry* is still the definitive treatment of his axioms for Geometry.

Non-Euclidean Geometry. A classic treatment of this topic is Roberto Bonola's *Non-Euclidean Geometry: A Critical and Historical Study of Its Development*. A modern (but still accessible) mathematical treatment may be found in Chapter 7 of Hartshorne's *Geometry*.

Peano Arithmetic. For readers interested in how arithmetic can be built rigorously from the ground up, Edmund Landau's *Foundations of Analysis* describes how to construct integers, rationals, reals, and complex numbers starting with Peano-like axioms. Peano's magnum opus *Formulario Mathematico* actually covered many areas of practical mathematics, not just the axioms that became famous. Unfortunately, this great book has never been translated from its original invented language. For more about Peano's work, see *Twelve Articles on Giuseppe Peano* by Hubert Kennedy.

Chapter 10

Aristotle's Organization of Knowledge. A good introduction to Aristotle's life and philosophy is Sir David Ross's *Aristotle*. There are several good editions of Aristotle's complete works, including the two-volume Bollingen Foundation edition and the multivolume Loeb Classical Library edition. Readers interested only in Aristotle's *Categories*, the work discussed in this chapter, can choose the appropriate volume.

Concepts. Chapter 1 of *Elements of Programming* by Stepanov and McJones covers this material more formally and in more detail.

Iterators and Search. Chapter 6 of *Elements of Programming* covers this material more formally and in more detail.

Chapter 11

Permutations and Transpositions. A good introduction to permutations is in Chapter XXIII of Chrystal's *Algebra*. Chapter 1 of Burnside's *Theory of Groups of Finite Order*, mentioned under Chapter 6, gives more details about these topics.

Rotate and Reverse. The algorithms in this chapter are described in more detail in Chapter 10 of *Elements of Programming*.

Chapter 12

Stein's Algorithm. Stein's original paper on the faster GCD algorithm is "Computational Problems Associated with Racah Algebra." Knuth describes the algorithm in Section 4.5.2 of *The Art of Computer Programming, Vol. 2*.

Recreational Mathematics. Many developments in mathematics came from studying seemingly frivolous problems, and many distinguished mathematicians became interested in mathematics through exposure to mathematical games. A classic book on the subject is *Mathematical Recreations and Essays* by W. W. Rouse Ball.

Chapter 13

Cryptography. An entertaining history of cryptography is David Kahn's *The Codebreakers: The Comprehensive History of Secret Communication from Ancient Times to the Internet*. To learn more about methods used in modern cryptography, a standard text is *Introduction to Modern Cryptography: Principles and Protocols* by Katz and Lindell.

Number Theory. A good modern introduction to number theory, which includes a discussion of the RSA algorithm, is John Stillwell's *Elements of Number Theory* (2003). It also includes some material that we cover in Chapters 5 and 8.

AKS Primality Testing. The deterministic polynomial-time algorithm for primality testing is described in Granville's paper "It Is Easy to Determine Whether a Given Integer Is Prime" (2005).

Notation

The following are symbols used in the book that may not be familiar to a non-mathematical reader and that are not explained in the main text. (Other new symbols are explained when they are introduced.) We'll list the symbols first, then give a few examples of their use.

$\neg p$

    Logical negation. Read "not p." If p is true, then $\neg p$ is false, and vice versa.

$p \vee q$

    Logical disjunction. Read "p or q." The statement $p \vee q$ is true if either p is true, or q is true, or they are both true.

$p \wedge q$

    Logical conjunction. Read "p and q." The statement $p \wedge q$ is true only when both p and q are true.

$p \implies q$

    Logical implication. Read "p implies q" or "if p, then q." Note that the statement $p \implies q$ is false only when p is true and q is false. It may not be intuitive that the expression is true when p is false, but one way to think of it is "you can make an argument for anything if you get to start by assuming something that isn't true." For more about logical implication, see "Implication and the Contrapositive" at the end of this appendix.

$p \iff q$

    Logical equivalence. Read "p if and only if q" and sometimes written "p iff q." The statement $p \iff q$ is true when both p and q are true, or when both p and q are false. This is exactly the same as saying $(p \implies q) \wedge (q \implies p)$.

$x \in S$

Set membership. Read "x is an element of S" or "x is in S."

$x \notin S$

Negation of set membership. Read "x is not an element of S" or "x is not in S."

$\forall x \in S$

Universal quantifier. Read "for all x in S" or "for any x in S." Sometimes membership in the set S is assumed from the context, so we just write $\forall x$.

$\exists x \in S$

Existential quantifier. Read "there exists an x in S" or "there is an x in S." Sometimes membership in the set S is assumed from the context, so we just write $\exists x$.

$S \cup T$

Set union. Read "the union of S and T." An element x is in the union of S and T if it is in either S or T or both.

$S \cap T$

Set intersection. Read "the intersection of S and T." An element x is in the intersection of S and T if it is in both S and T.

$S = \{x \mid \ldots \}$

Set definition. Read "S is the set of all x such that ..." (where the "..." could be any list of conditions about x).

$\mathbb{N}$

The set of natural numbers 0, 1, 2, 3, ...—numbers used for counting. (Some authors do not include 0 in the set of natural numbers.)

$\mathbb{Z}$

The set of integers, which includes all the natural numbers and (for all except zero) their negations.

$\mathbb{Z}_n$

The set $\{0, 1, 2, \ldots, n-1\}$ of remainders modulo n.

$\mathbb{Q}$

The set $\{\frac{p}{q}\}$ of rational numbers (the ratio of two integers).

$\mathbb{R}$

The set of real numbers.

$\mathbb{C}$

The set of complex numbers $a + bi$, where a and b are real numbers and $i^2 = -1$.

Examples

even$(x) \iff \neg$odd(x)
> "x is even if and only if x is not odd."

$S = \{x \mid x \in \mathbb{Z} \wedge$ even$(x)\}$
> "S is the set of all x's such that x is in the set of integers and x is even" or, more concisely, "S is the set of all even integers."

$\forall x \, \exists y : y = x + 1$
> "For any x, there is a y such that y equals x plus 1."

$x \in \{S \cap T\} \implies x \in \{S \cup T\}$
> "If x is in the intersection of S and T, then x is in the union of S and T."

Implication and the Contrapositive

The implication $p \implies q$ (also known as a *conditional*) is logically equivalent to a variant called the *contrapositive*, which has the following form:

$$\neg q \implies \neg p$$

Consider this example:

> If $n = 2$, then n is even.

Here our proposition p is "$n = 2$" and our proposition q is "n is even"; this conditional happens to be true. To form the contrapositive, we logically negate both sides and reverse the direction of the implication. So the contrapositive of the preceding statement is

> If n is not even, then $n \neq 2$

which is also true.

Since a conditional statement and its contrapositive are logically equivalent, we occasionally replace one with the other, in situations where the latter form is more convenient.

Don't confuse the contrapositive of $p \implies q$ with its *converse*, which is $q \implies p$. Just because an implication is true does not mean its converse is true; the two are independent. Continuing the earlier example, even though our original statement was true, its converse

> If n is even, then $n = 2$

is clearly false.

Common Proof Techniques

There are a few standard proof techniques that occur frequently in mathematics and computer science, and which we use in this book. If you are having trouble understanding the proofs in the main text, you may want to review this section.

B.1 Proof by Contradiction

Many things we want to prove have the form "if p, then q" (also sometimes written "$p \implies q$"), where p and q are two propositions. We always start with the premise that p is true; otherwise, we would be solving a different problem. The idea of proof by contradiction is to assume the opposite of what the original conjecture concludes (i.e., assume that q is *not* true), and then show that this assumption would lead to a logical contradiction—in particular, that proposition p would be false, which we know is not the case. This forces us to conclude that proposition q must be true after all, which is what we really wanted all along.

Let's look at an example. Suppose we want to prove that for all integers n:

If n^2 is odd, then n is odd.

Here "n^2 is odd" is our p and "n is odd" is our q. So let's assume the opposite conclusion is true, that n is **not** odd—that n is even. What does it mean for an integer n to be even? It means we can write it as twice some other integer m:

$$n = 2m$$

What happens if we square n?

$$n^2 = 2 \cdot 2 \cdot m^2$$

Let's introduce a new variable x, and set $x = 2m^2$. Then we can substitute:

$$n^2 = 2 \cdot 2m^2 = 2x$$

Now we see that n^2 can be expressed as twice some other integer x. But that's the definition of *even*, and our premise was that n^2 is *odd*. n^2 can't be both even and odd—that's a logical contradiction. So the assumption we made at the beginning that n is even must be false; n must therefore be odd, and we've proved the original result.

B.2   Proof by Induction

Some results we'd like to prove involve infinite sets of things. Obviously in these situations we can't enumerate all the cases, but we can often use mathematical *induction* to obtain our result. To prove something by induction, you need to do two things:

- Prove that it's true for the first element in the set. This is called the *basis*.

- Prove that if it's true for an arbitrary element in the set (the *induction hypothesis*), then it's also true for the successor of that element. This is called the *inductive step*.

For example, suppose we want to prove that for any positive integer n:

$$1 + 2 + 3 + \cdots + n = \frac{n(n+1)}{2}$$

Basis:

Does the equation hold if $n = 1$? In other words, is it true that

$$1 = \frac{1 \cdot (1+1)}{2}?$$

We can just do the arithmetic, and see that the answer is "yes."

Inductive step:

Assume that the equation is true for $n = k$. If that were true, would it also be true for $k + 1$? This is what it means to be true for k (i.e., this is our induction hypothesis):

$$1 + 2 + 3 + \cdots + k = \frac{k(k+1)}{2}$$

Let's add $k + 1$ to both sides:

$$1 + 2 + 3 + \cdots + k + (k + 1) = \frac{k(k + 1)}{2} + (k + 1)$$
$$= \frac{k(k + 1)}{2} + \frac{2(k + 1)}{2}$$
$$= \frac{(k + 1)(k + 2)}{2}$$
$$= \frac{(k + 1)((k + 1) + 1)}{2}$$

This is just $\frac{n(n+1)}{2}$, where $n = k + 1$. So we have proved that if the equation is true for k, it's true for $k + 1$.

Since we have shown both the basis and the inductive step, we have proved our original statement.

B.3   The Pigeonhole Principle

The pigeonhole principle (sometimes known as the Dirichlet principle) is very simple: if you have n pigeonholes and more than n pigeons, then at least one pigeonhole must contain more than one pigeon. There are lots of examples of this in real life. For example, if you have 367 people, at least two of them must have the same birthday. But the idea also turns out to be useful in some mathematical proofs. Often when you see a theorem that's trying to prove that two things will be the same, the pigeonhole principle is a good approach.

Here's an example:

> Prove that any set of 10 positive integers smaller than 100
> will always contain two different subsets with the same sum.

First, let's consider how many possible sums we can get. Since one of the subsets can be the empty set, the smallest possible sum is zero. The largest possible sum would come from the set containing the 10 largest numbers, i.e., $90 + 91 + 92 + \ldots + 99 = 945$. So no matter which numbers we pick, the subset sums must be somewhere in the range $[0, 945]$. That range contains 946 values, so that's the maximum number of possible sums. Next, let's see how many possible subsets of those 10 integers there are. We can represent each subset as a binary number where the ith bit is 1 if the ith integer in the set is in that subset, and 0 otherwise. There are 10 elements in the set, and we use one bit for each element, so there are $2^{10} = 1024$ possible subsets. Since there are only 946 possible sums, and there are 1024 possible subsets, by the pigeonhole principle, at least two of the subsets must have the same sum.

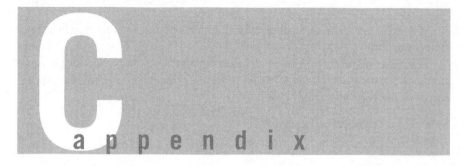

C++ for Non-C++ Programmers

This book generally uses a subset of C++ that should be easily understandable to most programmers who have used a language like C or Java. However, there are a few important features and idioms specific to C++ that we rely on. These are described in this Appendix. Except where noted, we use only features of C++ that have been available in the 1998 standard version of the language. For a good brief introduction to C++11, see *A Tour of C++* by Bjarne Stroustrup. For a complete reference, see Stroustrup's *The C++ Programming Language*.

C.1   Template Functions

One way C++ supports the generic programming paradigm is through the use of templates. Suppose you have a function like this:

```
int my_function(int x) {
    int y;
    ... do something complicated ...
    return y;
}
```

Now you want to do the same set of computations, but this time you want the function to take and return a double-precision floating-point number. C++ allows you to overload the function name, so you can write a whole new function with the same name that works with different types:

```
double my_function(double x) {
    double y;
    ... do something complicated ...
    return y;
}
```

But if everything is the same except for the type, writing a whole separate function is wasteful.

Templates avoid this problem. With templates, you can write a single function to work on any type that satisfies both the syntactic and semantic requirements of the code, like this:

```
template <typename T>
T my_function(T x) {
    T y;
    ... do something complicated ...
    return y;
}
```

Now we have a function that takes type T and returns type T, where T depends on how the function is called. On the one hand, if you say

```
int x(1);
int y = my_function(x);
```

then `my_function()` will be called with T set to `int`. On the other hand, if you say

```
double x(1.0);
double y = my_function(x);
```

then `my_function()` will be called with T set to `double`. This is done at compile time, so there is no performance penalty for using templates.

C.2 Concepts

Concepts are the essential part of generic programming, and we discuss them in some detail in Section 10.3. The following discussion is intended to be a quick reference.

Ideally, we would like to have a way to tell the programmer what the requirements are on a given template argument. For instance, we'd like to say

```
template <Number N>
```

and have that mean that whatever type this function gets called with must be a number. This means the code is intended to work for things `ints` and `doubles` and `uint64_ts`, but not, say, for strings. A restriction like "Number" is an example of a *concept*. Unfortunately, as of this writing, C++ does not support concepts as a built-in part of the language—that is, C++ does not have any way to enforce requirements on template types.

Despite this limitation, we will write our code examples as if concepts were present in the language. We can implement this by just defining our favorite concepts as aliases for `typename`:

```
#define Number typename
```

So when we write

```
template <Number N>
```

as far as the compiler is concerned, it's as if we wrote

```
template <typename N>
```

but the human programmer will understand the intended restriction.

C.3   Declaration Syntax and Typed Constants

C++ provides multiple ways to declare and initialize a variable. While the traditional C syntax

```
int x = y;
```

is legal, the common way to write this in C++ is

```
int x(y);
```

This is more consistent with the syntax used to construct arbitrary C++ objects. (Note: The current version of C++ supports an additional way to do initialization:

```
int x{y};
```

However, this usage is still less widespread, so we do not use it in our examples.)

When using numeric constants, we'll be very careful about types. For example, a traditional C program might contain a line like this:

```
if (something) return 0;
```

This is a bit sloppy. Which type is the 0 returned by the function? By default, it's an int, but suppose our program was supposed to return a specific kind of integer, like a 16-bit unsigned integer, or one specified by a template argument. Rather than rely on implicit type conversion, we'll try to be explicit about what we're returning by writing something like this:

```
if (something) return uint16_t(0);
```

or, in the case of a template argument:

```
if (something) return T(0);
```

where T is the type specified in the template.

C.4   Function Objects

Often we'd like to have a function that requires some initialization and maintains some state. A common way to implement this in C++ is by the use of a *function object*, also called a *functor*. A function object is an object that encapsulates a single (unnamed) function. Let's look at a simple example—a function object for doing currency conversion:

```
struct converter {
    double exchange_rate;

    converter(double ex) : exchange_rate(ex) {}

    double operator()(double amt) {
        return amt * exchange_rate;
    }
};
```

Note the use of the syntax operator() to declare the unnamed function that belongs to the object.

To use this function, we first construct an instance of our converter object (which initializes the exchange rate). In this example we want to convert euros to U.S. dollars, so we'll name our instance eur_to_usd. Then we can invoke the function by using that instance:

```
int main() {

    converter eur_to_usd(1.3043);

    double euros;
    do {
        std::cout << "Enter amount in Euros:  ";
        std::cin >> euros;
        std::cout << euros << " euros is "
                  << eur_to_usd(euros) << " dollars "
                  << std::endl;
    } while (euros > 0.0);
}
```

Function objects have the benefit that we can pass them as arguments to functions. (C++ does not allow passing functions directly, only function pointers, which requires the added cost of an indirect function call.) In addition, function objects can contain state information.

C.5   Preconditions, Postconditions, and Assertions

Given valid arguments, a function performs a certain computation. Another way to put this is that if its preconditions are satisfied, certain postconditions will be true. Sometimes we write these preconditions and postconditions as comments in our code, like this:

```
// precondition:  y != 0.0
double my_ratio(double x, double y) {
    return x / y;
}
// postcondition:  returned value is x/y
```

However, the library also provides a mechanism called `assert` for checking some conditions. So we could write:

```
double my_ratio(double x, double y) {
    assert(y != 0.0);
    return x / y;
}
```

If the `assert` expression evaluates to true, nothing happens. But if it evaluates to false, execution of the program halts and an error message is printed.

In production code, assertions are typically disabled to avoid a performance penalty.

C.6   STL Algorithms and Data Structures

The C++ language contains a library of standard software components, known as the Standard Template Library (STL). This library includes data structures, algorithms, and other utilities commonly used by C++ programmers. All STL components belong to the namespace `std`; we will explicitly use the prefix `std::` when we refer to them in our code examples.

STL is a generic library, meaning that each component can be used with any appropriate type. In the case of data structures, the types are specified as template arguments when the object is declared. For example,

```
std::vector<int> v;
```

declares a vector of integers, while

```
std::vector<bool> v;
```

declares a vector of Booleans.

The following STL components are used in this book:

Function objects for arithmetic operations and comparisons (see Section C.4 for explanation of function objects):

- `std::plus`—Computes the sum of its operator's two arguments.

- `std::multiplies`—Computes the product of its operator's two arguments.

- `std::negate`—Computes the negation of its operator's argument.

- `std::less`—Returns true when its operator's first argument is less than its second, false otherwise.

- `std:less_equal`—Returns true when its operator's first argument is less than or equal to its second, false otherwise.

Data structures:

- `std::pair`—A struct that stores two arbitrary objects; typically used to return two things from a function.

- `std::vector`—A container for a sequence of elements of a single type that supports constant-time random access.

Algorithms:

- `std::fill`—Fills the range specified by its first two arguments with the value specified by the third argument.

- `std::swap`—Exchanges the contents of its arguments.

- `std::partition_point`—Returns an iterator to the first element in an already partitioned range (specified by the first two arguments) for which the given predicate (third argument) is not true. See discussion in Section 10.8.

Other utilities:

- `std::advance`—Increments the position of an iterator (its first argument) by a distance (second argument).

For a more detailed description of these and other STL components, see Part IV of Stroustrup's *The C++ Programming Language*.

C.7   Iterators and Ranges

Iterators are an important part of generic programming, and we discuss them in greater detail in Section 10.4. The following discussion is intended to be a quick reference.

Iterators are an abstraction of pointers; an iterator indicates a position in a sequence. The examples in this book use these four types of iterators, each with its own iterator tag.

- *Input iterators* support one-directional traversal, but only once, as is found in single-pass algorithms. The canonical model of an input iterator is the position in an *input stream*.
  Tag: `std::input_iterator_tag`

- *Forward iterators* also support only one-directional traversal, but this traversal can be repeated as needed, as in multi-pass algorithms. The canonical model of a forward iterator is the position in a *singly linked list*.
  Tag: `std::forward_iterator_tag`

- *Bidirectional iterators* support bidirectional traversal, repeated as needed (i.e., they also can be used in multi-pass algorithms). The canonical model of a bidirectional iterator is the position in a *doubly linked list*.
  Tag: `std::bidirectional_iterator_tag`

- *Random-access iterators* support random-access algorithms; that is, they allow access to any element in constant time. The canonical model is the position in an *array*.
  Tag: `std::random_access_iterator_tag`

The iterator tags are special types that may be used in function signatures to ensure that the correct version of an overloaded function will be invoked when a given iterator is used; see Chapter 11 for an example.

*   *   *

STL functions often take two iterators representing the beginning and end of a range of data. By convention, the iterator for the end of the data (often called `last`) points to the position directly *after* the last element.

Iterators also have special attributes called *iterator traits*. The ones we use are:

- `value_type`: the type of the objects pointed to by the iterator.

- `difference_type`: an integral type large enough to express the number of increment operations needed to get from one iterator to another.

- `iterator_category`: the iterator tag, described earlier.

The syntax to access an iterator trait for a particular iterator type x is (for example)

`std::iterator_traits<x>::value_type`

For more information on iterators, see Chapter 10.

C.8 Type Aliases and Type Functions with using in C++11

C++11, the current standard version of C++, has a feature called using that allows programmers to provide aliases for types and other constructs. This is typically used to provide a short way to write a long and complicated type. For example:

```
using myptr = long_complicated_class_name*;
```

After writing this statement, programmers could refer to myptr in the code wherever they would have previously written long_complicated_class_name*.

Users of C and earlier versions of C++ may be familiar with an older aliasing mechanism, typedef, but using is more flexible. For example, the using feature allows us to write templatized type functions for iterator traits. If we write

```
template <InputIterator I>
using IteratorCategory =
        typename std::iterator_traits<I>::iterator_category;
```

then every time we want to know the category of an iterator, we can say

```
    IteratorCategory<I>
```

rather than

```
    std::iterator_traits<I>::iterator_category
```

C.9 Initializer Lists in C++11

In C and C++, you can conveniently initialize an array by enclosing the list of values in curly braces, like this:

```
char my_array[5] = {'a', 'e', 'i', 'o', 'u'};
```

C++11 extends this syntax beyond arrays, so now you can also write things like this:

```
std::vector<char> = {'a', 'e', 'i', 'o', 'u'};
std::pair<int, double> = {42, 3.1415};
```

C.10 Lambda Functions in C++11

C++11 includes support for *lambda functions*. These are anonymous functions that are needed only once, often as arguments to another function.

Suppose for some application, we wanted to take a function that computed the cube of its argument and pass it to another function. Traditionally, we'd have to implement this as a function object, declare it separately, instantiate it, and pass the instance, like this:

```
struct cuber {
    cuber() {}; // constructor

    int operator()(int x) {
        return x * x * x;
    }
};

int main() {
    ...
    cuber cube;
    int a = some_other_function(cube);
    ...
}
```

But if this is the only time we ever need the cube function, that's a lot of work. Why bother creating the function object, or even giving the function a name, when we're never going to use it again? Instead, we can write a lambda function inline and pass the whole expression as an argument:

```
int main() {
    ...
    int a = some_other_function([=](int x) { return x * x * x; });
    ...
}
```

The syntax for lambda functions is just like the syntax for implementing any other function, except that the name of the function is replaced by the expression [=], and the return type usually does not need to be specified; the compiler figures it out.

C.11   A Note about inline

The C++ directive inline before a function is a hint that tells the compiler that the programmer would like the body of the function to be included as part of the code of the caller, avoiding the usual function call overhead. In practice, many functions in this book would benefit today from being declared inline.

Inlining makes sense only for relatively small pieces of code. Larger inlined functions could end up increasing the size of the calling code enough to disrupt code caching or cause other performance problems. Compilers take this into account and ignore the `inline` request in those cases. At the same time, compilers are getting smart enough to inline code automatically when it makes sense. For these reasons, the `inline` directive will soon be obsolete, so we did not use it in our examples.

Bibliography

Adler, Mortimer J. (Ed.). (1991). *Great Books of the Western World*, Vol. 10: *Euclid, Archimedes, Nicomachus*. Chicago: Encyclopaedia Brittanica.

Aristotle. (1938). *Aristotle: Categories, On Interpretation, Prior Analytics*, Vol. 325. Translated by H. P. Cooke and Hugh Tredennick. Cambridge, MA: Loeb Classical Library.

Aristotle. (1984). *The Complete Works of Aristotle: The Revised Oxford Translation*. Edited by Jonathan Barnes. Princeton, NJ: Princeton University Press.

Backus, John. (1978). "Can Programming Be Liberated from the Von Neumann Style?: A Functional Style and Its Algebra of Programs." *Communications of the ACM 21*(8), 613–641.

Ball, W. W. Rouse, and H. S. M. Coxeter. ([1922] 2010). *Mathematical Recreations and Essays* (10th ed.). Reprint, New York: Dover Publications. Original edition published 1892.

Bonola, Roberto. ([1955] 2010). *Non-Euclidean Geometry: A Critical and Historical Study of Its Development*. Translated by H. S. Carslaw. Reprint, New York: Dover Publications. Originally published as *La Geometria non-Euclidea*, 1912.

Burnside, William. ([1911] 2004). *Theory of Groups of Finite Order* (2nd ed.). Reprint, Mineola, NY: Dover Publications.

Byrne, Oliver. (2010). *The First Six Books of the Elements of Euclid*. Taschen. Facsimile of 1847 edition.

Chrystal, George. ([1964] 1999). *Algebra: An Elementary Text-Book* (7th ed.). Reprint, Providence, RI: American Mathematical Society. Original edition published 1886.

Cohen, Morris R., and I. E. Drabkin. (1948). *A Source Book in Greek Science.* Cambridge, MA: Harvard University Press.

Corry, Leo. (2004). *Modern Algebra and the Rise of Mathematical Structures* (2nd revised ed.). Basel, Switzerland: Birkhäuser.

Dean, Jeffrey, and Sanjay Ghemawat. (2008). "MapReduce: Simplified Data Processing on Large Clusters." *Communications of the ACM 51*(1), 107–113.

Dedekind, Richard. (1996). *Theory of Algebraic Integers.* Translated by John Stillwell. Cambridge, UK: Cambridge University Press. Originally published as *Über die Theorie der ganzen algebraicschen Zahlen*, 1877.

De Millo, Richard A., Richard J. Lipton, and Alan J. Perlis. (1979). "Social Processes and Proofs of Theorems and Programs." *Communications of the ACM 22*(5), 271–280.

Dirichlet, P. G. L. (1999). *Lectures on Number Theory.* Supplements by R. Dedekind. Translated by John Stillwell. Providence, RI: American Mathematical Society. Originally published as *Vorlesungen über Zahlentheorie*, 1863.

Euclid. (1956). *Euclid: The Thirteen Books of the Elements.* Translated by Thomas L. Heath. (2nd ed.). New York: Dover Publications.

Euler, Leonhard. (1988). *Introduction to Analysis of the Infinite*, Vol. 1 and 2. Translated by John D. Blanton. New York: Springer. Originally published as *Introductio in analysin infinitorum*, 1748.

Euler, Leonhard. (2000). *Foundations of Differential Calculus.* Translated by John D. Blanton. New York: Springer. Originally published as *Institutiones Calculi Differentialis*, 1755.

Fibonacci, Leonardo Pisano, and L. E. Sigler (Trans.). (1987). *The Book of Squares: An Annotated Translation into Modern English.* Boston: Academic Press. Originally published in Latin as *Liber Quadratorum*, 1225.

Floyd, Robert W., and Donald E. Knuth. (1990). "Addition Machines." *SIAM Journal on Computing 19*(2), 329–340.

Fowler, David H. (1987). *The Mathematics of Plato's Academy: A New Reconstruction.* Oxford, UK: Clarendon Press.

Gauss, Carl Friedrich. (1965). *Disquisitiones Arithmeticae.* Translated by Arthur A. Clarke, S.J. New Haven, CT: Yale University Press. Original Latin edition, 1801.

Granville, Andrew. (2005). "It Is Easy to Determine whether a Given Integer Is Prime." *Bulletin of the American Mathematical Society 42*(1), 3–38.

Gries, David, and Gary Levin. (1980). "Computing Fibonacci Numbers (and Similarly Defined Functions) in Log Time." *Information Processing Letters 11*(2), 68–69.

Grimm, Richard E. (1973). "The Autobiography of Leonardo Pisano." *Fibonacci Quarterly 11*(1), 99–104.

Hartshorne, Robin. (2000). *Geometry: Euclid and Beyond.* New York: Springer.

Heath, Thomas. ([1921] 1981). *A History of Greek Mathematics.* Reprint, New York: Dover Publications.

Hilbert, David. ([1971] 1999). *Foundations of Geometry* (10th ed.). Translated by Leo Unger and revised by Paul Bernays. Chicago: Open Court. Originally published as *Grundlagen der Geometrie*, 1899.

Iverson, Kenneth E. (1962). "A Programming Language." In *Proceedings of the May 1–3, 1962, Spring Joint Computer Conference*, AIEE-IRE '62, pp. 345–351. ACM.

Iverson, Kenneth E. (1980). "Notation As a Tool of Thought." *Communications of the ACM 35*(1–2), 2–31.

Kahn, David. (1996). *The Codebreakers: The Comprehensive History of Secret Communication from Ancient Times to the Internet* (Revised ed.). New York: Scribner.

Kapur, D., D. R. Musser, and A. A. Stepanov. (1981a). "Operators and Algebraic Structures." In *Proceedings of the 1981 Conference on Functional Programming Languages and Computer Architecture*, FPCA '81, New York, NY, pp. 59–64. ACM.

Kapur, D., D. R. Musser, and A. A. Stepanov. (1981b). "Tecton: A Language for Manipulating Generic Objects." In *Program Specification, Proceedings of a Workshop*, pp. 402–414. Springer-Verlag.

Katz, Jonathan, and Yehuda Lindell. (2008). *Introduction to Modern Cryptography.* Boca Raton, FL: CRC Press.

Katz, Victor J. (2009). *A History of Mathematics: An Introduction* (3rd ed.). Boston: Addison-Wesley.

Keisler, H. Jerome. (1989). "Fundamentals of Model Theory." In J. Barwise (Ed.), *Handbook of Mathematical Logic.* North Holland.

Kennedy, Hubert. (2002). *Twelve Articles on Giuseppe Peano*. San Francisco: Peremptory Publications.

Knuth, Donald E. (2007). *The Art of Computer Programming*, Vol. 2: Seminumerical Algorithms. Boston: Addison-Wesley.

Landau, Edmund. ([1966] 2001). *Foundations of Analysis* (3rd ed.). Translated by F. Steinhardt. Reprint, Providence, RI: Chelsea.

McClenon, R. B. (1919). "Leonardo of Pisa and His *Liber Quadratorum*." *The American Mathematical Monthly 26*(1), 1–8.

Musser, David R., and Alexander A. Stepanov. (1988). "Generic Programming." In *Proceedings of the International Symposium ISSAC'88 on Symbolic and Algebraic Computation*, pp. 13–25. Springer-Verlag.

Peano, Giuseppe. (1960). *Formulario Mathematico*. Edizioni Cremonense. Original edition published 1908.

Plato. (1997). *Plato: Complete Works*. Edited by J. M. Cooper and D. S. Hutchinson. Indianapolis, IN: Hackett Publishing.

Robins, Gay, and Charles Shute. (1987). *The Rhind Mathematical Papyrus: An Ancient Egyptian Text*. London: British Museum Publications.

Ross, David. (2004). *Aristotle* (6th ed.). London: Routledge.

Russo, Lucio. (2004). *The Forgotten Revolution: How Science Was Born in 300 BC and Why It Had to Be Reborn*. Translated by Silvio Levy. New York: Springer. Originally published as *La rivoluzione dimenticata*, 1996.

Sarton, George. (1934). "Simon Stevin of Bruges." *Isis 21*(2), 241–303.

Sigler, Laurence. (1987). *Fibonacci's Liber Abaci: A Translation into Modern English of Leonardo Pisano's Book of Calculation*. New York: Springer. Original Latin edition, 1202.

Stein, Josef. (1967). "Computational Problems Associated with Racah Algebra." *Journal of Computational Physics 1*(3), 397–405.

Stepanov, Alexander, and Meng Lee. (1995). *The Standard Template Library*. Hewlett-Packard Laboratories, Technical Publications Department.

Stepanov, Alexander, and Paul McJones. (2009). *Elements of Programming*. Boston: Addison-Wesley Professional.

Stillwell, John. (1994). *Elements of Algebra*. New York: Springer.

Stillwell, John. (2002). *Elements of Number Theory*. New York: Springer.

Stillwell, John. (2010). *Mathematics and Its History*. New York: Springer.

Stroustrup, Bjarne. (2013a). *The C++ Programming Language* (4th ed.). Boston: Addison-Wesley Professional.

Stroustrup, Bjarne. (2013b). *A Tour of C++*. Boston: Addison-Wesley Professional.

van der Waerden, B. L. (1983). *Geometry and Algebra in Ancient Civilizations*. Berlin: Springer-Verlag.

van der Waerden, B. L. (1988). *Science Awakening: Egyptian, Babylonian, and Greek Mathematics*. Translated by Arnold Dresden. Dordrecht, Netherlands: Kluwer Academic Publishers.

Weil, André. (2007). *Number Theory: An Approach through History from Hammurapi to Legendre*. Cambridge, MA: Birkhäuser Boston.

Index

* (operator), mathematical convention
    for, 115
+ (plus sign), mathematical convention
    for, 115
α. *See* Aliquot sum
φ. *See* Euler totient function
σ (sum of divisors) formula, 31

A

Abelian group, 86, 108, 153
Abstract algebra
    birth of, 85, 140–145
    Euclidean domains, 150–151, 153
    fields, 151–153
    groups, 85–88, 92–95, 108, 152
    ideals, 226–228
    modules, 151, 154
    monoids, 89, 108–109, 152, 154
    and programming, 2, 141, 249
    principal ideals, 227–228
    rings, 142–145, 153
    semigroups, 90–91, 108–109, 152
    semirings, 145–149, 153
    vector spaces, 152, 154
Abstraction
    Aristotle, 177, 180, 196
    in mathematics, 84, 85–109
    and programming, 2, 5, 249
Academy (Plato's), 41–44, 178
Addition
    associativity of, 9, 156, 174

commutativity of, 155–156,
    174–175
definition, 173
Addition chains, 11
Additive groups, 86
Additive monoids, 89, 109
Additive semigroups, 90, 109
Address, 181
Adleman, Len, 239
advance, 190
Agrawal, Manindra, 244
Ahmes, 8–9, 57
Ahmes algorithm. *See* Egyptian multi-
    plication, Egyptian division
AKS primality test, 244–245
Alexander the Great, 43, 178–179
Alexandria, 43–44
Algebraic integers, 140
Algebraic structures, 85. *See also*
    Abstract algebra
Algorithms
    in ancient Egypt, 7–11
    definition, 7
    domain or setting, 150
    first recorded, 8
    generalizing, 111, 119–123, 126–
        127, 151
    history of, 7–11
    in-place, 215–216
    memory adaptive, 216–217
    polylog space, 215–216
    space complexity, 215–216
    performance in practice, 211

Photo Credits

inform**IT**.com THE TRUSTED TECHNOLOGY LEARNING SOURCE

Learn**IT** at Inform**IT**

Looking for a book, eBook, or training video on a new technology? Seeking timely and relevant information and tutorials. Looking for expert opinions, advice, and tips? InformIT has a solution.

- Learn about new releases and special promotions by subscribing to a wide variety of monthly newsletters. Visit **informit.com/newsletters**.

- FREE Podcasts from experts at **informit.com/podcasts**.

- Read the latest author articles and sample chapters at **informit.com/articles**.

- Access thousands of books and videos in the Safari Books Online digital library. **safari.informit.com**.

- Get Advice and tips from expert blogs at **informit.com/blogs**.

Visit **informit.com** to find out all the ways you can access the hottest technology content.

Are you part of the **IT** crowd?

Connect with Pearson authors and editors via RSS feeds, Facebook, Twitter, YouTube and more! Visit **informit.com/socialconnect**.